Entrepreneurship in the Global Economy

Entrepreneurs have long been drivers of innovation in developed countries. They start companies and create new industries that keep economies strong and prosperous. Today, however, in developing nations such as China, state-controlled economies are building robust industries at stunning speed and siphoning off jobs from the West. How can entrepreneurs function in the face of this challenge? Can they continue to create economic value in a globalized business environment? This book addresses the crucial issue of state planning vs. free enterprise and examines specific problems surrounding entrepreneurship in the global economy through nine case histories of entrepreneurial companies. It also looks at how and why government gets involved in economic growth and how entrepreneurs contribute to economic value. Based on this analysis, the authors argue that companies can succeed, even in controlled economies, by understanding the customs and policies of countries where they do business.

HENRY KRESSEL, a senior partner of Warburg Pincus LLC, has been responsible for investments in technology companies in the US, Europe, and Asia. He began his career at RCA Laboratories where he pioneered the first practical semiconductor lasers. He was the founding president of the IEEE Photonics Society and co-founded the IEEE/OSA *Journal of Lightwave Technology*. He is the recipient of many awards and honors, a Fellow of the American Physical Society and the IEEE, was elected to the US National Academy of Engineering, and is holder of thirty-one issued US patents for electronic and optoelectronic devices. He is the co-author of three previous books, *Semiconductor lasers and heterojunction LEDs* with J. K. Butler (1977) and *Competing for the future: How digital innovations are changing the world* (Cambridge University Press, 2007) and *Investing in dynamic markets: Venture capital in the digital age* (Cambridge University Press, 2010), both with Thomas V. Lento. He also edited *Semiconductor devices for optical communications* (Springer-Verlag, 1987).

THOMAS V. LENTO is founder and President of InterComm, a corporate communications consultancy specializing in technology companies. He has been a university professor, an ad agency executive, and Director of Communications for Sarnoff Corporation. In addition to collaborating with Henry Kressel on three books, he was editor of *Inventing the future: 60 years of innovation at Sarnoff* and co-authored Gregory H. Olsen's *By any means necessary: An entrepreneur's journey into space* (2009).

Other Cambridge University Press books by the same authors

Competing for the future: How digital innovations are
changing the world (2007)
ISBN 9780521862905

Investing in dynamic markets: Venture capital in the digital age (2010)
ISBN 9780521111485

Entrepreneurship in the Global Economy

Engine for Economic Growth

HENRY KRESSEL

THOMAS V. LENTO

CAMBRIDGE
UNIVERSITY PRESS

CAMBRIDGE UNIVERSITY PRESS
Cambridge, New York, Melbourne, Madrid, Cape Town,
Singapore, São Paulo, Delhi, Mexico City

Cambridge University Press
The Edinburgh Building, Cambridge CB2 8RU, UK

Published in the United States of America by Cambridge University Press,
New York

www.cambridge.org
Information on this title: www.cambridge.org/9781107019768

First published 2012

Printed in the United Kingdom at the University Press, Cambridge

A catalogue record for this publication is available from the British Library

Library of Congress Cataloguing in Publication data
Kressel, Henry.
  Entrepreneurship in the global economy : engine for economic
growth / Henry Kressel, Thomas V. Lento.
    pages   cm
  Includes bibliographical references and index.
  ISBN 978-1-107-01976-8
  1. Entrepreneurship.   2. Economic development.   3. Free trade.
  4. Industrial policy.   5. Economic policy.   6. Globalization–Economic
aspects.   I. Lento, Thomas V.   II. Title.
  HB615.K74 2012
  338′.04–dc23
  2012013671

ISBN 978-1-107-01976-8 Hardback

For
Bertha Kressel
and
Takako Lento
with love

Contents

Figures

Tables

Acknowledgments

This book had its genesis in a lecture regarding the future of venture capital in the global economy that I gave at Columbia University in 2010 at the invitation of Professor Graciela Chichilnisky. However, this book would not have been possible without the experience I gained as a senior partner at Warburg Pincus, one of the largest private equity and venture capital firms in the world. Since the 1980s, Warburg Pincus has expanded internationally with offices in London, Frankfurt, Hong Kong, Beijing, Shanghai, Mumbai, and Tokyo. The firm has invested over $30 billion in companies located in thirty countries in a wide range of industries. The companies it has funded have ranged from startups to some having revenues in the billions of dollars.

A hallmark of the firm is the outstanding teamwork of its international professional staff, which brings to bear the required skills from all parts of the world as needed by its portfolio companies. As a result, the firm's partners work as a single entity and with a common purpose in promoting the success of its investments wherever they are located.

Lionel I. Pincus and John L. Vogelstein led the firm from the 1970s to 2002. Succeeding them in 2002, Co-Presidents Joseph P. Landy and Charles R. Kaye have continued its record of success. As Vice-Chairman of the firm, Dr. William Janeway had a major role in directing the firm's investment in technology businesses. All three have been involved, along with other partners, in the companies discussed here, which were Warburg Pincus investments. The partners who participated in one or more of these investments include Dr. Frank Brochin, Julian Cheng, Dr. Nancy Martin, Bilge Ogut, Chang Q. Sun, Barry Taylor, and Beau Vrolyk.

In addition, I have also had the pleasure of collaborating over the years with Scott A. Arenare, Alex Berzofsky, Christopher Brody, Dr. Harold Brown, Mark M. Colodny, Timothy J. Curt, Cary J. Davis, Andrew Gaspar, Patrick T. Hackett, Jeffrey A. Harris, Julie Johnson Staples, Kewsong Lee, James Neary, Dalip Pathak, Dr. Stan Raatz, Henry Schacht, Steven G. Schneider, Dr. Joseph Schull, Patrick Severson, Christopher Turner, and Jeremy Young.

Valuable discussions helped in writing this book. We are indebted to Dr. Bart Stuck, Dr. William Janeway, Dr. Peter Scovell, Dr. Alexander Magoun, and Paula Parrish, the Commissioning Editor at Cambridge University Press, for valuable discussions.

Finally, I am very grateful to Tina Nuss for her extraordinary work in preparing and proofreading the manuscript.

Henry Kressel

Introduction

> Innovation is a primary engine of economic growth ... The innovation process involves the invention, commercialization, and diffusion of new ideas. At each of these stages, people are spurred to action by the prospect of reaping rewards from their investment. In a free market, innovators vie to lower the cost of goods and services, to improve their quality and usefulness, and – most importantly – to develop new goods and services that promise benefits to customers ... Successful innovations blossom, attracting capital and diffusing rapidly through the market, while unsuccessful innovations can wither just as quickly. In this way, markets allow capital to flow to its highest-valued uses.[1]

President Bush's 2005 report on the economy (quoted above) identifies innovation as the prime driver of economic development. And while Democrats and Republicans might disagree on how to promote it, innovation is officially a bipartisan cause. The Obama administration trumpets the need to foster innovation if America is to maintain its leading position among the world's economies.

Joseph Alois Schumpeter would be gratified. The great twentieth-century Austrian-American economist was the foremost theorist of innovation as the source for economic growth in the industrial world. Schumpeter knew that all technologies eventually became obsolete, and according to his theory this presented an opportunity for change and growth that could only be realized with innovation. In his view the decline of older technologies makes room for new ones. Through a process he called "creative destruction," innovation enables vibrant new enterprises to replace obsolete industries.

As the creator of new companies, the entrepreneur is innovation's true agent of change. By "entrepreneur" we do not mean the many founders of small businesses with modest ambitions. Such

---

[1] *Economic report of the President* (Washington, DC: United States Government Printing Office, February 2005), p. 135.

entrepreneurs undoubtedly create many valuable jobs, but they do not *individually* generate enough industrial growth to be meaningful in a modern economy.

In Schumpeter's vision, true entrepreneurs are the rare leaders capable of building revolutionary enterprises and new industries on the basis of technological innovation.

> Schumpeter's hero ... is the creative daring entrepreneur, the captain of industry who makes the innovations that introduce new products, embody resource discoveries and technological improvements, and open new markets, and in the process, build new industrial empires ... The dynamic innovations of the entrepreneurial class constitute a powerful competitive force in economic development.[2]

Every new wave of technology has seen entrepreneurs build great companies. In the US, in the second half of the twentieth century, many of the entrepreneurs who helped lay the foundations for the new digital age have been venture capital funded. Venture capital has played a central role in the growth of such trillion-dollar industries as computers, telecommunications, software, and Internet-based businesses, which lie at the heart of modern commerce. This wave of innovative entrepreneurship occurred in a period of dramatically increasing world trade that opened new markets for companies created in the developed countries, including the US, industrialized Europe, and later, Japan.

That now feels like ancient history. The world economic order has shifted since the beginning of the twenty-first century. With the rapid industrialization of the Asian economies outside of Japan, a massive amount of industrial diffusion has occurred, and developing countries are assuming leadership roles.

---

[2] J. E. Elliott in J. A. Schumpeter, *The theory of economic development* (New Brunswick, NJ: Transaction, 1983), pp. xxxvi–xxxvii.

Whereas once the US, the EU, and Japan were practically the only highly industrialized countries, new Asian competitors, notably China, South Korea, and Taiwan, have joined the club. As a consequence the highly successful industrial model of the US, which encourages open markets and individual entrepreneurship, finds itself challenged by economic models where the state has a much stronger influence on industrial development. To varying degrees these emerging countries practice various forms of mercantilism, a policy that favors the development of their local industries. At the same time, the developed countries have policies for protecting their industries as they are increasingly concerned about their health. So every country works to promote or protect its own industries in various manners, which makes for a world with increasing trade restrictions.

The degree of state intervention in national economies varies widely from one country to another, and businesses must learn to deal with it in each country where they operate. They have little choice, because the biggest growth markets are global. They must establish international operations in order to grow and stay competitive. What this means is that entrepreneurs with global ambitions face additional challenges when they start companies. Government favoritism has a marked effect on all aspects of commerce, and strongly influences the creation of businesses and the ability of foreign companies to operate in local markets. Today's entrepreneur must think globally and learn to master new relationships in order to build a big business. In this book we will see how modern innovators and entrepreneurs have built important new businesses in this new world economic order.

Many factors have contributed to the alteration of the global economic landscape: the fluidity of industrial "know-how," the worldwide easing of the movement of capital, and the widespread industrialization of countries with economic models dominated by the state. All of them make the task of the ambitious entrepreneur, in Schumpeter's sense, harder.

How has the world been transformed so quickly? There are a number of causes, but the rapid development of technology lies at the heart of the revolutionary changes this age has witnessed. Once upon a time industries were protected by proprietary knowledge in the hands (and heads) of craftsmen. Today this knowledge is most often embedded in computer software that travels at the speed of light. That makes it easier and faster to move jobs than it was in the days when relocating factories also meant relocating workers.

So the industrialized countries that emerged as economic leaders in the nineteenth and twentieth centuries are watching their mature, established industries and associated manufacturing migrate to China and other developing countries. By sending work overseas, companies get the advantages of lower costs and plentiful capital for easing industrial relocation. But such relocations leave behind unemployed citizens who clamor for new jobs. It takes innovative new industries to generate such jobs, because the old industries will not come back.

To put this in a larger perspective, a half-century of ceaseless innovation and global industrial development and diffusion has irrevocably altered the world's economic landscape, lifting billions of people out of poverty and conferring on them the benefits of a modern society. It has also put the developed world in the uncomfortable position of watching former client nations turn into competitors. Developed countries must rely on innovation to create new industries, while older, commoditized technology migrates to countries with lower wages and costs.

One can't blame developing countries for wanting to benefit from the outsourcing of jobs. These nations have turned to rapid industrialization as the surest way to foster economic growth and provide for the wellbeing of their citizens. They are now competing for the factories that drive jobs and exports. They also want to move to the forefront of industrial innovation, recognizing that this is essential for maintaining their competitive position. Having joined the industrialized world, developing economies realize that they must support innovation to create the industries of the future, or risk falling behind. The result: a race among practically all industrialized countries, developed and developing, to encourage innovative entrepreneurship with varying degrees of state support.

This drive for innovation is especially urgent for the developed world. It would be comforting to think that innovative entrepreneurship will quickly fill the industrial void in those countries, but skeptics say this will not happen fast enough.

> "There's been this assumption that there's a global hierarchy of work, that all the high-end service work, knowledge work, R&D work would stay in the US, and that all the lower-end work would be transferred to emerging markets," said Hal Salzman, a public policy professor at Rutgers and a senior faculty fellow at Heidrich Center for Workforce Development. "That hierarchy has been upset, to say the least," he said. "More and more innovation is coming out of the emerging markets, as part of this bottom-up push."[3]

With the focus on sustaining economic growth, there are two diametrically opposed approaches. At one extreme we have pure "state capitalism," where the state is the source of capital and provides competitive protection to major new enterprises. On the other extreme we have "pure" free-market capitalism, where private capital finances enterprises and they compete in an unregulated market.

Free-market theorists, such as the people who wrote the report for President Bush quoted at the start of this Introduction, would say that the government should not intervene in the market in any way at all. They would point to incentives from developing nations to attract factories, for example, as an unfair practice.

---

[3] C. Rampell, "Once a dynamo, the tech sector is slow to hire," *The New York Times*, September 6, 2010, p. 1.

However, their call for no government "interference" in the market is misguided. In fact most countries exercise varying levels of control over the environment in which important businesses operate. Entrepreneurs need access to resources and markets to succeed, and this is where national policies play a vital role.

Proponents of the other extreme often base their argument on China's policy for most industries, which is the closest approach we have to "state capitalism." Since China has demonstrated remarkable success in rapid industrialization, moving from an agrarian nation to the world's second largest economy in less than four decades, its economic model has a profound influence in shaping industrial policies around the world. Other fast-growing Asian economies have largely adopted a model of strong state control, quite contrary to the pure free-market economic theory beloved of economists.

But China's leaders seem to understand that ideological purity never jump-started the creation of a successful national economy. Although they have adopted the model of state capitalism, they also encourage entrepreneurs in selected sectors of the economy.

All of this creates a dilemma for developed economies. They are losing industries to the developing world, and need dynamic new businesses that can compete in international markets. Unfortunately, the newcomers are racing to develop the same kind of businesses. Developed countries have to get there first if they are to maintain their prosperity.

How can developed countries promote the creation of innovative companies charting new markets? That is the question with which their leaders are grappling. Politicians and financiers would love to discover a magic formula that would enable Schumpeter's kind of entrepreneurs to appear and create new industries faster than the old ones can migrate overseas.

Entrepreneurship is essential to a growing economy in large part because its innovations create demand for new products and services that were not previously available. People only know they want a specific product when someone shows it to them.

Many economists argue as if the only thing that matters for a buoyant economy is rising demand from the great mass of consumers. Nothing can happen until demand increases, we are told. Well, demand is crucial. But to look only at one side of the ledger is disturbing. Demand side economists fail to recognize that supply is critical in the creation of demand. That's why restaurants, for example, offer new supply in the form of updated menus and new dishes and why businesses of all kinds constantly offer products "new and improved." What was the market for an iPad in 1985? Zero: the product didn't exist. Demand cannot exist until the supply is brought to market, which is why incentives to undertake risk are so important ... The main goal should be to create wealth. We're better off if entrepreneurial risk is richly rewarded. Every private sector job depended at one time or another on someone willing to take a risk.[4]

Promoting entrepreneurship and seeing it succeed are not the same thing. There are no sure-fire recipes for entrepreneurial success in a world where increasing government interference is to be expected as nations struggle to maximize their economic performance – more often than not at the expense of other nations. But there is much to be learned from the example of successful innovators in key industries. That is what we provide in this book. In our exploration of their achievements we will focus on the motivations of ambitious entrepreneurs, factors that have an impact on their behavior, and the national and international conditions that can affect their success, including the role of government and the availability of capital.

We will also discuss how governments affect entrepreneurship. This is an important topic, because the success of China, a huge country under tight economic control, is forcing other countries to

---

[4] E. T. McClanahan, "Americans are better off when risk is richly rewarded," *Austin American-Statesman*, August 24, 2011, p. A9.

take a much stronger stance on government's role in their economy as a defensive move, if nothing else.

This book approaches these complex issues in three sections. In the first part (Chapters 1 and 2) we set the stage for the exploration of entrepreneurship in the global economy. We discuss the effects of national policies and international conditions on industrial development, and look at some factors that promote entrepreneurship. We also discuss regional innovation clusters and the nature of the Silicon Valley model in promoting entrepreneurial success.

In the second part of the book (Chapters 3 to 9) we present the stories of entrepreneurs who successfully mastered the complexities of international operations. We draw our examples from various industries, and cover businesses created both in the US and in other countries, including successful startups in China founded by US-trained entrepreneurs and a startup in Israel. Some are based on innovative technologies while others involve bringing new services, enabled by new technologies, to the market. Each of these companies provides lessons that bear on the success of new companies in the global market. At the end of each chapter, we offer comments on the key success factors of the company or companies involved. We hope these analyses will be helpful to other ambitious entrepreneurs.

Each of the companies we discuss exemplifies Schumpeter's definition of the entrepreneur in that it opened a new market. Of course, the scale and impact of these businesses varied greatly. Some companies, such as SanDisk and Transammonia, became multibillion-dollar enterprises; others had smaller revenues. However, all represented businesses that changed the landscape in their market sector.

We begin with David Sarnoff, an entrepreneur of an earlier generation who ranks among the first of the great entrepreneurs of the electronic age. In Chapter 3 we describe how he built RCA into a dominant electronics company, and created the radio and television broadcast industry. He also set the pace for managing intellectual property as a key foundation for corporate success in the electronic age.

In Chapter 4 we discuss Ron Stanton and the founding of Transammonia, a leading international commodity trading company. He built a big global company on the basis of an innovative business model rather than a novel technology.

Chapter 5 focuses on RMI, a Silicon Valley startup that pioneered a new family of computing processing chips to greatly improve the data capacity of communication networks. Its initial success came from developing the market in Asia. This example of entrepreneurship evolved over two generations of CEOs, starting with a visionary founder, Atiq Raza, followed by Behrooz Abdi, an outstanding executive who possessed a remarkable combination of technological and managerial skills.

The story of SanDisk and its founder Eli Harari, told in Chapter 6, demonstrates how an outstanding entrepreneur can adapt truly innovative technology to create a whole new industry segment. The Silicon Valley company is a world leader in flash memories. It is equally notable for the exceptional skill with which it developed and managed intellectual property, and for how it addressed the problem of low-cost manufacturing in a highly capital-intensive industry by partnering with Toshiba, a Japanese company.

Chapter 7 discusses Ness Technologies, an information technology services company that was started up in Israel and became a successful global provider. It was selected for discussion because it illustrates the importance of building an international corporate culture. Raviv Zoller, the entrepreneur who launched the company, built an organization that was able to operate in many countries, and could leverage resources from Israel and elsewhere to deliver an outstanding level of service in all geographies.

By covering three China-based startups, Chapter 8 demonstrates that there is a role for venture-capital-backed entrepreneurship, even in a huge state-controlled economy. It also shows that there are ground rules for operating companies in this environment that entrepreneurs must learn if they are to be successful. Two of these startups prospered as independent companies and became publicly traded on NASDAQ. The third was acquired by a local company.

Chapter 9 discusses Aicent, a Silicon Valley company founded by Lynn Liu, an entrepreneur born in Taiwan and educated in the US. This company's success was not built on inventing technology but on providing a mission-critical service to the global wireless telecommunications industry. Aicent also serves as a model for companies with their origins in the US, but destined from the start to go global. It was focused on Asia, where it became a dominant player in its niche market.

As we discuss what it takes for entrepreneurs with global ambitions to succeed in the current economic and political environment, it becomes evident that the hurdles they face are higher than ever. This translates into the requirement for more capital to build valuable businesses and perhaps lower chances for building big businesses with private capital. The companies that we selected made it, but how often will others follow? A fair question is whether privately funded entrepreneurship can be counted on in the future as an important engine for growth based on innovations. This would leave governments as the most important patrons for building innovative new industries.

This is the subject of our concluding Chapter 10. We believe that the answer lies in between the views propounded by pure free-market advocates on one extreme, and by proponents of state control on the other. History has shown that, while governments are not equipped to drive innovation into the market, neither can entrepreneurs operate in a state-free vacuum. Or, to put it in positive terms, governments play an important role in industrial development, but they are no substitute for the ambitious entrepreneur provided with the right level of resources and a dependable legal environment.

1 Government: Boss, financial partner, regulator – Entrepreneurs in mixed economies

> Nothing has been more important since the beginning of my reign than increasing the prosperity of my people. The introduction of certain new manufacturing industries ... enables thousands of my people to gain their bread honorably, the raw material stays in the country ... and my subjects can easily pay their taxes. While previously money left the country, it now stays within, making the country richer and more populated. Leopold I, Emperor of Austria (1640–1705)[1]

We quote Emperor Leopold here because his touching concern for his subjects' welfare (and their ability to pay their taxes) communicates a clear message: the government needs to play a big role in expanding his country's economy. Instead of issuing a proclamation encouraging local entrepreneurs to innovate, he instituted an active policy, backed by state funds, to create important new industries. The idea of depending solely on local entrepreneurs to build such industries would not have entered his head.

Leopold was neither the first nor, certainly, the last head of state to hold such views. Rulers of his era were well aware that building a country's economic prosperity had the desirable side-effect of increasing its power in international affairs, and many acted on that realization. In the late 1600s Sir Walter Raleigh observed, "Whosoever commands the sea, commands the trade, whosoever commands the trade of the world commands the riches of the world and consequently the world itself."[2] As a result, the competitive race

---

[1] J. Berenger, *Histoire de l'empire des Habsbourg 1273–1918* (Paris: Librairie Arthème Fayard, 1990), p. 331.
[2] A. Herman, *To rule the waves* (New York: HarperCollins, 2004), p. 150.

to industrialize and sustain national trade advantages was a constant source of international friction, sometimes leading to war.

Statesmen have been involving themselves in their countries' economies for centuries. They know that building and maintaining a healthy industrial base is the key to growing national wealth and sustaining prosperity. They are not about to leave the outcome of this high-stakes game to chance. Naturally, the economic purists who advocate totally free markets are perpetually distressed by this state of affairs.

But these purists ignore the lessons of history. Free enterprise cannot prosper without the infrastructure, investments, and rule of law that government provides. Likewise, governments sabotage economic growth – and their global influence in the bargain – when they try to impose too many controls on business, or establish rigid plans for its direction.

In other words, government and entrepreneurs need each other. This does not imply that Emperor Leopold's command-and-control mode of economic planning is a model for our times. Economies have evolved toward more open, mixed systems with complex interplay between the public and private sectors. Entrepreneurs may exploit opportunities to build new companies or industries, but governments still play a major role in charting the overall course of an economy and supporting its growth. The only "pure" systems are failed systems. Plenty of evidence is available to back this up.

HISTORICAL ANTECEDENTS

National economic development programs have historically relied on several stratagems:

- investments in education and infrastructure;
- subsidies for exporters;
- state funding to help or even create new companies;
- erection of trade barriers to limit imports;
- establishment of local monopolies or cartels to reduce domestic competition and increase the ability to export.

This is as true for free-market countries as for nations with controlled economies. A nation's official commitment to free enterprise has never stood in the way of a little cheating to help its preferred industries.

For entrepreneurs, such government involvement – or "meddling," as the purists would have it – is a decidedly mixed blessing. Government influence over the economy can have a decisive impact on the success of individual ventures, and decisions made at the highest levels can foster or stifle entrepreneurial efforts.

Problems usually start for entrepreneurs when political leaders are looking to jump-start their country's industrialization process. Politicians typically believe that national programs to promote rapid industrial development (and exports) work faster than independent entrepreneurial enterprises acting in their own perceived best interests.

It follows that the establishment of state-owned corporations to address critical industrial needs has been a recurring theme in countries that are seeking to accelerate their industrialization. Clearly, the heads of these state-owned enterprises are bureaucrats, not entrepreneurs, in the context of our discussion.

But real entrepreneurs who build new industries with direct or indirect state help have also emerged in most industrializing countries. Entrepreneurs have learned to live with whatever hand the government deals them and find ways to prosper, which is part of the definition of being an entrepreneur.

For example, during Leopold's reign Austria began producing textiles and arms in privately owned factories. At the start of the process, the country lacked the knowledge and expertise to build and operate these industries. So it set about attracting the talent it needed.

Its appeal was simple. The government promised to grant local monopolies, place import restrictions on competitive products, and give business people access to some state capital to establish their industries. These incentives lured experienced entrepreneurs and skilled technicians from elsewhere to set up shop in Austria. If you were an entrepreneur, seventeenth-century Austria was a good place to be, not in spite of government meddling, but because of it.

England, the birthplace of the Industrial Revolution, may have led the way in the race to industrialize in the seventeenth and eighteenth centuries, but over the next 200 years its increasing prosperity encouraged others to follow its example. France, the US, Germany, Russia, Japan, and other countries industrialized in turn, each at its own pace, and with varying degrees of government oversight and support.

Since the 1960s it has been the turn of Asian countries to join the ranks of industrialized nations, and they have done so with a high level of government involvement. These newcomers have learned from history, and have no hesitation in using aggressive national economic strategies to hasten their growth. China, India, South Korea, and Taiwan have all emerged as industrial powers, with exports that compete successfully with the most sophisticated products of the developed world. Their emergence has revolutionized the world economy and trade patterns.

China has been the most closely watched of all the Asian success stories, because of both its size and its extraordinary industrial progress. It launched its industrial program in earnest only in the late 1970s, but by 2010 it moved from the back bench to second place in the world economy, displacing Japan. It now has prospects of surpassing even the US.

China's industrialization process has been a forced march, controlled by an omnipotent Communist Party. Individual entrepreneurship has played a minor role. The term "state capitalism" has been applied to the current Chinese model because of its combination of state and private capital. But this policy is actually a modern form of an old system called mercantilism. It should be seen in that context.

Early mercantilism

Mercantilism has a long history. The term is commonly applied to national economic policies that encourage exports and discourage imports. The ultimate goal is to produce a trade surplus. Such policies were roundly condemned as long ago as 1776 by Adam Smith in *The Wealth of Nations.*

Smith advocated free trade of complementary products among nations. But as we have already noted, very few statesmen are willing to leave economic development hostage to the vagaries of the free market when vital national interests are at stake.

Mercantilism as a policy was widely practiced from the seventeenth to the nineteenth century, particularly as countries with agrarian economies sought to industrialize. It protected fledgling domestic industries from being crushed by outside competition. Governments would provide state support to build locally important industries where the market risk was very low and the technology well established. Once these industries had succeeded in replacing imported products, the state could then promote exports and hopefully generate a trade surplus.

Does this sound familiar? It should. Classic mercantilism bears a striking resemblance to policies being pursued by developing countries to this day, including China.

Colbert launches modern French industry

Mercantilist policy was first deployed on a large scale by Jean-Baptiste Colbert (1619–1683), finance minister of France for twenty-two years under Louis XIV.

Leopold I expressed pride in the growing prosperity of his Austrian subjects. Whether Colbert worried much about the welfare of his fellow Frenchmen is highly debatable. What is certain is that Colbert's big problem was financing the aggressive wars of his king.[3]

Four years after Louis XIV personally took over the reins of government in 1661, he chose Colbert to rescue France from near

---

[3] For a summary of Colbert's career and influence, see I. Murat, *Colbert* (Paris: Librairie Arthème Fayard, 1980), pp. 225–263.

bankruptcy, mostly brought on by previous military adventures. But this did not stop the "Sun King" from enmeshing France in conflicts of his own making. In the succeeding fifty years of his reign France was involved in three major and two minor wars, creating a nearly constant need for cash.

During this era soldiers and foreign allies had to be paid in gold and silver. Since France lacked mines for precious metals, the only way to accumulate bullion was by building a trade surplus, and the structure of the economy made that impossible. French industry was underdeveloped and backward, in the hands of small craft enterprises that simply could not compete in international markets.

Colbert decided to fix the problem by building industries such as glass and textile manufacturing. His plan was to restrict competitive imports and promote exports of exceptionally fine products. In this way he could generate a trade surplus that would bring a net inflow of foreign gold and silver into France.

Ruthless, determined, able, and in full control of the finances of France, he poached craftsmen and entrepreneurs from various countries by offering highly attractive incentives to set up shop in France. Many of the resulting businesses were granted "Royal Privilege," which meant that they received state funding, paid no taxes, and were guaranteed government orders for their products.

Colbert expected that such new businesses would become independent of state support as their products became commercially successful. But this was a slow process. He was known to complain of continuing demands by entrepreneurs for new funds to cover operating losses. If you were a favored entrepreneur in Colbert's France, you did very well. Why not hold onto your perks as long as you could?

The new companies built large factories with over 1,000 workers – something new in France at the time. Their workers lived in dormitories and were paid minimal wages. The working day was between fourteen and sixteen hours, and the only days off were religious holidays. Colbert complained to the Roman Catholic authorities that there were simply too many of those.

Labor was cheap because France was blessed, if that is the word, with a large population and significant unemployment in its rural economy. Colbert had enough foresight to ensure a continued supply of cheap labor by encouraging early marriages – women were expected to marry before the age of twenty.

Having pirated technical expertise from other countries, Colbert worried about losing what our era calls "intellectual property" by the same means. He took draconian steps to prevent it. Once in France, skilled craftsmen could not leave the country. Severe punishments awaited those caught fleeing – from a sentence of rowing in one of the King's galleys to the death penalty.

For Colbert's program to succeed, French products had to win international customers. To ensure that the new industries produced the highest quality goods, Colbert established a corps of state-funded industrial inspectors who were tasked with checking the quality of products. Delinquent producers were penalized and publicly punished for repeated lapses in quality.

At the same time he made sure that the industries he was building were protected from outside competition until they were ready to compete in the international market. For example, the importing of Venetian glass was forbidden in 1672. And woe to the entrepreneur who attempted to evade his trade and quality controls. His technocrats were said to have had over 15,000 small entrepreneurs executed for the crime of importing or manufacturing cotton cloth in violation of French law.

Colbert did not limit his attention to manufacturing. He was also anxious to compete with the Dutch in international trade, which they dominated. To that end Colbert promoted the construction of a merchant navy, and gave preference to its ships for French trade. To discourage competitive transport, high fees were placed on foreign vessels visiting French ports.

By most measures Jean-Baptiste Colbert was a thoroughly nasty man, widely hated within and outside France. But he launched the country on the path of large-scale industrialization. Under his compulsion French industry became renowned for its quality, particularly in such luxury products as silk fabrics, tapestries, and fine glass. In these areas French products came to surpass any goods previously available on the international market.

Many famous company names in France date from this era, including the tapestry maker Gobelin and the glass maker Saint-Gobain. In 1688 a Venetian ambassador wrote that "such is the quality of the French products that they are the best in the world and attract orders from all countries." Colbert's policies were successful in at least sustaining the finances of France in spite of the country's being in an almost continuous state of warfare.

Colbert's basic approach held sway in France for some time after his death. In the eighteenth century French industry benefited from government attempts to attract English technicians and entrepreneurs. France sent agents on undercover missions to England to recruit people and collect commercial secrets, particularly those dealing with production machinery and metallurgical processes. For example, the first English steam engines were secretly imported into France.

In 1779 the ice between France and England thawed considerably as the two countries signed agreements allowing the French to import steam engines openly. Bilateral agreements covering other products were also negotiated, but true free trade was far in the future. Entrepreneurs who followed the rules had done well under tight government control, but free trade was something better to look forward to.[4]

In fact, it was in 1846 that England led the way to a national free-trade policy by removing the restrictive Corn Laws and easing its control of the export of advanced technology. By the 1860s practically all restrictions on imports were gone. At that time England

---

[4] This presentation draws on the wealth of historical information found in J.-C. Asselain, *Histoire économique de la France du XVIII siècle à nos jours* (Paris: Éditions du Seuil, 1985), pp. 77–105; A. Malet and J. Isaac, *XVII and XVIII Siècle* (Paris: Librairie Hachette, 1923), pp. 190–194; and Murat, *Colbert*, pp. 249–261.

had such a huge industrial lead on other countries that it could afford to be generous and open its market. It did not anticipate that imports would ever threaten domestic industry. Other countries trying to catch up continued to play by more restrictive trading rules – and are doing so still.

MODERN MERCANTILISM

You might ask why we are spending so much time on mercantilism and its history in a book on the modern global entrepreneur. The simple answer is that today's entrepreneurs operate in a world where governments increasingly control economies, a defining feature of mercantilism over the centuries and one that will not disappear quickly.

This reality shapes the economic decisions made by business people and entrepreneurs as they seek markets and business partners in countries with diverse economic agendas. To fully understand its implications, it is necessary to see it in a historical perspective.

For the same reason we must also take some time to discuss China, by far the most prominent of modern countries with controlled economies. China has the second largest – and fastest growing – economy in the world. What happens there, in consumer or industrial markets, has a huge impact on the direction of all global business.

Industrializing Asia

We are witnessing an economic revolution in Asia, affecting billions of people. Countries in that region are striving to industrialize as quickly as possible. Given the pressure to make rapid progress and the top-down structure of many of their economies, it is not surprising that Asian countries would adopt mercantilist methods.

Indeed, we are living in the golden age of broadly defined mercantilism. It is currently being practiced in a highly developed form, on a scale unprecedented in history, by China. The world's most populous country has embarked on a path to industrialization that in some ways mirrors the journey of France under Colbert, using some of the same strategies. Its astonishing success has prompted other countries to learn from its example and shape their trade policies accordingly.

Long relegated to the ranks of a "third-world" country with a primarily agrarian economy, China has vaulted into a position of economic leadership in just forty years. The ruling Communist Party still controls the land, much of the economy, the military, foreign policy, and whatever else is of major importance to the country. But the highly pragmatic Party has abandoned some communist practices and embraced a number of capitalist methods without relinquishing political control.

Perhaps the biggest difference between China and the developed West is that the state owns all of the country's banks, either in part or in whole. It also controls their activities, and can therefore channel capital to meet its industrial objectives.[5] China's reluctance to allow banks to operate outside of government control is as much a matter of history as it is of ideology. The country suffered through a long period of weakness and foreign intervention, and its government is determined to keep it free of foreign economic domination.[6]

Within China the most obvious sign of the success of these policies is plain to see. Visitors are frequently amazed at the quality and quantity of public facilities that have been built in the past couple of decades. Indeed, the development of a modern infrastructure is a key element of comprehensive state plans for industrial development.

Of course the government of China had some powerful advantages in its rapid construction of the infrastructure to support a modern economy. In addition to absolute control of the country's

---

[5] For an excellent review of the Party's role, see D. Shambaugh, *China's Communist Party: Atrophy and adaptation* (San Francisco, CA: University of California Press, 2010). Also, R. McGregor, *The Party: The secret world of China's Communist rulers* (New York: HarperCollins, 2010).

[6] H. Jones, *Chinamerica: Why the future of America is China* (New York: McGraw-Hill, 2010) contains a good overview of Chinese economic practices and policies.

finances, the government owns all the land. Hence it can develop roads, airports, railways, and public structures without the legal restrictions found in countries where land is in private hands. It can also set arbitrarily low lease rates for land to stimulate the building of factories and other facilities wherever and by whomever it chooses.

China's emergence as an economic power is not accidental. It is based on long-term development plans drawn up by government authorities in order to

- preserve Chinese control over key domestic industries and the economy;
- promote exports and create a trade surplus;
- acquire modern technology; and
- build a domestic industrial base capable of innovation.

Developing nations are watching China's amazing progress very closely. As more countries adopt various aspects of its approach, entrepreneurs in the global marketplace will have to make adjustments to economic systems in which mercantilism is flying high and the government is in the pilot's seat. It is worth looking more closely at what they face in China, and may encounter in the other countries that it influences.

Mixed ownership, tight control

China's economic policy permits a mix of ownership models: privately owned businesses, joint ventures with foreign investors and corporations, and businesses that are fully government owned and funded. Regardless of ownership, foreign trade by all of these businesses is controlled by the government. Needless to say in a country where the currency is tightly regulated, access to foreign exchange is also strictly controlled.

Some businesses in non-strategic consumer industries, such as textiles, services, and retail, may be fully owned by foreign investors, but restrictions exist on investment and capital repatriation. Large companies in industries deemed critical, including telecommunications services and banking, are either fully government-owned or have majority government ownership. Even when these vital companies are publicly traded, the government maintains significant ownership and ultimate control.

Fifty-four state-owned enterprises, including China Mobile, Petro China, Sinopec, and China Electronics Corporation (CEC), are considered "backbone" companies. To get an idea of the scale and scope of these enterprises, consider the fact that CEC, which was established only in 1989, today has 70,000 employees.

While control remains with the parent company, CEC owns fourteen subsidiaries that are publicly listed and have some degree of public ownership. These businesses cover software, computers and computer components, and consumer electronics products. Some of these companies rank among the world leaders in their product categories. They include joint ventures with foreign companies such as HP, IBM, and Philips who contribute their technology. With revenues in excess of $10 billion annually, CEC is a big technology conglomerate with the resources to address new business areas.

As would be expected in such an economy, exporting for the purpose of acquiring foreign exchange is a key objective of state planners. In this they have been markedly successful. Much to the chagrin of its trading partners, China runs a large trade surplus. A major reason for this success is the number of foreign companies that have moved their production to China. The products from these transplanted factories are exported under their original brand names.

Like Colbert's France, China's government offers significant incentives to attract foreign manufacturing: a modern infrastructure, a disciplined low-cost labor force, and significant financial inducements for companies that locate factories in areas of the country designated for development. It is enough to convince many companies that previously manufactured in Europe, Japan, or the US to move their equipment into Chinese plants.

China benefits from its new status as the world's factory in three ways.

- Transplanted manufacturing plants churn out products for which there is already worldwide demand, building exports at minimum risk.
- These plants provide employment for many millions of Chinese workers.
- Last but not least, they bring the latest technology into China, helping it acquire the skills and knowledge to compete on its own in the international market.

By some estimates as much as 70 percent of the exported products from China are from such transplanted manufacturing plants.

To take one prominent example, most Apple® products are assembled in China, using imported and locally manufactured components. In some cases the factories where they are produced are joint ventures with local companies; in other cases the manufacturing is done by contractors such as Foxconn. Either way, it is estimated that over 100,000 workers are employed in manufacturing Apple products alone. These wildly popular products are sold worldwide under the Apple brand, helping boost China's burgeoning trade surplus.

Foxconn, a huge company ($80 billion of annual revenues in 2009) of Taiwanese origin, exemplifies the importance of transplants to the development of China's economy and its workforce. Foxconn is a contract manufacturer of electronic products not only for Apple, but for HP and other major international brands.

The company has built virtual dormitory cities for its Chinese workers. One such location, in Shenzhen, houses over 300,000 workers in a sprawling compound. Since factories draw their low-wage workers from rural areas, owners have to provide the workers with access to affordable housing near the plants.

Building domestic industries

Infrastructure, employment, exports: all are prerequisites for a modern industrial economy. But other bricks are needed to build a stable industrial base. While transplants contribute to growth, they are no substitute for home-grown industry.

China's leaders, anxious to make sure that foreigners do not control key industries, made the development of domestic industry a state policy, as one analyst has noted. "In the late 1990s increasing dependence on foreign companies led Beijing to build strong national industries in the protected shell of the domestic market. But then excess capacity and reliance on foreign consumer markets impelled Beijing to strive to make its national champions truly global and to back them with an assertive trade policy."[7]

Its success in turning these companies into effective global competitors was and is helped by the use of foreign-developed technology from foreign firms seeking access to the potentially large Chinese market. Since many are restricted from doing business on their own in industries deemed critical to the state, foreign companies have to participate in joint ventures within China, which involves a sharing of their expertise.

It works like this. As noted above, China may allow minority foreign ownership in a China-based company. There is a better chance of this happening if the local company can acquire state-of-the-art technology as part of the deal. In this scenario foreigners benefit economically from the domestic market, but without having total control of the venture or of their intellectual property.

For example, GE has made minority investments in local companies that produce wind turbines for power generation – an industry that Chinese authorities deem critical as they seek to build world leadership in this new technology. GE is expected to contribute its own technology to the joint venture.[8]

Chinese authorities have also targeted electric automobiles as a crucial product for the country's industrial future. Here, too, they are looking to foreign firms for technology that could give them a leadership position. "China's government is considering plans that could force foreign auto makers to hand over cutting-edge electronic-vehicle technology to Chinese companies in exchange for

[7] J. Holsiag, "China's flexing of its muscles is a sign of weakness," *Financial Times*, September 28, 2010, p. 13.

[8] See P. Glader, "GE in China wind-power venture," *The Wall Street Journal*, September 28, 2010, p. B3.

access to the nation's huge market, international auto executives say."[9]

But the imported technology does not generate products strictly for domestic consumption. For example, Japanese and European companies that pioneered high-speed train technology and shared it with Chinese companies are now facing competition from the Chinese products in international markets.[10]

Overseas companies find access to China's immense and increasingly affluent market a powerful argument for sharing their expertise, but the country needs to develop its own technology if it is to build a competitive industrial sector. To that end, government planners are working to generate domestic innovation by funding research institutes and universities.

In addition, the authorities are pushing local companies to invest in research and development. This investment rose from 0.5 percent in 2004 to 1.8 percent in 2009. When a new industrial activity needs to be developed to meet a market need, state funds are available and every effort is made to build plants for mass production. This ensures that new technologies are not neglected.[11] China now ranks among the top four largest generators of patents after the US, Japan, and Germany.[12]

The effort is paying off. Some newly created corporations in technology sectors have already become world leaders. For example, Huawei Technologies, established in 1988, is now one of the leading manufacturers of advanced telecommunications and networking equipment, with over \$30 billion in annual sales in 2011. Huawei successfully competes globally against established vendors such as Alcatel-Lucent and Ericsson.

[9] N. Shirouzu, "China spooks auto makers," *The Wall Street Journal*, September 17, 2010, p. A1.

[10] N. Shirouzu, "Train makers rail against China's high-speed designs", *The Wall Street Journal*, November 18, 2010, p. A1.

[11] J. Dean, A. Browne, and S. Oster, "China's state capitalism sparks a global backlash," *The Wall Street Journal*, November 16, 2010, p. A1.

[12] *IEEE Spectrum*, July 2011, p. 68.

Follow the leader

You can debate whether a top-down, controlled economy can continue to prosper into the indefinite future. It is easy enough to point to basic weaknesses including a neglect of environmental conditions and overbuilding of certain industries. We can point to plenty of examples in other countries where bureaucratic incompetence sooner or later impedes progress.

However, the emergence of China has changed global trade patterns. It is hard to think of an industry that is not affected by competitors from China or by the promise of sales of its products to China. Hence the importance of China to entrepreneurs with ambitions to become global players.

China's success also encourages other industrializing countries such as Malaysia, India, Brazil, Thailand, and Vietnam to step up their own national initiatives to woo manufacturing sites from the developed countries with subsidies and other incentives.

Vietnam's case is especially interesting. It too is a country controlled by a monolithic Communist Party but open to foreign capital and technology importation. Foreigners are investing in the country, setting up factories that once upon a time would have gone to China. Two-thirds of the economy is now in private hands (but with state supervision); the remaining third consists of state-owned corporations in industries deemed vital by the authorities. In general terms Vietnam is closely emulating the Chinese model.

However, the government is dealing with the same problem that has bedeviled other mercantilist countries, starting with Colbert's France: state-owned companies can easily become unprofitable, forcing taxpayers to cover their losses. This has been the case with the Vietnam Shipbuilding Industries Group, which ran up multi-billion dollar debts while its operating losses ballooned.[13]

---

[13] J. Hookway and P. Barta, "A troubled state flagship makes waves in Vietnam," *The Wall Street Journal*, September 22, 2010, p. C1.

In spite of this risk, the model of combined state and private ownership is spreading. For example, Brazil is funding the construction of dams to generate power through such companies. A dam built to generate 11,200 megawatts, begun in 2010, is 49 percent owned by the government-controlled Eletrobras. Its total cost will be BRL 20 billion. The rest of the funds came from non-direct state sources and private investors. The demand for power is stimulating the interest of investors, with the government coming in when such generating capacity or transmission needs are not met by private capital.[14]

Heavy-handed government doctoring of the economy, administered with an (un)healthy dose of good old-fashioned mercantilism, can act as a quick tonic for an underdeveloped industrial sector. It is not only developing countries that are tempted to self-medicate in this way. In developed countries where jobs are disappearing, disgruntled citizens are alarmed, and political pressure is building to "do something," politicians are equally susceptible to the lure of more government intervention. We return to this subject in Chapter 10.

Among the public, a commitment to free trade is usually the first victim of the malaise. The call for tariffs to deter low-cost imports has become ever louder in countries that, like the US, have suffered a loss of industry. A recent survey shows a marked deterioration in US public opinion regarding free trade agreements, according to *The Wall Street Journal*. In 1999, only about 30 percent of the people polled believed that free-trade agreements hurt the US economy, while in 2010 over 50 percent thought such agreements hurt the country. Even more significant is that only about 15 percent of the people believed that such agreements were helpful.[15]

Given this level of disapproval on the part of the public, we should not wonder if politicians engage in ever louder saber-rattling over tariffs and trade deficits in the coming years.

---

[14] P. Winterstein, "Brazil power will still see state pressure under Roussseff," *Dow Jones Newswires*, September 2010.

[15] S. Murray and D. Belkin, "Americans sour on trade: Majority say free trade pacts have hurt the US" *The Wall Street Journal*, October 4, 2010, p. A1.

IMPLICATIONS FOR ENTREPRENEURSHIP

The changing world economic order has enormous implications for entrepreneurs everywhere. The greater the degree of government control and willingness to finance and protect industries, the harder the task is for independent entrepreneurs reliant on private funding. Such policies affect access to markets and capital. And, most troublesome, government-protected competitors can behave irrationally, as they are not subject to normal market forces.

We live in a world where the fastest-growing economy is the one where the government has the most control. This has encouraged other governments to become more involved in their economies in the hope of encouraging competitive new industries and defending established ones. Ours is also a time when trade barriers are likely to grow.

How do entrepreneurs feel about building their businesses in this environment? It depends on where they are, and where the best market for their products is located. We look first of all at the effects on a Chinese entrepreneur.

While China's planners are not dependent on domestic entrepreneurs to build the country's economic muscle, there is ample opportunity for entrepreneurship in industrial sectors that don't compete head-on with state enterprises. There is even a growing venture capital industry there to finance such new businesses. Some of this activity is financed by foreign capital looking for high returns in a fast-growing economy.

Indeed there are investment opportunities available. A growing number of independent entrepreneurs, as opposed to state-appointed managers, are now creating big businesses. For example, the largest group of Chinese electronics retail stores, Gome, was started by a private entrepreneur. He was reputed to be the richest man in China after the company had a public offering of its securities in the Hong Kong exchange. We will discuss three other Chinese startups in Chapter 8.

As an independent entrepreneur in China, you would welcome the government's financial help. In fact, a survey of entrepreneurs in China suggests that many count on some kind of government support for their success.[16] But you would have to learn to deal with state planning policies.

For example, 2010 was the last year of a national Five Year Plan that called for a 20 percent reduction in energy use per unit of GDP to reduce pollution. As a result, if you are an entrepreneur running an energy-intensive manufacturing business, you might find that the power available to your factory has been reduced or even shut down by the local power utility. Such cutbacks actually occurred in 2010, reducing the production of materials such as polysilicon used to manufacture solar cells.

Your only alternative would be to buy diesel-powered electrical generators. Of course, their exhausts will add to air pollution – directly negating the intent of the Five Year Plan. But that is not your problem.

Now, let us imagine that you are an entrepreneur in the US. You are likely to wish for freedom from all government interference. Here is a classic statement of this position from two US entrepreneurs, published as a letter to the editor in *The Wall Street Journal*: "In our experience [as entrepreneurs] the very last group we would appeal to for help with a new venture would be a federal bureaucrat. We thus feel the best way to revive the US economy and revitalize the past ability to innovate would be to cut government spending, regulation, and taxation."[17]

While such total independence is praiseworthy in principle, it simply isn't practical in the real world. Entrepreneurs aiming to build major enterprises have no choice but to have a global strategy and they cannot do it just on the merits of their products. This

---

[16] R. Steeter, "Asian entrepreneurs are bullish on the future," *The Wall Street Journal*, August 6, 2010, p. A13.

[17] Letter to the editor by R. Gamblin and K. Borgh, *The Wall Street Journal*, September 18, 2010, p. A14.

means they may have to accept from the US government such "help" as tax rebates, licenses, access to loans, or financial assistance with exports if they are to succeed.

For example, if you want to sell your products in a country where government restrictions limit imports, you will certainly welcome US government help in opening such markets. You will also be happy to accept its help in protecting your intellectual property. And you will also welcome new business opportunities created by government mandates.

Here is an interesting example of how a US government mandate helped launch a new business. Telnet was arguably the first commercial packet switching network service provider. In the mid-1970s, it started offering dial-up modem access to central packet switches that provided email and, later, file transfer services.

Telnet subscribers accessed these services through local wire-line telephone networks, which created a problem. In some states the telephone rates are flat or fixed, while in other states they are priced on usage. There were long holding times for data sessions, amounting to tens of minutes or even hours, and customers who paid by usage complained about their charges. Telnet lobbied for relief with the Federal Communications Commission (FCC).

Eventually the FCC created what it called Special Access, which mandates that third-party service providers can pay the local telephone carrier to provide space in the telephone end office for their equipment (modems, multiplexers, routers, and management equipment). In return they got local phone numbers at that end office and a flat rate for these services. AOL was arguably the most successful of all Internet service providers in exploiting special access, mailing tens of millions of CDs to potential customers, and signing up millions of subscribers.

Special access is now offered in over fifty countries around the globe, with other countries adopting what was arguably a great success in the US in stimulating novel data communication services. Today it is being used increasingly for voice communications via packet switching, a development unforeseen in the 1970s.

All of the companies that benefit from this cost structure owe a debt of gratitude to a government agency for creating it. It is an excellent example of how, instead of crying about government "interference," smart entrepreneurs learn to take advantage of such actions. They adapt in ways that allow them to profit from all opportunities, including government assistance, which support innovative business models and help pay for new technologies. That is what they have done throughout history. (We will return to these issues later in the book.)

Working with the system

Just because countries have restrictive industrial policies does not mean that there is no market in those countries for innovative products from abroad.

For example, advanced semiconductor devices essential for the manufacture of electronic products are freely imported into China and other countries that lack internal competitive resources. This policy enables new companies from other countries to build their sales at attractive prices. We will discuss one such entrepreneurial company, RMI (Chapter 5), which became a leading exporter to China of advanced chips for its communications industry. We will also discuss Aicent (Chapter 9), a Silicon Valley-based company, which sells telecommunications services in China.

It is always satisfying to declaim about freedom from government intrusion, but it should not be forgotten that, even in the US, government programs have generated opportunities that spurred the creation of major new industries. US government policies have enabled huge investment opportunities in telecommunications, the Internet, and alternative energy production, to name only the most important recent examples.[18]

---

[18] For a fuller discussion of this topic see H. Kressel and T.V. Lento, *Investing in dynamic markets: Venture capital in the digital age* (Cambridge: Cambridge University Press, 2010), especially chs. 1, 4, and 6.

In telecommunications, for example, the deregulation of the US industry in 1996 and the opening to newcomers of what was once a monopoly field enabled the formation of entrepreneurial companies that eventually grew to be worth many billions of dollars. Similar deregulatory steps in other countries also led to the growth of extremely valuable businesses in services and in advanced hardware and software products. Following deregulation, the US government played a key role in allocating wireless spectrum to companies and regulating its use. This in turn impacted the development of technology to use this spectrum in wireless communications.

The growth of the Internet is, if anything, a more striking instance of beneficial government support. Originally developed with government funding, its implementation, coupled with nearly universal access to broadband communications by consumers, enabled an almost infinite number of new businesses offering products and services on the Web. The opportunities ranged from commerce (Amazon.com, for example), to auction sites (eBay), software on demand (Salesforce.com), and social networks (Facebook.com).

Our third example of a government initiative in the US (and many other countries) that holds promise for entrepreneurs is the fostering of energy generation that uses non-fossil fuels. Hundreds of new companies have been formed to develop and manufacture solar energy sources, wind-driven generators, and biomass sources. They depend on subsidies created by government policies to insure the commercial viability of these alternative energy sources. Without government "meddling" many of these new businesses would not exist. Whether these investment opportunities are good ones depends on many factors, and we return to this subject in Chapter 10.

Of course government involvement in the economy has a downside as well as an upside. The bounty of opportunities opened through government initiative is accompanied by legal challenges with the potential to kill new businesses.

Nowhere is this more apparent than in the case of the Internet, where enormous business potential exists side by side with obstacles for entrepreneurs to overcome.

To name one such challenge, the issue of Internet privacy pits new businesses against government regulations. One of the commercial services enabled by the Internet, now being widely exploited by new entrepreneurial companies, is the ability to track the online behavior of individual consumers for the purpose of improving the ability to sell them products.

Its use is being challenged as an intrusion of privacy: "Since July 2010 at least six suits have been filed in the US District Court for the Central District of California against websites and companies that create advertising technology accusing them of installing online tracking tools that are so surreptitious that they essentially hack into users' machines without their knowledge."[19]

SUMMING UP

The world order is being fundamentally changed and entrepreneurship must adjust accordingly.

Here is a comment by one observer regarding our new situation.

> Two-thirds of the world's people live in countries that are growing fast. Unfortunately, the one-third of the world's population living in [relative] stagnation includes the US, Japan, and Western Europe, which contribute disproportionately to world GDP – for the time being. The source of the growth is the great migration from rural poverty to urban prosperity, perhaps the greatest engine of economic expansion in history. But this sort of growth implies great disruptions in the economic life of many countries; it arises from a shift in the world

---

[19] J. Valentines-DeVries and E. Steel, "Cookies cause bitter backlash: Spate of lawsuits shows user discomfort with latest innovations to online tracking technology," *The Wall Street Journal*, September 20, 2010, p. B1.

economic structure, not incremental expansion of the existing structure.[20]

Under such conditions, entrepreneurs need to learn to succeed in international markets, where each government has its own set of rules. And, rules there will be, as countries intensely compete to defend their industries and nurture new ones on the basis of innovation.

National industrial policies have historically been condemned by many people as infringing on their liberties within countries founded on the principles of "free enterprise," such as the US. Yet today political pressure in these same countries is intensifying to build import barriers, promote exports, and find new ways for governments to promote the creation of new, innovative industries to replace the mature ones that have migrated to countries with lower labor and capital costs.

This is precisely the situation in which, more than ever, we need entrepreneurs to stimulate economic growth. Calling for more entrepreneurship in an era of big government may seem counterintuitive, but it is actually the most desirable way to generate economic growth in the developed countries of the world.

In short, we need both private entrepreneurial and public initiatives to advance economic goals. In the next chapter we discuss the role of entrepreneurship in achieving that objective.

[20] D. P. Goldman, *The Macro Strategist,* from dgoldman@macrostrategy.com – September 19, 2011.

2 Standing still is not an option: On promoting entrepreneurship and economic growth

> The secret to maintaining a robust economy centers on more than
> efforts to modernize existing plants and equipment. The secret
> is creativity, allowing new firms with new ideas to rise up, while
> existing firms work every day to reinvent themselves to compete on a
> global scale.

D. S. Smick[1]

Forty years ago China had one of the most strictly controlled economies in the world, with all major businesses owned by the state.
Now the government permits private ownership of companies, and
seeks a higher level of innovation to keep its economy growing.

In other parts of the world individuals rather than politicians
and strategists are driving the creation of enterprises. One striking
outcome of the Egyptian uprising in early 2011 was the emergence
of young entrepreneurs rushing to form new businesses. It seems
that, in the aftermath of Hosni Mubarak's overthrow, the new
business registration process had become easier. So these aspiring
businesspeople, with guidance from experienced American entrepreneurs, took advantage of the opportunity and launched their own
enterprises.[2]

Before Mubarak's departure they would have faced forbidding
barriers all too common in the Middle East: copious red tape, bureaucratic foot-dragging, bribery demands from officials, and a protec-
tionist stance that worked in favor of the politically well-connected.
Many of the entrepreneurs-in-waiting would have gone abroad to

---

[1] *The world is curved: Hidden dangers to the global economy* (New York:
Portfolio/Penguin Group, 2008), p. 81.

[2] H. Seligson, "Arab Spring, start-up summer?" *The New York Times*, July 17, 2011,
p. BU1.

pursue their dreams. Now, with a government that, if not helping, was at least not hindering, they had a chance to control their economic destinies in their home country and help build a new, more prosperous Egypt.

There is no question that the "Arab Spring" uprisings were fueled at least in part by public resentment over stalled economies. Barely a year before the Middle East exploded in revolt, Ahmed Mohammed Lukman, Director General of the Cairo-based Arab Labour Organisation and a top labor expert, warned that regional unemployment, which had been rising for years, had "reached an alarming level, exceeding 20 million people."[3] This amounted to a 17 percent unemployment rate. Educated young people made up 26 percent of the total. It is not surprising that when the winds of freedom began to blow through Cairo's ancient streets, many of the protesters who assembled in Tahrir Square to demand regime change were young people without jobs or prospects. While it is too early to say if the Arab Spring will produce any lasting effect, it holds out the promise of more open governments and increased economic opportunity for the people of the Arab world. It also highlights a couple of facts about the age we live in.

First, the global economy is moving so fast that standing still means falling behind. Unfortunately for governments that resist change, economic stagnation is a sure formula for producing popular unrest. People won't tolerate declines in their economic wellbeing for very long.

Second, no country can afford to ignore the value created by entrepreneurs. Even in Cairo, hardly a hotbed of pro-American sentiment, young Egyptians looked to American-style entrepreneurism as a remedy for their country's economic ills. Total government control of the economy had failed them, and they decided to become

---

[3] Nadim Kawach, "Arab unemployment at alarming levels: ALO," www. emirates247.com, December 6, 2009.

entrepreneurs, agents of change and innovation who could spur the creation of dynamic businesses.

Their faith is not misplaced. Entrepreneurs can have significant economic impact. In this chapter we will survey the positive effect entrepreneurial innovations have had on job creation and GDP growth in the US. Then we will explore the conditions that create and support an entrepreneurial culture, including funding sources and regional centers of innovation. We will also discuss intellectual property management and certain government regulations and activities that affect international business operations.

ENTREPRENEURSHIP AND INNOVATION

Many countries are in a race to build and maintain industries that can compete successfully in international markets. With the emergence of the Asia-Pacific countries, the race is hotter than ever, and the stakes are huge.

Asia has taken over industries in which the developed countries once ruled supreme. As a result, developed countries must create the industries of tomorrow and get their economies growing. But the newcomers are trying to find the same magic formula so that they can keep their own momentum going. Everybody knows what is needed. The challenge lies in its execution.

Technology industries help to drive GDP growth

That magic formula has to include a heavy dose of new technology, which seeds industrial growth. Sooner or later all technology becomes either a commodity or obsolete. Commodities don't spur growth, and industries built around obsolete technology eventually have to be replaced – preferably by something developed domestically. This is the process of "creative destruction" as described by economist Joseph Schumpeter.

Several studies bear out the economic importance of new technology. For example, several years ago, in the wake of the "dot-com" crash of 2000–2001, the consulting group Global Insight analyzed

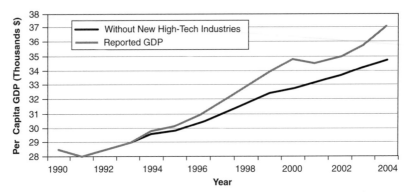

FIGURE 2.1 GDP of the US with and without new technology industries between 1990 and 2004 (ref. 4).

the impact of high-technology industry on per capita GDP in the US between 1990 and 2004.[4] As Figure 2.1 shows, in 2004 per capita GDP would have been about 7 percent lower without the rapid growth of the technology industries, many of which were funded by venture capital.

Increased per capita GDP implies the creation of many jobs, and other figures bear out the importance of new companies in improving the employment picture. An analysis of US census data by economists at the Kauffman Foundation shows that new companies have been the major driver for new jobs created in the US between 1980 and 2005. Nearly all net job creation has been in businesses that are less than five years old.

In the year 2007, for example, of the 12 million jobs added, 8 million were added by young companies.[5] Without these companies, the US economy would have *lost* jobs during those years – not a pleasant prospect, and one with severe political consequences. That was when massive shifts were occurring in the US manufacturing

4 "Venture impact 2004: Venture capital benefits to the US economy," www.ihsglobalinsight.com/publicDownload/genericContent/07–20–04_fullstudy.pdf (accessed May 6, 2011).

5 D. Stangler and R. E. Litan, "Where will the jobs come from?" *Kauffman Foundation Research Series: Firm foundation and economic growth,* November 2009.

base as Asian countries became industrialized. Imagine the outcry if jobs were not only being shipped overseas, but people were suffering an overall net decline in employment at the same time.

While this study proved the importance of new companies in creating jobs, it did not identify how those companies were being funded. Other evidence shows that the vast majority of new companies start with limited private funding or family loans and remain small. They generally operate in the service sector and may employ only a few people; hence their large-scale economic impact is limited in generating economic growth.[6]

Among these startups, however, are the future giants that pioneer new markets. Although relatively few new companies qualify as business innovators in the Schumpeter sense, those that do have an enormous economic impact. They are often initially backed by private venture capital, later access public markets for growth capital, and are headed by the most ambitious class of entrepreneurs. Among US technology startups that became household names are Intel, Apple Computer, Microsoft, Yahoo!, eBay, VMware, Cisco Systems, Amazon, and BEA Systems.

In addition to these giants, thousands of pioneering startups of the past few decades made major contributions by creating new markets, yet did not reach the billion-dollar revenue run rate. Many were acquired by other corporations. VMWare is a recent example. As a 1999 startup it revolutionized the computer industry, but its revenues had only reached $219 million in 2004 when it was acquired by EMC Corporation for $635 million. (VMWare revenues for 2010 were $2.8 billion.)

The study by Global Insight cited above details the contribution of venture-capital-backed companies to the US economy.

- In the period from 2000 to 2003, venture-capital-supported company employment increased by 7 percent even though the US economy as a

[6] C. Kenny, "Small isn't beautiful," *Bloomberg Businessweek*, October 3, 2011, pp. 10–11.

whole produced a net loss in US jobs. These data were collected from a total of 26,494 venture-capital-funded companies.

- These companies employed 10,130,807 people and had revenues of $1.769 trillion in 2003, representing about 15 percent of the total US GDP.
- California, the home of Silicon Valley and the biggest source of venture capital, was by far the largest beneficiary of these dynamic companies: 8,416 were located there, employing 2,470,557 workers, and boasting combined revenues of $438 billion.

These results would be welcomed by any country and its leaders. The big question is how to replicate the conditions that produced this outburst of innovation. The US, and developed nations in general, continue to search for answers to overcome fears of economic stagnation. As a recent review of the US economy noted, "Americans' worries stretch well beyond the next couple of years about stagnating living standards and a dark future in an economy slow to grow jobs, saddled with government deficits and under threat from China".[7]

Going forward, greater emphasis is needed on fostering the migration of new technology into the domestic and international marketplace through entrepreneurial activities. As one recent observer put it, "Economic success stems from ongoing innovations by a risk-taking entrepreneurial class that allows an economy to continually reinvent itself."[8]

Technology needs entrepreneurs

In his 2011 State of the Union address, President Barack Obama described what he saw as the major elements needed for economic growth: "We need to out-innovate, out-educate and out-build the rest of the world."[9]

Like his predecessor, George W. Bush, the President stressed innovation as necessary to the nation's economic health. Both

---

[7] "What's wrong with America's economy?" *The Economist*, April 30, 2011, p. 11.

[8] Smick, *The world is curved*, p. 125.

[9] "Hard choices for a soft people: The State of the Union can be stronger if government intervenes less in the economy," *Barron's*, January 31, 2011, p. 47.

leaders were correct, as far as they went. New industries cannot be developed without new technology. But in developed economies the problem of weak growth is rarely caused by a lack of new technologies. Governments fund research and development at universities and in other institutions to develop new technology, and most large corporations maintain their own product development organizations to generate the next big success.

To prove the point, consider the fact that the US invests more in R&D than any other country in the world. The level of this investment has remained between 2½ and 3 percent of GDP since about 1960. One-quarter of the total is government funded.[10]

The problem that is limiting the impact of innovations on the economy is not too little R&D; it is the inability to make more of the investment in R&D industrially productive. New technologies are being developed, but they are not making an impact on the market in the form of commercially successful new products, novel manufacturing technologies, or popular services. Competition is what drives businesses to risk new product introductions and startups play a key role as instigators for such activities.

It was the rapid migration of new technologies into products by entrepreneurial new businesses that fueled important past successes in industrial development. During the 1950s and 1960s companies in the Boston area received significant US government dollars to develop defense-related products and services. Once established, many of these companies then transitioned to commercial markets. Bose Corporation in the Boston area is a good example. The same pattern repeated itself in the 1960s and 1970s in Silicon Valley.[11]

Venture capital financed the entrepreneurs who created the industries now underpinning the digital age, and it continues to play

---

[10] Figures quoted in "Still full of ideas, but not making jobs," *The Economist*, April 30, 2011, p. 32.

[11] A. Saxenian, *Regional advantage: Culture and competition in Silicon Valley and Route 128* (Cambridge, MA: Harvard University Press, 1996) is an excellent study of the Boston area and Silicon Valley.

a key role in supporting entrepreneurship. But the task of building big businesses is becoming harder. Entrepreneurs and venture capital investors must think more broadly today. For US-based startups, for example, there was a time when just concentrating on the big US market was enough. That is no longer true. Now, startups with big ambitions need to focus on global markets in addition to the more familiar domestic ones. This means that such companies need to learn to play a much more complex competitive game in order to grow and thrive. Hence the importance of encouraging entrepreneurial efforts that are tuned to international opportunities. All of the companies selected for discussion in this book meet that criterion.

But before focusing on how to instill the global outlook that is practically a prerequisite for success, we should consider how entrepreneurs are created in the first place.

FACTORS IN PROMOTING ENTREPRENEURSHIP

It is not hard to convince skeptics of the economic value created by ambitious entrepreneurs. It is far more difficult to identify the factors that drive economically important entrepreneurship. Unfortunately there is no sure-fire formula. Though government policies and resources play a big role in encouraging and supporting entrepreneurship, they certainly aren't sufficient to make it an important economic asset. Programs to "out-innovate, out-educate, and out-build" other nations may be noble in their ambitions, but they take time, and they may not produce the desired results.

If entrepreneurial activities cannot be mandated by politicians or bureaucrats, neither can they be stimulated solely by individual ambition. Dreams of success are motivators for budding entrepreneurs, but on a more practical level they are not enough to generate broad-based value creation. In fact, there is another major determinant in attracting the most talented people into an entrepreneurial career: the cultural environment. Here the US experience can serve as a guide.

Since the 1970s Silicon Valley has been the epicenter of the entrepreneurial world, the place where some of the most successful technology companies of modern times were founded and developed. Similar innovation centers have arisen in the US and other countries in the past few decades. This is an area where the US has set the pattern and reaped the rewards.

The article from *The Economist* on worries about the American economy, cited above, crystallizes one aspect of this cultural advantage: "Are these worries justified? On the plus side, it is hard to think of any large country with as many inherent long-term advantages as America: what would China give to have Silicon Valley?"[12]

Other factors – the presence of educational institutions, the availability of capital and the level of rewards that entrepreneurs can expect for their efforts – do have an impact. However, expertise and money can be found in countries that have not had as much success as the US in generating industries based on innovative technology as a result of entrepreneurial efforts.

Cultural orientation in all its aspects seems to be a deciding factor in entrepreneurial activities. Moreover, that culture is concentrated in specific geographic areas. We will look at these so-called innovation clusters to see how they function.

Silicon Valley: Model innovation cluster

Silicon Valley developed in the 1970s, and became the recognized center of the digital revolution in the 1990s. Many people have asked what makes the Valley so special, and whether it can be replicated. I am familiar with the area because Warburg Pincus has maintained an office there for many years.[13] Several of our most successful technology companies were headquartered in the area. My personal experience persuades me that Silicon Valley boasts an unparalleled combination of talent, industrial relationships, and venture capital

---

[12] "What's wrong with America's economy?," *ibid.*

[13] When the narrative shifts to first person singular (I, me, my, mine) here and throughout this book, the speaker is Henry Kressel.

investment professionals that is extremely well adapted to fostering entrepreneurial innovation. Needless to say, I am not the first person to come to this conclusion.

We have already said that while technology forms the raw material for new industries, it is entrepreneurial innovation that actually creates them. The Valley is the living proof of this observation. While it has an enviable track record for developing new technology, it did not invent many of the fundamental breakthroughs that made its own innovations possible in the first place. Neither did the great research universities that surround the Valley, though they did contribute to the deep pool of talent that finds its way into its industries.

For example, the UNIX operating system and its offshoots and the software languages C and C++ were developed at Bell Labs in Murray Hill, New Jersey. Relational databases and reduced instruction set computers were invented at IBM Yorktown Labs, New York. Semiconductor devices and integrated circuit manufacturing were developed at Bell Labs, Western Electric, and RCA Labs (later Sarnoff Corporation). As for the Internet, while Paul Baran (Palo Alto, California), Len Kleinrock (University of California at Los Angeles), Vint Cerf (Stanford University), and Donald Davies (UK) were instrumental in its development, the project to create it was funded by DARPA, a US government agency, in 1967–1969, thanks to Larry Roberts and others of BBN (now Raytheon BBN Technologies) of Cambridge, Massachusetts, who built the original hardware platforms.

What makes Silicon Valley and the surrounding area an outstanding center of industrially valuable innovation, apart from its deep research capacity? I asked Dr. Curt Carlson, CEO of SRI International, to define its special mystique. SRI, formerly called the Stanford Research Institute, located in the heart of Silicon Valley in Palo Alto, is one of the leading independent research laboratories in the world. "In the San Francisco Bay Area there is an unusual concentration of technologists able to create compelling commercial value," Carlson noted. "These are among the most valuable professionals anywhere."

Innovation, business savvy, access to capital
Give such professionals what they need and they become driven with the ambition to create great companies. A few succeed in creating businesses that change the world. Unfortunately many more fail, but, as my partner Dr. William Janeway keeps reminding everyone, waste is an unavoidable part of the Darwinian process of creating innovative industries.

Silicon Valley's fame attracts exceptional people from around the globe to try their hand at entrepreneurship. We will meet some of these in the case histories we discuss later in the book. Those who become successful garner immense prestige in the local culture, and serve as role models for others.

Everybody there knows someone who has made money in a startup. Over the years, as the number of companies has grown, so has the pool of trained people eager to assume the risk and challenge of working in young companies in anticipation of the rewards to be gained. Most interestingly, there is no stigma for failure in the Valley, as there is in most other business centers. People who fail are credited with having undergone an educational experience, and they get a second chance. Everybody understands how risky it is to build a new company, and how important experience is to doing so successfully.

Talented young people are drawn to the region more for what it promises than for the certainty of employment. I asked a young MIT-trained engineer why he left the Boston area. "What brings you to Palo Alto?" I asked. "Did you have a job lined up here?" "No," he answered. "I've always dreamed of starting my own company and I believe that the Valley is the best place to get the right training and build the relationships I will need to get started." To tide him over until then, he found a job at Cisco.

It is not just people who relocate to Silicon Valley; some established startup companies do it too. One twenty-seven-year-old entrepreneur moved his startup software company from Boston to the Valley because the chance of being acquired there is better than it is in Boston. "Here it's happening all the time," he said, "and it's something we'd definitely consider."[14]

Another attraction of Silicon Valley is its bias toward action. In this respect the Valley is following in the footsteps of IBM. Thomas Watson Jr. said that the single most important idea that IBM tried to inculcate into its management and culture is to do something, because if you do something, you learn from it – either success or failure – but if you do nothing, you learn nothing.[15]

There is usually no shortage of good business ideas in a region that can boast of an abundance of talented scientists and engineers. But the people who combine deep technological knowledge and the business talent to build a successful company are a scarce commodity. In the Valley, however, you find a significant number of seasoned managers capable of taking companies from the startup stage to the global market.

Given the thousands of companies that have emerged in or migrated into the region, the area around San Francisco has probably the highest concentration of technology-savvy business talent in the world. What is also remarkable about the region is its leadership in developing new industrial ideas. The Internet focus is the most prominent current example.

Finally, Silicon Valley's concentration of venture capital firms has been an essential part of its economic success story from the start: good ideas get funded. In order to gain access to promising new deals, hundreds of venture capital firms small and large maintain offices in the area. When a new company needs a higher level of investment, local venture capital firms will often jointly fund it. Even foreign companies such as Siemens hire local professionals to develop sources of new technology, build relationships with local

---

[14] M. Helft, "Big tech firms pay top dollar for start-ups, when they just want the bodies," *The Global Edition of The New York Times*, May 19, 2011, p. 15.
[15] T. Watson Jr., *Father, son, and company* (New York: Bantam, 2000), p. 77.

companies, and provide investment capital. What is particularly important is that young companies can get access to substantial amounts of growth capital from local firms after a successful startup stage – an essential requirement to build valuable companies.

It all adds up to an environment where good ideas get access to capital, management talent, and international partners. By contrast, Boston-based venture capital firms are much fewer in number, with far fewer assets under management. This situation has forced those firms to set up operations in Silicon Valley, or simply to move their whole operation there.

Building an innovation cluster

Given the success of Silicon Valley, it is not surprising that other regions aspire to replicate it. While no innovation cluster comes close to it in terms of economic value created, some that have emerged in the US and overseas have produced a significant number of successful entrepreneurial companies.

How do you build an innovation cluster?[16] It takes both infrastructure, present in abundance around Silicon Valley, and cultural development. After major efforts, successful innovation clusters have emerged in the past thirty years in the US, Europe, and Asia, usually at the initiative of local government authorities.

These locations usually start with excellent universities and a concentration of specialized industry. They also benefit from supportive state organizations, a modern infrastructure, and ready access to funding sources. Once past the take-off stage, such regions attract entrepreneurs and new as well as established companies because of the ease of recruiting experienced employees and building corporate partnerships.

Successful clusters all exhibit one overriding virtue: they are self-sustaining. Competition and collaboration among local

---

[16] A number of studies of regional innovation clusters have been published under the auspices of the Council on Competitiveness, 1500 K Street, NW, Washington, DC, 20005. See www.compete.org.

organizations in a cluster enables new technologies to reach the market in the form of successful products. This activity accelerates as the cluster gets bigger, increasing the cluster's value to new and established businesses as it expands.

Relationships with the local universities likewise become a self-regenerating activity. Typically, professors become consultants. They find outlets for their creative ideas in the form of new companies or relationships with established ones, making a lot of money over and above their academic salaries. The universities reap financial rewards in the form of industry grants and participation in license income from intellectual property. This allows them to strengthen their programs, attract more students, and even bring in more professors.

Prominent long-standing clusters around universities include the Boston area (Massachusetts Institute of Technology and Harvard University); North Carolina (Duke University, University of North Carolina, and North Carolina State University); San Diego (University of California at San Diego); and Puget Sound (University of Washington). In Britain, the area around the University of Cambridge has gained a great deal of prominence.

Cluster success stories
Rochester, New York, is an interesting example of how a small city that has seen its industrial base collapse has revived its economy thanks to entrepreneurial endeavors. Rochester lost its major source of jobs through the restructuring of three major employers in rapid succession: Kodak, Xerox, and Bausch & Lomb.

In the 1970s, the city's big three accounted for 60 percent of its employment. In 2011 they employed only six percent of the workforce. The rest work for small companies, 97 percent with fewer than 100 employees. These new companies emerged in an unexpected burst of entrepreneurship, enabled by the presence of a workforce with technology skills and the participation of the University of Rochester and the Rochester Institute of Technology. Because of the turnaround, in 2011 Rochester's unemployment rate was 7.2 percent, compared to about 9 percent for the US as a whole.[17]

Chicago is another example of a region that developed an entrepreneurial cluster by leveraging its industrial base in manufacturing and financial services. The city has a long history as a trading center in commodities. It once boasted many trading organizations with outstanding communications links with the rest of the world. As these "floor"-based manual trading exchanges withered away, they were replaced by computer-based trading facilities. In many cases these used proprietary technologies developed by startup companies in the immediate area. These facilities are staffed by local computer science graduates of the University of Illinois, the University of Chicago, and the Illinois Institute of Technology. These novel business strategies require massive computer power and clever algorithms to allow ultra-high-speed trading that takes advantage of short-lived market discontinuities. Chicago's 12,000 technology companies rank it as the third largest concentration of such businesses in the US. Many of them, though small, are leaders in their niches.[18]

Other regions in the US have developed new industrial hubs that have attracted entrepreneurs and investors. These include the following: Ogden, Utah, for sports gear; Indianapolis, Indiana, for life science companies; Albany, New York, for nanotechnology; and Nashville, Tennessee, for healthcare companies.[19] In each case industry specialization is what produces value for startups and investors, because it creates a concentration of talent and access to established companies in the industry.

---

[17] "Spotlight on Rochester, NY: Small businesses saved the city. It's a model for other turnarounds," *Forbes*, July 18, 2011, p. 77.

[18] H. Weitzman, "High-tech savvy helps Chicago shrug off its rustbelt image: The way to success is letting traditional business strengths converge with technology," *Financial Times*, December 29, 2010, p. 3.

[19] E. Maltry, "Where the action is," *The Wall Street Journal*, August 22, 2011, pp. R1–R2.

But, needless to add, there is no shortage of failed attempts. For example, Las Vegas, Nevada, had a grandiose plan for the Harry Reid Research and Technology Park. Six years and $2 million in development funds later, it remains an empty 122 acre lot.[20]

The Silicon Valley model has inspired international activity. A very successful innovation cluster has developed around England's renowned Cambridge University. Having served as a consultant to the Cambridge University Investment Committee, which provides seed capital to startups based on University innovations, I can claim some personal familiarity with the area.

Since the 1970s the Cambridge area has attracted many research laboratories from companies such as Microsoft. It has also been the site of a large number of startups, which have created 250,000 new jobs in the local region since 1971. This rate of job creation is substantially larger than that of the UK as a whole.

Many of these startups were built around technology developed at the University, and a small local venture capital industry has helped to fund them.[21] Noteworthy are three world-class technology companies, each with public valuations in excess of one billion dollars, all created as a result of technology spin-offs.

ARM Holdings is the world's leading developer of intellectual property for integrated circuits. The success of this company is truly amazing. It shows that there are no permanent monopolies in the world of technology if entrepreneurial innovations are allowed to bloom. It is a major challenger to Intel in specialized microprocessor design for wireless handsets, and is beginning to move into PCs. According to several sources, "rumors are swirling that by the second half of 2013, Apple will switch to ARM in its MacBook and MacBook Pro lines, and [at the 2011 Consumer Electronics Show]

---

[20] *Bloomberg Businessweek*, September 5–11, 2011, p. 87.
[21] For an overview see "The Cambridge Phenomenon, Main Report 2003," prepared by PACEC on behalf of Greater Cambridge Partnership, Cambridgeshire County Council and East of England Development Agency.

Microsoft had a rough, but working version of Windows running atop ARM processors."[22]

The other two major technology companies are also in the digital space. Cambridge Silicon Radio is one of the world's biggest vendors of Bluetooth radio connectivity chips. Autonomy Corporation is a world-leading search software company with novel data analysis capabilities (it was acquired by Hewlett-Packard in 2011).

However, many Cambridge companies are small and face limited growth opportunities, largely because they address niche markets. Others suffer from inadequate access to new capital or management resources. For example, business surveys in the area found that between 25 percent and 35 percent of firms indicated that their growth was being restricted by the difficulty of recruiting sales and marketing professionals. This kind of talent is not rare in Silicon Valley, but the Valley has an abundance of big companies. As Cambridge becomes home to more sizable companies, perhaps it will overcome both this limitation and the small pool of entrepreneurial talent.

Other countries anxious to develop entrepreneurial activity also face a dearth of experienced management willing to join new companies. People familiar with entrepreneurship in Germany consider the technical talent pool to be very good, and experienced people there seem prepared to take the risk of working in a young company. Their big deficiency is in entrepreneurs with international experience capable of building major companies – the kind of entrepreneurs we discussed earlier, many of whom originate in the Silicon Valley culture.

Cultural factors and entrepreneurship

Some people think that building an entrepreneurial culture is a simple matter of familiarizing the general population with its attractions. "Entrepreneurship is infectious," one writer claims. "The

[22] P. Escallier, "Armed and Dangerous?" *Maximum PC*, September 2011, pp. 42–44.

more young people are exposed to it, the more they will embrace it as a lifestyle and philosophy."[23]

That may be. But embracing it and doing it are two different things. Many of those young people will have neither the desire nor the skills to start a new business. Margaret Thatcher, the former British prime minister known for her championing of private enterprise, noted that "however pervasive an enterprise culture is, most people are not born entrepreneurs."[24]

Thus a central task in building an entrepreneurial culture is motivating people who are not entrepreneurs themselves to take professional risks and join innovative companies – or to develop a commitment to new ideas even if they join big corporations. Yet we can't afford to ignore the real entrepreneurs. Recognition that entrepreneurship needs to be promoted as a societal goal is growing internationally, but the success of efforts in that direction is hard to gauge.

In Europe, annual awards are given to successful entrepreneurs who have taken university-generated technology into the market. These awards are given by the Science Business Innovation Board (AISBL), which is sponsored by a Belgian not-for-profit organization.

France, which has a tradition of state industrial planning that stretches back to Colbert in the eighteenth century, now takes great pride in the 622,000 new private businesses created in 2010 with the support and encouragement of private groups. One of those groups, *Entreprendre Paris*, maintains regional organizations to promote new business formation.[25]

Even in the US, which already has a solid tradition of entrepreneurism, there is a growing demand for instruction in the subject. For example, 90 percent of the engineering majors at North Carolina

---

[23] L. Johnson, "The bug for creating a business is incurable," *Financial Times*, March 23, 2011, p. 12.

[24] J. Belrau, "The entrepreneur's process," *The Wall Street Journal*, April 28, 2011, p. A19.

[25] Y. Le Gales, "Création d'entreprises: Le trou d'air," *Le Figaro*, May 19, 2011, p. 21.

State University take a formal three-course entrepreneurship sequence taught by alumni who have built successful businesses. Such courses are offered at 90 percent of all accredited US colleges. This represents a sixteen-fold increase over the past decade.

One reason for this interest might be that students read about successful startups, and want to learn more. On the other hand, there are plenty of stories in the media about large, well-established firms being less willing to hire inexperienced college graduates and train them to be productive, or about companies laying off older staff in favor of younger, less experienced workers. Students who are reading these articles could be thinking that sooner or later they may be working in a small company, so they had better be informed about what this means!

How have these courses influenced the behavior of students? Results at North Carolina State University suggest that students who take the entrepreneurship sequence are 75 percent more likely to start their own businesses than those who don't. They are also 59 percent more likely to believe that they can lead a new business and 23 percent more likely to develop new products even if they don't start their own business.[26]

Though few people actually start a new business, even in a social environment as favorable as Silicon Valley, the exposure to such an environment does have a direct effect on entrepreneurship. Talented people are more willing to join startups or young companies with uncertain futures because there is no stigma attached to that experience if the business fails. As J. Berenson, editor of *Inc.* magazine, has noted, "America, they say, is the land of second chances. No one knows this better than our readers, many of whom have started businesses and failed. True entrepreneurs never leave it at that, however."[27]

[26] T. K. Miller III, S. J. Walsh, S. Hollar, E. C. Rideout, and B. C. Pittman, "Engineering and innovation: An immersive start-up experience," *Computer*, April 2011, pp. 38–46.

[27] *Inc.*, April 2011, p. 13.

Immigrant power

No discussion of the cultural aspects of entrepreneurship can ignore the role of immigrants. It is no accident that nearly all of the entrepreneurs we discuss in this book, starting with David Sarnoff in the next chapter and including some of the Chinese entrepreneurs discussed in Chapter 8, are immigrants or people who worked or were educated in a foreign country before they started their companies. One study suggests that more than half of Silicon Valley companies were started by immigrants.[28]

This is not a situation peculiar to the US. An astute observer of the social scene in the UK finds the same phenomenon there: "The fact that so many fast-growing companies were built up by immigrant families [in Great Britain] confirms the belief that entrepreneurship is always most evident among 'outsiders.'"[29]

Professor Tibor Barna, the well-known Hungarian-born economist, thought the reason that more immigrants were attracted to entrepreneurism was their outsider's point of view: "The outsider is likely to be strongly activated by the profit motive; for him the accumulation of wealth may bring social recognition. He may also see more clearly the unsatisfied wants of consumers and he may be more ready to experiment with new products, new techniques and new forms of organization."[30]

Immigrants may have another advantage over native entrepreneurs: they are comfortable in international business relationships. Learning languages and adapting to local conditions is easier if you have already done so once.

Israel provides further proof that immigration can boost a nation's innovation quotient. As the story of Ness Technologies

---

[28] R. T. Herman and R. L. Smith, *Immigrants Inc.: Why immigrant entrepreneurs are driving the new economy* (Hoboken, NJ: John Wiley & Sons, 2009).

[29] A. Sampson, *The new anatomy of Britain* (New York: Stein & Day, 1972), p. 602.

[30] T. Barna, *Investment and growth policies in British industrial firms* (Cambridge: Cambridge University Press, 1996), pp. 56–57.

in Chapter 7 illustrates, by any measure it has built one of the world's most successful entrepreneurial economies.[31] Part of this achievement must be credited to the country's several world-class universities. It is also a prolific producer of technology. It ranks as fourteenth out of 125 countries in its capacity for innovation. Its population has an exceptionally high ratio of technologists to non-technologists, and it generates one of the highest numbers of patents per capita in the world.

These are great advantages, but the fact that Israel is a country of immigrants must also be weighed in the equation as a driver for entrepreneurship. The country has attracted educated immigrants from all over the world, not least the former Soviet Union, which has supplied about one million of its most industrious and educated citizens since the 1970s.

If there is a lesson to be learned from these observations, it is that a country that welcomes immigrants and offers them educational opportunities along with integration into its society will benefit from an addition to its population that can actively promote its industrial growth.[32]

Looking for a new direction: Entrepreneurship in Japan
Japan's amazing rise from postwar devastation to the status of economic superpower has long been a model for other Asian nations. Japan proved that the quality of industrial innovations can provide the basis for industrial growth. But its economic stagnation since the 1990s presents a cautionary example of how growth can turn to stasis. There are many causes cited for this problem, but in the search for renewed growth the Japanese government is turning to

---

[31] D. Senor and S. Singer, *Start-up nation: The story of Israel's economic miracle* (New York: Twelve, Hachette Book Group, 2009).

[32] B. Sherwood, "Taking talent across borders: As governments tighten immigration rules, businesses fear they might lose out on skills," *Financial Times, Mastering Growth*, June 1, 2011, p. 4.

the promotion of entrepreneurship. This initiative is worthy of discussion here.

At its height, Japan's economy was amazingly successful, with a model that favored big corporations over small entrepreneurial endeavors. Its companies came to dominate industrial sectors such as consumer electronics, shipbuilding, and semiconductor memories. Japan accumulated vast foreign reserves as its exports grew at the expense of the established companies in the Western world. Japan's corporate prowess was attributed to magical long-term planning accomplished through the combination of the brilliance of the management of its biggest companies and the wise guidance of highly competent state bureaucrats. Admirers of the model ignored the impact of its protective policies, including making cheap bank capital available to favored companies and limiting imports while promoting exports. They also neglected the inevitable problem of industrial ossification when industries are protected from competition.

As a result, Japan never promoted its entrepreneurial culture on a wide scale. In fact, among those who compared the Japanese and American ways, the devotion to entrepreneurship was regarded as a crippling deficiency in the US economic model.

> The United States is fertile ground for the start-up of small
> entrepreneurial companies. That is where the nation's economic
> dynamism rests ... So when it makes the best economic sense
> to sell the company and cash in on what you have created,
> [you] cash in on what you have, a phenomenon known as the
> American Dream. If, however, you grow your company to five
> thousand or so employees, everything changes. You face a whole
> new set of problems with which as an entrepreneur, you do not
> usually have any special expertise ... When companies reach this
> kind of initial steady state, the leverage of individual decisions
> on market value plummets ... In Japan, by contrast, the national
> soil is much less nourishing for start-ups but much more so

for established, steady-state companies. Once such a company is in existence both managers and workers know that drastic, discontinuous changes are not really in the cards.[33]

This observation sounds quaint today. Try to convince the management of "established, steady-state companies" like Apple or Google that they are not dealing with "discontinuous changes" all the time.

Meanwhile, some of the giant Japanese companies (such as Sony) that established global leadership in their glory years have failed to adapt to new technologies and new market trends. They seem to be in search of the energy and creativity that brought them fame. They are still substantial enterprises, but they no longer return the results they once proudly proclaimed, and the Japanese economy as a whole has been stuck in low-growth mode since the 1990s.

There is no question that Japan has done, and still does, a lot of things right. The country invests a great deal of money in the development of new technology. In 2008 it spent $149 billion on R&D, second only to the US, and well ahead of China's $121 billion (in currency-adjusted purchasing parity).

However, as most research is done in established companies, it is mainly focused on incremental improvements to products and processes. Furthermore, it does not percolate through the industry. Since engineers in Japan are not as mobile as they are in the US, ideas don't move around with their creations. When an idea developed in the research laboratory doesn't address a company's immediate needs, it is often dropped for good, because the lack of staff turnover means it won't find a new champion to run with it.

Traditionally the more basic research has been conducted in universities with government funding. It is of a generally high caliber, but until recently little of it has moved into the marketplace, in part because there are so few entrepreneurs (and so little venture

[33] K. K. Ohmae, *The borderless world: Power and strategy in the interlinked economy* (New York: Harper Business, 1990), pp. 205–206.

funding) to build new companies around it, and in part because universities, especially the state-supported ones, were reluctant to collaborate with industry. "Particularly after 1945, [the universities] harbored strong anti-business sentiment, believing that large business had been responsible for driving Japan into the painful Pacific War ... It was only as late as the 1990s that Japanese society became serious about establishing mutually supportive relations between the two communities."[34]

Japan once benefited from remarkable entrepreneurs. In the turbulent years after World War II, when the country was rebuilding its industry, daring entrepreneurs contributed mightily to the Japanese economic miracle by creating great new companies such as Honda, Sony, Sharp, and Matsushita Electric (Panasonic). They often did so in the face of disapproval from government officials who thought they were better at strategizing for the future development of technology, and usually opted to protect big, established companies.

For example, when Soichiro Honda's motorcycle company began producing cars in 1957, "the Japanese government tried to strong-arm Honda into merging his company with one of the country's stronger automakers. He refused and set out to make stylish vehicles with high quality handling and engineering."[35] Sony's founders Akio Morita and Masaru Ibuka, convinced that transistors would transform electronics, "licensed the rights to the transistor from Bell Laboratories, after overcoming resistance from the Ministry of International Trade and Industry [MITI]."[36]

[34] R. Nezu, *Technology transfer, intellectual property and effective university-industry partnerships: The experience of China, India, Japan, Philippines, the Republic of Korea, Singapore and Thailand* (New York: World Intellectual Property Organization, 2007), p. 5. Available at www.wipo.int/freepublications/en/intproperty/928/wipo_pub_928.pdf, accessed February 12, 2012.

[35] M. J. Brewster, "Soichiro Honda: Uniquely driven," August 17, 2004, http://businessweek.com/bwdaily/dnflash/aug2004/nf20040817_3267_db078.htm, accessed Februrary 12, 2012.

[36] A. Pollack, "Akio Morita, key to Japan's rise as co-founder of Sony, dies at 78," October 3, 1999, http://.nytimes.com/1999/10/04/business/akio-morita-co-founder-of-sony-and-japanese-business-leader-dies-at-78.html?pagewanted=all&src=pm, accessed Februrary 12, 2012.

However, as the country's economy grew to become the second largest in the world after the US, the climate for entrepreneurial ventures became less favorable. There are a number of reasons why this happened.[37]

- Japan's venture capital industry is very small and averse to risking its money with unproven management teams.
- People who fail in business in Japan lose status, and rarely get a second chance. This discourages would-be entrepreneurs.
- At the national level, the strategy is to support established companies rather than new ones.
- New companies face high regulatory hurdles, so talented people tend to join and stay with big employers – the bigger the better. Without vibrant new enterprises to develop and market the good ideas generated in universities, big companies overwhelmingly control new product introductions.
- Unlike Silicon Valley, Japan does not attract talent from around the world. Immigration is strictly controlled, and foreign entrepreneurs are not welcome.

In short, while the Japanese public professes admiration for successful entrepreneurs, both its political and business establishments favor conventional corporate leaders. Even though the media often tout entrepreneurial successes, the overall environment is not favorable to risk takers. This means that talented people tend to choose lower-risk careers with established companies over risky new ventures. In a country where the Confucian precept "Harmony is to be valued" is taken seriously, and group effort is preferred to individual action, this is an easy choice to make.

To be fair, the bursting of Japan's real estate bubble and the subsequent banking crisis had a lot to do with its economic malaise. Unfortunately, it served to exacerbate the weakness of venture creation there. Since Japanese banks provide most of the

---

[37] See "Japan: Technology and innovation," Special section, *Financial Times*, December 9, 2010 for a full analysis.

funding for startups, the drying up of capital has directly impacted entrepreneurial endeavors.

In response, the Japanese government has taken a number of steps to open up the system and encourage new ventures. Several of its actions affected university/industry collaboration.

- To jump-start collaboration between business and both public and private universities, in 2002 the government proposed that universities create 1,000 new venture companies in three years. This goal was exceeded, with Tokyo University alone establishing sixty-four spin-offs. By 2008 it could boast of 125 sustainable venture businesses. Including that number, the top ten universities spawned a total of 679 such firms.
- In 2004 the government changed the legal status of Japan's prestigious national universities to give them the freedom to chart their own course and to "make them more accountable for creating value in Japanese society."[38] The mandate freed researchers from regulations that had prevented them from working with the private sector.
- Earlier the universities had demonstrated increasing interest in protecting their inventions through patent filings as part of a technology transfer strategy. Their patent filings rose from seventy-six in 1996 to 1,355 in 2002.
- The Development Bank of Japan, a government institution formed in 1951 to finance Japan's industrial expansion, began a privatization process in 2008 to separate it from the government. Its new charter will be to "provide integrated investment and loan services to domestic and *international* [emphasis added] clients."

It remains to be seen whether such steps will help in revitalizing Japan's industrial sector, or if they will stimulate the creation of entrepreneurial companies. However, it might be unwise to bet against a country that has transformed itself twice in the past 150 years: from a feudal agrarian society in 1868 to a modern industrial power with a market economy in 1900; and again from a defeated and impoverished nation in 1945 to the world's second largest economy four decades later.

---

[38] Nezu, *Technology transfer*, p. 14. Information in this and the previous bullet point is drawn from this document.

In the early 1990s Taichi Sakaiya, a leading economic analyst and former MITI official, made this very point. He published a book[39] that was critical of Japan's exclusive focus on manufacturing, and the conformist attitudes it produced, which he ascribed to the military regime in control before the war. However, he maintained that its group mindset could help Japan reverse course quickly, because everyone within a group changes at once.

Indeed there are stirrings of a desire for wholesale change. In the face of continuing political and economic turmoil, and in the wake of the disasters of earthquakes, tsunami, and nuclear power meltdowns, opinion makers and the mass media are calling for a "return to the spirit of post-WWII." It has almost become a slogan for driving Japan forward.

Other nations with highly structured societies, no matter what their level of economic development, face problems similar to those of Japan. Challenging the incumbent economic powers in such societies is difficult at best. South Korea has also been cited as a country with highly successful, big established companies that is having major difficulties in developing an entrepreneurial culture.[40]

Contract R&D for small and mid-sized companies: A key role for government support

I frequently meet heads of small and mid-sized technology product companies. When asked about their biggest worry, they mention the difficulty of staying competitive with new international competitors leveraging new technologies in their products.

This is not surprising. Starting a new company is easier than making it successful over the long term. Companies usually launch with a single idea, and then concentrate on getting the first products to market while managing cash flow. All attention is focused

---

[39] T. Sakaiya, *What Is Japan? Contradictions and transformations* (New York: Kodansha America, 1995).

[40] "South Korean entrepreneurs: Young, gifted and blocked," *The Economist*, May 14, 2011, p. 82.

on near-term product features. Long-term R&D is relegated to the future owing to its cost and its delayed payback.

Some entrepreneurs, as we will see in our case studies, do manage to get access to enough capital and other resources to grow through product innovations. But all too many small and mid-sized companies find themselves unable to adapt to market needs fast enough, both because they don't have the money to invest in R&D, and because their talent needs keep shifting in light of new technologies.

Historically small businesses address this problem by finding a market niche that is defensible, establishing themselves with solid products and reference customers, and then moving into adjacent or bigger market segments. But it is hard to do this successfully, for two reasons.

First, many startups do not have a disruptive technology that would allow them to fortify a niche. Second, many do a poor job of executing on their original strategy and wind up with no resources to invest in lateral growth. Whatever the cause, their growth, their profitability, and even their viability are threatened.

There must be a better way of supporting ongoing businesses that have limited resources. Germany appears to have developed an approach that works.

German industry has managed to stay competitive in the world market in spite of having higher costs than the developing world. The country continues to generate large manufactured product trade surpluses in the face of new Asian competitors. Well-managed small and mid-sized companies, many of them family-owned for several generations, are a source of great strength for the German economy. It helps that exports are their lifeblood. But these are not giant conglomerates with infinite resources. In the face of accelerating technology development, how can such companies afford the ever-changing development resources needed to stay in the game?

The solution that Germany has developed to help its industry is centered on the Fraunhofer Gesellschaft. Fraunhofer was founded in 1949 as a non-profit research institution with the mission of undertaking applied research to drive economic development. This is accomplished through fifty-nine Institutes, mostly in Germany, which support the innovation needs of major domestic German industries ranging from solar energy and software to wood products. The staff of 17,000 consists mostly of engineers and scientists who work with an annual budget of about 1.6 billion euros (2009).[41] In an interesting twist, the Institutes also function as training grounds for technologists who eventually move into industry. They also act as conduits to academic research of commercial importance.

The government pays for Fraunhofer's infrastructure costs (one-third of the budget). The rest of the revenues come from license fees and product development contracts from companies or government agencies. While companies pay the direct cost of the work performed on their behalf, and own the results, costs are indirectly shared with other customers of an Institute in the same industry. With the government infrastructure subsidy reducing overhead costs and customers benefiting from independent research, this is a productive arrangement.

Two of the biggest advantages that businesses derive from working with Fraunhofer are access to specialized talent familiar with their industry and exposure to the latest technology. In effect, such cooperative work substitutes for a lot of the in-house R&D that a small or medium-sized business would have to conduct. For example, the Institute devoted to solar energy development has facilities that are of commercial scale. As a result, device research goes from concept to production in record time, and companies that contract with the Institute can quickly move the new products to production scale and into the market.

The Fraunhofer Institutes are well known for their leading-edge technology development. Given the breadth of the work they conduct,

---

[41] Data from *Fraunhofer Annual Report*, 2009.

it is hard to single out one accomplishment to represent their influence, but in our media-obsessed culture it is noteworthy that one of the Institutes is responsible for the MP3 music compression software technology used by virtually every music player in the world market.

SOURCES OF CAPITAL

It is almost too obvious to say: you can't start a new company without money. But you also cannot hope to grow beyond the startup phase without access to capital on favorable terms. Hence, entrepreneurs need both seed capital and follow-on growth capital to build economic value. For that reason one of the basic necessities of a healthy entrepreneurial environment is the availability of capital to finance startups and their growth. There are several potential sources for this kind of funding, and which one(s) you use can depend as much on what country you're in as on such factors as your company's stage of development and its industry.

Access to public markets has been the preferred way to raise growth capital. Thousands of companies initially funded with venture capital, such as Apple, Microsoft, Intel, and Google, raised their capital that way. Among the companies we discuss later in the book, RCA, SanDisk, Ness Technologies, RDA, and AsiaInfo were able to access public markets. But as we note below, public markets are a fickle source of funding and cannot be relied upon within defined time limits.

In the absence of access to public markets (or other sources of growth capital including bank financing), business growth becomes problematic and companies may be forced into mergers with other companies to access the needed capital. As we will see later, RMI (Chapter 5) and Harbour Networks (Chapter 8) were in that situation when their IPO (initial public offering) opportunities temporarily disappeared in a market crash.

Government grants and bank funding

Because small businesses create jobs, governments regularly provide direct financial support or encourage other entities to do so. Here are some examples.

In the UK, Project Merlin was designed to make bank loans available to small and medium-sized business. The amount targeted in 2011 was £19 billion.

In the US, the Small Business Jobs Bill, signed into law in May 2011, includes a $30 billion lending fund that community banks can use to make loans to small businesses. The bill also increases the guarantee by the US government through the United States Small Business Administration of up to 90 percent of the loans extended by local banks using their own funds. The purpose of the loans is "to help start-ups and existing small businesses obtain financing when they might not be eligible for business loans through normal lending channels." There are also $12 billion in tax incentives for small businesses.[42]

Unfortunately, US government-backed funding carries a significant drawback for small businesses. It requires very detailed reports and accounting documents to be filed on a regular basis to assure compliance with the law. Small companies are ill-equipped to do this without taking time away from their regular business activities or spending money to have someone else handle the filings. That goes against the reason for seeking the funding in the first place. Furthermore, many regional banks are not anxious to deal with small business loans that carry government-mandated requirements with them.[43]

Germany has a program designed to attract venture capital and promote the movement of innovations from universities into the market. The Federal Ministries of Economics and Technology and of Education and Research provide funds to startups, typically about 1 million euros or less, in the form of matching grants – that is, they match any funds provided by private capital. Another agency, the KfW Bankengruppe, a Federal and State-owned development finance organization, also provides either equity or loans to startups on a

---

[42] *Source:* www/growthink.com/category/blogs/entrepreneurship, May 3, 2011.
[43] E. Maltby, "The credit crunch that won't go away," *The Wall Street Journal*, June 21, 2010, p. R1.

matching basis. For example, a startup requiring 3 million euros can get 1 million from private funds, 1 million from the Ministries, and 1 million from KfW.

Singapore is another country striving to achieve a consistently high economic growth rate. It has a stated policy of attracting leading-edge industries and helping them acquire the innovations they need to stay competitive over the long term. To this end, the government funds research that is related to the country's industrial activities. In order to move innovations into products, strong ties exist between government-funded research organizations and local industry. A strong manufacturing sector is part of the national economic strategy.[44]

Funding to help small businesses export their products

There has been a notable shift in the attention paid in the US to exports by small companies. This represents a recognition of the importance of globalization and the fact that the US now represents a shrinking portion of the world market.

That is a positive development, but it comes with a built-in set of problems. Once a small business reaches the stage where it has products to sell in a global market, it faces the problem of financing not only its regular operations, but its export activities. Lacking the financial and logistical resources of large corporations, small businesses often find it difficult to wait for payment from overseas customers – or, sometimes, to collect their money at all.

Mindful of the need to help small US businesses go global, the Export-Import Bank of the United States, an independent Federal Agency, offers valuable services to bolster their export capabilities. The Bank is self-funded (i.e. not supported by the taxpayer) and relies on fees for its services as a source of revenues. Its historic focus has been on supporting big companies, but small business is now on its

[44] C. Day, "Singapore applies itself to science," *Physics Today*, June 2011, pp. 20–21.

radar screen. New programs launched in 2010 provide insurance to protect exporters and lenders from nonpayment for commercial or political reasons. They also allow exporters to extend credit to international customers. Another service guarantees up to 90 percent of an exporter's working capital that gets tied up with outstanding inventory or accounts receivable.

These programs helped relieve the financial strain of building an export business for 900 small companies in fiscal 2011. During that year the amount of export financing covered by these initiatives exceeded $2.4 billion.

Private funding

Before the advent of venture capital firms most entrepreneurs were funded through banks and private investors – what are now called angel investors.[45] Angel investors are still a large source of capital in the US, with an estimated $20 billion invested in 2010, but today professionally managed venture and private equity funds finance the most ambitious young companies. Furthermore, angel investors rarely have the capital (or appetite) needed to provide the large amounts commonly needed to finance the growth of promising startups after their initial development phase.

Angel investors continue to be crucial to small business funding in many countries. Certainly this is true in India and China. But given how dispersed such funding sources are, there are no reliable figures on how much money is invested annually by angel investors. There is clearly a need for such a funding source in the absence of others.

In China, for example, the number of private companies tripled between 2000 and 2009, from 120,000 to 340,000. Professional venture capital was and is relatively scarce there, and it is only available to businesses in very high growth sectors not dominated by

---

[45] For an excellent review of funding mechanisms see N. R. Lamoreax and K. L. Sokoloff, eds., with a foreword by W. Janeway, *Financing innovation in the United States: 1870 to the present* (Cambridge, MA: The MIT Press, 2007).

state-owned companies. Banks are state-controlled too, and their lending policies are set by government planners who target favored industries. So how do private companies get financed in this kind of economy? The answer is that rich individuals in the emerging economies, who are looking for big profits in fast-growing companies, are anxious to invest.

This puts small-business funding in the hands of financial intermediaries who channel investment money from rich individuals. There are also companies that guarantee the loans (with the blessing of the authorities) to help manage the risk to individual investors. It remains to be seen how this insurance works out in bad times, because the amount of money guaranteed is likely to be far in excess of the capital covering these guarantees.[46]

The terms of these investments vary with the perceived risk. Access to capital to finance growth is, however, a big problem for many small companies because interest rates on loans can be very high. Press reports suggest that many of the small companies in China with fewer than 300 employees are operating well below their potential because capital is so hard to get.[47]

However, for ambitious entrepreneurs who need many millions of dollars to build major enterprises, angel investors are not an adequate source of money. Only access to professional equity capital and bank financing will meet that need. This level of funding is now available in many countries around the world, but on a highly selective basis. In addition to funding US-based companies, professional investors are moving capital to high-growth emerging economies like Brazil or certain Asian countries, which have growth rates sometimes double or triple those in the developed countries. In the Asia-Pacific market, the number of private equity funds grew by 60 percent between 2005 and 2010. In 2010 alone $34 billion of

---

[46] H. Sender, "A shadowy presence: Chinese finance," *Financial Times*, April 1, 2011, p. 9.

[47] *Bloomberg Businessweek*, August 15–28, 2011, p. 13.

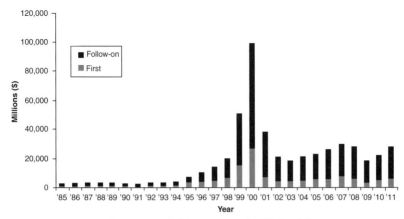

FIGURE 2.2 Venture capital investments by US funds by year, 1985–2011.
Source: Based on data from Thomson Reuters.

new capital was committed there.[48] The three Chinese companies discussed in Chapter 8 were funded by Chinese and US venture capital.

In any period of time, the amount of money available for investment by private investors depends on their willingness to commit long-term capital. That willingness depends in turn on the anticipated rate of return of venture capital compared to other asset classes, such as public securities. Because the rate of return of US venture capital (as a group) has lagged since 2000, the *total* amount of capital available in US-based funds has declined over the past several years.[49] It is important to note that the best-performing funds are getting an increasing share of the funding because the top-performing 25 percent of venture capital funds account for practically all of the industry's profits. Poorly performing funds go out of business. However, the net result is that the total venture capital funding has declined from its peak years as shown in Figure 2.2.

---

[48] C. Meads, "Opportunities for private equity in a changing world," *Financial Times*, April 4, 2011, p. 6.

[49] See H. Kressel and T. V. Lento, *Investing in dynamic markets: Venture capital in the digital age* (Cambridge: Cambridge University Press, 2010), pp. 41–61 for an overview of the world of venture capital.

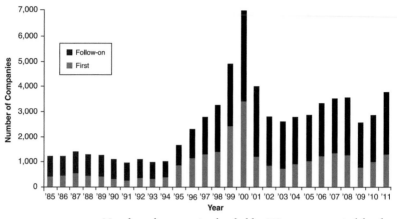

FIGURE 2.3 Number of companies funded by US venture capital funds, 1985–2011.
Source: Based on data from Thomson Reuters.

Clearly, with less money to go around, a smaller number of companies are getting funded – both in the startup stage and to finance growth (see Figure 2.3.) As Figure 2.2 shows, follow-on investments in established companies dwarf startup funding. Whether the reduced venture capital availability is necessarily detrimental is unclear. Investors will clearly be more selective about where they put their money and hence improve the success rate of ventures. Note that Figure 2.2 shows that, despite the drop in funding level from the peak years, the amounts invested are still high by historical standards, assuming the Internet "bubble" period around the year 2000 is considered an aberration – which it clearly was.

Given the high failure rate of new companies around the peak of the Internet-driven investment bubble in 2000, one can speculate that not many good new business ideas are being left behind at current funding levels. There may even be a silver lining: with venture capital funds being better managed, the profitability of the venture capital industry is likely to improve, which will stimulate an increased inflow of capital.

PUBLIC MARKETS AND FINANCIAL REWARDS
FOR ENTREPRENEURS

Ask any ambitious entrepreneur about his or her dream, and you will be told that the hallmark for success is an IPO on NASDAQ or even the New York Stock Exchange. There are two factors that drive this desired event:

- the ability of the management team and investors in the company to sell some of their stock; and
- the ability to raise growth capital at attractive rates – instead of bank loans, for example.

In fact, US exchanges are viewed by investors as well as entrepreneurs as the most desired place for a listing. Of venture capitalists polled globally in 2011, 87 percent selected NASDAQ as the preferred market to list.[50]

The joys of pioneering a new business are stimulating, but the expectation of big financial returns is still a major driver for entrepreneurial endeavors. Ultimately, these rewards can come either from selling the business, selling shares in an IPO, or harvesting profits over a long period of time. Harvesting profits is how family businesses that dominate the small and medium-sized business environment in many countries are built. Transammonia, covered in Chapter 4, is a good example of such a business.

In a Silicon Valley-style venture capital mentality the priorities are different. Investors and entrepreneurs are looking at a time frame that is much shorter than that found in the development model for a traditional family business. Venture capital funds that finance companies are generally pools of capital with a ten to twelve year life. At the end of that period the limited partners expect to get their money back, with profit. Hence, by definition, their portfolio companies must somehow return capital. This liquidity can only be

---

[50] M. Davis and S. Ingram, "Getting ready for an IPO window," *XConomy*, September 22, 2011.

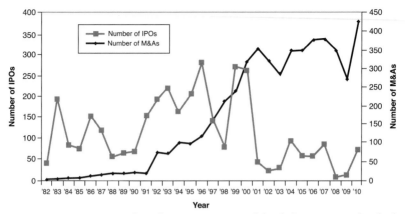

FIGURE 2.4 Number of US venture capital-funded companies that had an IPO and the number of companies that merged or were acquired since 1982.
Source: Based on data from Thomson Reuters.

generated by a public offering of stock in the company, which then makes it possible for employees and investors to sell their stock over time, or by its outright sale.

Taking the IPO route allows a company to continue on its independent way while rewarding its investors and entrepreneurs. This obviously requires that young companies be valued for substantially more than the capital invested in them. On the negative side of IPOs, public markets are notoriously fickle and unpredictable. Furthermore, government regulations regarding reporting rules are enormous and very costly for public companies, so an IPO is not necessarily the right choice, especially for companies too small to support such costs.

As Figure 2.4 shows, the number of venture capital-backed company IPOs in the US has fluctuated over the years, but the activity in outright sales or mergers of these companies tends to increase as the number of IPOs decline.

While an IPO is still a cherished objective, regarded as the gold standard of success for a new company, the reality is that an acquisition by or merger with another firm can be a better outcome under the right circumstances. This holds especially true for a company that is starving for growth capital, and can't wait for frozen public markets to once again welcome an IPO. Naturally, it also includes companies that never get big enough to warrant a public offering.

A merger or sale under such circumstances can actually enhance the economic value created. Such an event creates liquidity to management and investors, thus providing the looked-for return for risk-taking.

Sales of promising startups benefit buyers as well. By buying an innovative new company, a larger firm can acquire needed new products and technologies much faster than if it had to develop them on its own. This process of absorption is actually healthy for a national economy. It puts entrepreneurial innovations in the hands of firms with the resources needed to successfully commercialize them, rather than allowing them to languish in an under-capitalized startup.

GLOBAL CONSIDERATIONS

Throughout this chapter we have discussed the major conditions under which entrepreneurship can be effective in building valuable companies. These include appropriate government support, a culture of risk-taking, and access to risk capital and markets.

We must remember, however, that this whole process is effective only in a legal and economic system that supports and rewards individual initiatives. Entrepreneurship cannot bring out the best and most creative people in a country where there is no respect for the rule of law and there is no reliable legal system to protect private property rights. Corruption, excessive state control, and the inability of entrepreneurs and investors to reap the financial rewards of risk taking are all enemies of entrepreneurial achievement as we understand it in this book.

As more and more entrepreneurial companies enter the global market, they find themselves challenged by unfamiliar, and in some cases unfair, policies and practices in certain countries where they would like to do business. Entrepreneurs also operate under the constraints of their countries of origin. While none of these are insurmountable obstacles, they do increase the business risk when operating in certain geographies.

Here is a summary of some of the issues and pitfalls entrepreneurial firms may face as they go global.

Government restrictions on trading technology products

International commerce is rife with limitations imposed by various governments on the sale of technology products. Keeping track of them not only keeps companies out of trouble – it can keep entrepreneurs out of jail!

For example, the US government places restrictions on the export of certain products, technology or software, nominally non-defense in nature, to select countries. The controlled items are in the category of "dual use," which means that they can be adapted to strategic applications as well as commercial ones. These regulations fall under the grouping of Export Administration Regulations, which are administered by the Department of Commerce. You need special licenses for the export of such items. For example, one instance with which I am familiar involved the export of cameras able to view in the infrared. Such cameras can be used in defense applications for night vision in addition to being used for commercial security systems.

Having to keep track of which countries are embargoed complicates matters. And sometimes the restrictions seem arbitrary, since companies in other countries can and do sell similar products to those very same countries. But the government is very serious about enforcing these prohibitions. The US is not alone in enforcing such regulations. The EU has restrictions on trading with certain countries. Breaching its rules can entail criminal sanctions on the individuals involved.

Needed: Tight financial controls

Every business person understands the need for stringent control over its company's finances. This is doubly important in international business.

Fraud is always a big risk. Examples of questionable business practices are found everywhere, but newcomers to countries with weak legal systems should be ready for surprises. Anecdotal stories circulate of sweetheart arrangements between suppliers and competitors designed to keep out newcomers; bribes paid for government licenses; and such scams as local managers running their own little businesses by using corporate personnel as their staff.

Incidents of accounting irregularities are common. There are documented horror stories about Eastern European countries formerly part of the Soviet Union.[51] Fast-growing markets in any geography are prime locations for irregularities, as they attract shady business people.[52] Young companies with limited resources are particularly vulnerable if they have not established strong local business relationships with trustworthy organizations. Such relationships take time to develop. They are based on mutual trust established between senior executives, and sustaining these relationships requires frequent meetings.[53]

Well-managed international companies implement centralized financial controls, so that local controllers report to headquarters as well as to local management. They unify financial systems to ensure timely reporting and problem discovery. In addition, internal auditors periodically check local systems and purchasing policies. Uniform financial reporting is particularly important for companies hoping to become publicly traded in the US. Accounting standards

[51] "From Bolshevism to backhanders," *The Economist*, April 16, 2011, p. 57.
[52] R. Cookson and H. Sender, "Carlyle suffers China setbacks: Two investments hit by fiscal allegations," *Financial Times*, May 6, 2011, p. 13.
[53] G. Colvin, "The biggest problem for developing economies: corruption," *Fortune*, May 2, 2011, p. 48.

are extremely stringent here, and inaccurate reporting can have severe legal implications.

Pay a bribe, go to jail

There is no lack of official attempts to eliminate bribery. The Organization for Economic Cooperation and Development sponsored an Anti-Bribery Convention in 1999 to curb bribery of foreign officials. Thirty-eight countries subscribed to the Convention, but a recent report indicates that only thirteen of the signatories (with the US being most active) have actually imposed sanctions on individuals or corporations caught in bribery. Of the thirteen, the most active in applying sanctions has been the US.[54] Reports of bribery of foreign public officials by employees of some big US corporations surface periodically.[55] The consequences are severe. A recent conviction involved a US company selling products to a Mexican utility where bribes were paid to officials to enable the sale.[56]

Collecting the bill

While you can guard yourself against fraudulent business practices, timely collection of receivables can be a huge problem. Stories periodically surface of companies totally reliant on a single customer when a dispute arises. One publicly traded company was unable to collect from a customer because of a price dispute.[57] The incident affected its public market standing.

To avoid getting local courts involved in settling such disputes, a common practice is to agree up front to binding arbitration in a

---

[54] P. Hannon, "Few nations punish bribery," *The Wall Street Journal*, April 21, 2011, p. A8.

[55] E. Byron, "Avon's stock is hit by widening bribery probe," *The Wall Street Journal*, May 6, 2011, p. B4.

[56] S. Rubenfeld, "Conviction in foreign bribery case is first in US trial," *The Wall Street Journal*, May 11, 2011.

[57] E. Crooke and L. Hook, "American Superconductor misses new filing deadline," *Financial Times*, June 21, 2011, p. 13.

neutral country. Singapore is a popular location in the Asia-Pacific region for arbitration proceedings.

Unfortunately, the collection problem is not restricted to exotic locations. Hard times can make even the most honest customer in the most law-abiding country look for creative ways to delay payment and conserve cash. If it happens in the European Union the problem can be as troublesome as in any other geography. There are 27 different national legal systems in the EU, each with its own procedures for handling claims and bankruptcies. So it is not surprising that it is hard for a small foreign company to legally challenge its customers on payment claims.[58]

MANAGING INTELLECTUAL PROPERTY

Managing intellectual property is an essential part of technology business management and the greater the dependence on international operations, the more challenging this task is. The simple reason is that laws protecting intellectual property vary widely in different countries, as do the criteria for patent issuance and protection. In some countries, little or no legal protection is available as a practical matter, and doing business in such countries is a risk that companies can avoid only by going elsewhere.

In a world where few industrial secrets stay secret for long, protecting a competitive edge is not getting any easier. Bitter patent fights among corporations in leading-edge technologies are nothing new (as the history of RCA in Chapter 3 shows), but it does feel like the amount of litigation has been increasing steadily as companies jockey for position in fast-growing international markets.[59]

We should not be surprised by this state of affairs. Product costs are disappearing as real differentiators around the world for

---

[58] S. Daley and S. Castle, "Slow payers hinder cross-border trade in Europe," *The New York Times*, April 19, 2011, p. B1.

[59] "LED makers wage patent war," *Photonics Spectra*, August 2011, p. 76. "Intellectual property: inventive warfare – Battles over patents are becoming fiercer and more expensive," *The Economist*, August 20, 2011, pp. 57–58.

most technology products, and software is an ever-increasing part of what differentiates technology products. It is natural that corporations are looking to their intellectual property as a prime defensive and offensive tool in their competitive wars.

Ironically, however, a strong IP position can expose a company to risk of government action. Governments try to help their domestic champions. If your startup becomes too successful, as in the cases of Microsoft or Qualcomm, for example, don't be surprised if some government brands you a monopolist. The motivation for such actions is usually to protect or help domestic companies unable to compete. Such can be the price of building new industries on the strength of strong patents.

With accelerating technological evolution producing more innovations all the time, the ferocity with which companies protect their turf while attacking their competitors has escalated. The increase in the number of lawsuits has been partly fueled by the number of questionable patents issued, a side effect of the relatively recent decision to allow patents on software. It is very difficult to decide the novelty of conflicting claims on software without a court fight.

The trouble really starts at the patent offices, where the sheer volume and specialization of patents overwhelms the staff charged with deciding the merit of patent claims. But IP battles can also involve claims that employees have violated patents or used trade secrets from their former employer at a new company. So protecting intellectual property has two components: retention of productive employees, and a vigorous patent filing and legal protection strategy.

Whoever is not prepared to do legal battle need not bother to file patents. Unfortunately, while legal protection may be available, the legal costs can kill a small company because such protracted battles can last years and cost millions of dollars. The basic problem is that too many patents are ambiguous and overlapping, leaving each side of the argument believing that they have the upper hand.

What makes matters more difficult is that the number of patents is increasing rapidly around the world. Each country has its own way of dealing with claims of patent infringement, so the global cost of patent filing and protection continues to rise.

Visions of monetizing intellectual property through licensing agreements are common among entrepreneurs with a patent portfolio and badly in need of cash. They are frequently disappointed, because collecting license fees is never easy, particularly in developing countries. For example, a US government report surveyed 5,051 companies in various industries regarding their ability to collect license income.[60] Many reported difficulties in fee collection.

Each business needs to develop its own intellectual property strategy, but looking at some successful examples is worthwhile. We selected for discussion two companies that can be viewed as "poster children" of the industrial intellectual property battlefield, RCA and SanDisk. David Sarnoff at RCA (Chapter 3) was one of the dominant masters of the art of intellectual property management in the past century.

SanDisk, the subject of Chapter 6, is a remarkable story of leveraging patents on an international scale by a smart licensing strategy, backed by relentless legal action. The company used license income to fund a great deal of its technology development. In effect, SanDisk's competitors financed the innovation engine which fueled the growing market strength of the company. It is a strategy that David Sarnoff, the subject of the next chapter, developed and worked to perfection. There is much to learn from these examples.

[60] US International Trade Commission, "China: Effects of intellectual property infringement and indigenous innovation policies on the US economy," May 2011; reported by M. J. Slaugher, "China, patents and US jobs," *The Wall Street Journal*, June 6, 2011, p. A19.

3   Electronic innovation and the government: David Sarnoff creates the RCA empire

I hitched my wagon to an electron rather than the proverbial star.[1]

David Sarnoff

INTRODUCTION

Entrepreneurs, inventors, and innovations have driven the electronics revolution since its chaotic beginnings in the early years of the twentieth century. Unfortunately, the astonishing advances of the last thirty years have obscured the contributions of the pioneers of that era. These men laid the foundation for today's wired and wireless society, but they rarely get the credit they deserve.

Case in point: David Sarnoff of the Radio Corporation of America (RCA), the company he built and directed for a half-century. Sarnoff was the Bill Gates or Steve Jobs of his day, a visionary who pushed his company to develop or adopt new communications technology, create a market for it, and become the dominant player in that market.

Under his leadership RCA successfully commercialized both radio and television, either inventing the technology or licensing others' intellectual property (IP) as needed. At Sarnoff's urging RCA later invented most of the technology for color television, from the cameras to the displays. It was also the first company in the world to successfully commercialize these innovations. He also understood that he couldn't commercialize major innovations alone, so he licensed RCA's IP to competitors. They helped him create market

---

[1] *The New York Times*, April 4, 1958.

momentum, and the license fees generated a handsome revenue stream.

Sarnoff combined an ability to foresee commercial applications for technology with the business savvy to make them economically viable. More than eighty years ago he created the National Broadcasting Company (NBC) subsidiary of RCA to build the world's first radio and TV broadcasting networks. He financed them with an innovative advertising-supported business model. Electronic mass media, including websites and Internet search engines, still use this model.

His contemporaries stood in awe of his achievements. For much of his career he was ranked as a colossus of world industry. In 1975, four years after his death, he was named one of fifteen "Laureates from Two Centuries" in *Fortune* magazine's inaugural Hall of Fame for Business Leaders. Other nominees included Henry Ford, John D. Rockefeller, J. P. Morgan, and Andrew Carnegie.

Yet today few people remember who he was or what he did. He established no foundations to carry on his name, and his fame and influence began to wane after he officially retired in 1969. RCA, once one of America's largest and most powerful corporations, was acquired by GE in 1987 and sold off in pieces.

Sarnoff deserves better. He was present at the birth of electronic technology, and maintained a prescient vision of its potential to the very end of his career. In 1965, at the age of seventy-four, he gave a speech[2] predicting that one day satellites would broadcast TV directly to homes, and mused about the political and social consequences.

Telstar, the first satellite to relay TV among broadcasters, had been launched only three years before. Direct-to-home analog satellites would not be announced for more than a decade, and it took until 1994, nearly thirty years after his speech, for the launch of the

[2] David Sarnoff, *Looking ahead: The papers of David Sarnoff* (New York: McGraw-Hill, 1968), pp. 184–87.

DirecTV digital satellite TV system to presage the fulfillment of his prophecy.

In many ways Sarnoff was the archetypal globally oriented entrepreneur, sparking innovation and driving economic growth. For that reason his career makes a good starting point for our survey of entrepreneurial ventures in the global economy. But his example is important for another reason. The history of Sarnoff and RCA demonstrates the delicate balance between entrepreneurship and government goals and policies.

This cuts against the romantic view of early entrepreneurs as swashbuckling builders of industry who didn't have to worry about government regulations and interference. But the fact is that there has always been plenty of government involvement in areas that affect national security and economic policy. Government agencies essentially dictated the creation of RCA. They continued to monitor and restrict its business activities, and periodically reshaped the communications industry through antitrust suits and other actions against the company they had sponsored. Sarnoff proved to be as skilled in navigating the uncertain waters of governmental intervention as he was in grasping the commercial implications of technology.

As we review his achievements as a global entrepreneur, however, we must not let his knack for dealing with governmental concerns obscure the true dimensions of his legacy. His work was a significant spur to the development of today's electronics industry, an industrial sector that continues to create a staggering amount of economic value. To take just the most recent figures, the Telecommunications Industry Association reports that telecommunications revenues for 2009 were $3.7 trillion worldwide. The figure for the US alone was $1.2 trillion. A substantial portion of those revenues comes from mobile phones. These devices are essentially radio receivers/transmitters, making them direct descendants of RCA's original products. Another heir to RCA's legacy, the US cable TV industry, also accumulates huge revenues – $93.7 billion in 2010.[3] In the same year digital satellite TV had 195 million subscribers in 73 countries, producing $71 billion in revenues.[4]

In the area of job creation, a primary concern of all governments, the numbers are just as impressive. The US Bureau of Labor Statistics estimates that the telecommunications industry alone employed 975,000 US workers during 2010.[5]

Sarnoff's company also produced innovations that made the growth of the computer and electronics industries possible. RCA Laboratories (later Sarnoff Corporation), a monument to his faith in R&D, invented both the color CRT (cathode ray tube) and the LCD (liquid crystal display). Originally designed as TV displays, these devices are also one of the foundations of the computer industry.

RCA made many other fundamental contributions to the electronics industry. For example, while it did not "invent" the integrated circuit, it did pioneer the CMOS process used to manufacture over 90 percent of today's processors and memory chips. My group at RCA Laboratories created the first practical semiconductor lasers, today enabling fiber-optic communications systems, medical devices, computer printers, and CD and video disc players.

David Sarnoff was one of those rare entrepreneurs who made a successful transition to corporate executive. As head of RCA he displayed remarkable managerial skill in growing a fledgling company into a world leader. But his major contribution to the global economy came from his entrepreneurial activities. Few other entrepreneurs have helped create industries that have generated so much economic value, employed so many people, and improved so many lives.

---

[3] www.ncta.com/StatsGroup/OtherIndustryData.aspx, accessed August 19, 2011.

[4] *Source:* www.digitaltvnews.net/content/?p=19886, accessed August 19, 2011.

[5] Figures compiled from original sources by Plunkett Research, accessed June 10, 2011 at www.plunkettresearch.com/telecommunications%20market%20research/industry%20statistics.

ENTREPRENEUR IN WAITING

We focus on David Sarnoff because in many ways he prefigured today's global entrepreneur. It is true that business conditions were different during his heyday, which extended from 1915 through the 1950s. But our world grew out of his, and as a pioneer in his industry, he faced challenges that were remarkably similar to what innovators encounter in today's internationalized economy.

He was at his most entrepreneurial early in his career. From 1915 to 1932 he shaped RCA and broadcasting to his vision of the future of electronics and electronic media. In doing so he often had to spar with government agencies over the ground rules of electronic communications and industrial practice. During his later career, with RCA firmly in the ranks of major corporations, Sarnoff became what we now call an "intrapreneur," driving internal projects such as the development of television and the invention of color TV. We will cover this period in somewhat less detail.

We will start with a brief look at the events of his early life. This biographical information is crucial to understanding how he became a major figure in the development and growth of the electronics industry. It also puts his achievements in their proper historical context.

Struggling immigrant stumbles on a career

David Sarnoff, like so many other American entrepreneurs, was an immigrant. This accounts in part for his single-minded striving after success.

Sarnoff was born in 1891 in Uzlian (Uzlyany), a tiny *shtetl* or Jewish village in Russia. He arrived in New York with his family in 1900. We can only imagine the shock he felt at suddenly being in the middle of a teeming city filled with massive buildings. Carl Dreher brings the abrupt dislocation into perspective: "In the thousands of villages like Uzlian, such amenities as telephones, the telegraph, gas, and electric light were entirely unknown; as fate would have it, the foremost entrepreneur in modern communications came from a place where the only communication was by direct word of mouth."[6]

In America he entered a society where information and communication were open, free, and abundant. He was amazed at this – and turned it to his advantage. His father's health was so poor that he could not work steadily, and so from almost the day he arrived, David supplemented his family's meager, often non-existent income by selling newspapers. He worked morning and evening, before and after school at the Educational Alliance. There were other odd jobs as well, including singing as a boy soprano at a local synagogue.

Ultimately his family's parlous financial situation made it impossible for David to continue his formal education. In 1906, at the age of fifteen, he left school for good to look for a full-time job.

Today we marvel at people who drop out of college and start successful companies. But Sarnoff never attended high school, let alone college. The man who gained fame for his grasp of technology, who became a proficient public speaker and precise writer in his second language, and who conversed and negotiated with world leaders and prominent intellectuals on an equal footing, was essentially self-educated.

Undaunted by his youth and lack of formal schooling, Sarnoff was determined to pursue a career as a reporter. He had sold newspapers, so why not write them? He went to the *New York Herald* building to apply for work. There, by sheer accident, he found his true vocation: a career in electronic communications. When Sarnoff entered the *Herald* building he asked a man he saw behind a window in the lobby for a job. But the man was not a *Herald* employee. He worked for the Commercial Cable Company, an undersea telegraph business that was renting space in the building. The company had an opening for a messenger boy, and young David took it.

[6] C. Dreher, *Sarnoff: An American success* (New York: Quadrangle/The New York Times Book Co., 1977), p. 10.

Entrepreneurial beginnings

Within a few months Sarnoff would leave Commercial Cable because the company would not give him (unpaid) time off to sing at a synagogue during the Jewish holidays. But while he was there he had taught himself Morse code. Another telegrapher, with whom he had exchanged messages, referred him to the Marconi Wireless Telegraph Company of America in downtown Manhattan, a subsidiary of the British firm.

Marconi had no junior operator positions, but it could use an office boy and file clerk. Sarnoff took the job and used the opportunity to learn all he could about the company and the industry. In six years he worked his way up to telegraph operator and, eventually, station manager in such places as Nantucket Island and Sea Gate in Coney Island, as well as on a Canadian sealing expedition.

In 1912 he was named manager of the American Marconi station on the top floor of Wanamaker's department store in New York. There he had a brush with history, which he would later inflate to promote the image of himself as the dauntless executive.

On April 14, 1912, the *Titanic* famously hit an iceberg and began to sink. Thanks to its wireless SOS signals, it was able to attract help from the *SS Carpathia*, which rescued over 500 survivors hours after the sinking. However, in part because no operators were on duty on other nearby ships, 1,700 other passengers perished in the cold Atlantic waters.

Fourteen years later Sarnoff and the publicists at RCA floated the story that he was the first wireless telegrapher to get the *Carpathia*'s message reporting the sinking. They also claimed he had gotten national recognition for receiving all the names of the victims and survivors. In fact, the story asserted, President William Howard Taft had ordered all wireless stations on the East coast off the air so that the young telegrapher would have clear access to messages from the site of the tragedy.[7]

---

[7] See Sarnoff, *Looking ahead*, pp. 22–23, which reproduces the whole fabricated tale as reported in *The Saturday Evening Post* for August 7, 1926.

This PR fairytale was obviously a near-total fabrication, yet it gained wide acceptance. To this day it is occasionally trotted out by careless writers. Even historians who dismiss the claim that Sarnoff was the first to get the news of the *Titanic*'s sinking have gotten caught up in the legend. In Carl Dreher's account, for example, Sarnoff is depicted as sitting at his receiver for three days straight, receiving the names of survivors from the *Carpathia* while VIPs peer over his shoulder and police restrain crowds of relatives and curiosity seekers outside the station.[8]

In fact David Sarnoff was not even on duty at the time of the tragedy. He is mentioned in contemporary news accounts as manager of the station, but credit is given to his assistant J. H. Hughes for picking up "direct communication with Siasconsett, Sagaponack, Cape Cod, Hatteras, Sable Island and many other stations along the coast."[9]

According to historian Alexander B. Magoun, Sarnoff did have some involvement in the aftermath of the *Titanic* sinking. However, it was limited to "working with two other operators at the Wanamaker station to obtain the number of survivors and then in trying to get their names from the Marconi Seagate station before the *Carpathia* arrived with the survivors in New York."[10] Nevertheless the *Titanic* incident had a powerful effect on his future – and that of everyone else in wireless.

On July 23, 1914, US President Taft responded to the tragedy by signing a bill "requiring ships carrying 50 or more persons to carry at least two radio operators, with one on duty at all times."[11]

---

[8] Dreher, *Sarnoff*, p. 29.

[9] From *The Boston American*, April 16, 1912, p. 4, as quoted by http://earlyradio-history.us/amwana.htm, accessed August 23, 2011.

[10] A. Magoun, "Pushing technology: David Sarnoff and Wireless Communications, 1911–1921," presented at IEEE 2001 Conference on the History of Telecommunications, St. John's, Newfoundland, July 26, 2001, p. 3. Available at www.ieeeghn.org/wiki/images/1/1c/Magoun.pdf, accessed February 12, 2012.

[11] www.davidsarnoff.org/rca01.html. Davidsarnoff.org was the official website of the recently closed David Sarnoff Library. Still available online as of this writing, it contains useful facts, timelines, and perspectives on Sarnoff and RCA.

Wireless had arrived as a necessary technology. The government had taken an interest, and "American Marconi expanded its business by a factor of twenty over the next two years."[12] It would not be the last time a government action determined the future of radio and, later, of Marconi and RCA.

Thwarted entrepreneur

In 1915 Sarnoff's talent for recognizing and commercializing promising new technology was brilliantly demonstrated in the famous "Radio Music Box Memo" he submitted to American Marconi management. The recent emergence of continuous wave transmission technology made it possible for radio stations to transmit voice and music, not just the dots and dashes of Morse code. In his memo the young manager proposed that Marconi exploit this capability by building and selling receivers for a voice and music service, which it would provide.

Radio transmission of voice and music was not new. It dated from Reginald Fessenden's experiments of 1900 and 1906 – the world's first "broadcasts." By May 1914 Frederick M. Sammis, American Marconi's chief engineer, had set up a transmitter that could send voice and music to Marconi-equipped ships.

Lee De Forest, a noted if controversial electronics pioneer, used the audion amplifying vacuum tube he had invented in 1906 to run an experimental voice-and-music radio station for a while, then sold the rights to the device to the American Telephone and Telegraph Company (AT&T) in 1913. Two years later the telephone giant used it to start transcontinental wired telephony and to send wireless telephone messages to distant receivers. No one took voice and music radio seriously.

Poor reception was one reason: static frequently obliterated the weak radio signals of the day. But in late 1913 Sarnoff got a glimpse of the future of radio. Edwin H. Armstrong, a major figure in radio

---

[12] Magoun, "Pushing technology," p. 3.

and electronic technology, had developed a regenerative receiving circuit that miraculously captured and clarified weak signals. On hearing a public demonstration Sarnoff raved about its capabilities to management. In London, however, Guglielmo Marconi himself read the memo and decided that the invention was nothing special.

To confirm his initial impressions, Sarnoff had Armstrong conduct another demonstration at the Marconi receiving station in Belmar, New Jersey. He reported that the receiver reliably logged signals from Clifden, Ireland; Honolulu; and Nauen, Germany. His conclusion: "The results obtained with Mr. Armstrong's invention are sufficiently convincing to warrant our most careful investigation of his patents and circuits, etc., for ... I am of the opinion that it is the most remarkable receiving system in existence."[13]

It was a revelatory demonstration, which he recalled years later in a letter to Armstrong. "Whatever chills the air produced," he said, "were more than extinguished by the warmth of the thrill which came to me at hearing for the first time signals from across the Atlantic and across the Pacific."[14] Sarnoff's reward for his initiative was a reprimand for misuse of Marconi facilities.

Undaunted, Sarnoff experimented with transmitting music from Wanamaker's that he received on a ship sixty miles away. And the next year he returned to the topic in the "Radio Music Box" memo. Others had previously recognized the technical importance of continuous wave transmission, but few understood its commercial potential. Only Sarnoff envisioned a new industry based on the technology.

---

[13] Sarnoff, *Looking ahead*, pp. 7–8. Years later, when two Supreme Court cases awarded the patent for Armstrong's regenerative circuit to De Forest, Sarnoff and RCA did not come to Armstrong's defense, possibly because the company stood to profit from the decisions. However, RCA's staff was among those who affirmed Armstrong's priority in the invention when he tried to return the Institute of Radio Engineers (IRE) Medal of Honor he had been awarded for this achievement.

[14] Quoted in D. Stashower, *The boy genius and the mogul: The untold story of television* (New York: Broadway Books, 2002), p. 4.

> I have in mind a plan of development which would make
> radio a "household utility" in the same sense as the piano
> or phonograph. The idea is to bring music into the house by
> wireless ...
>
> The "Radio Music Box" can be supplied with amplifying
> tubes and a loudspeaking telephone, all of which can be neatly
> mounted in one box.... Within such a [transmission] radius [of 25
> to 50 miles] there reside hundreds of thousands of families ...
>
> The manufacture of the "Radio Music Box," including
> antenna, in large quantities would make possible their sale at a
> moderate figure of perhaps $75 per outfit [around $1,600 in 2011
> dollars]. The main revenue to be derived would be from the sale
> of "Radio Music Boxes," which, if manufactured in quantities of
> a hundred thousand or so, should yield a handsome profit ...
>
> There are about 15 million families in the United States
> alone, and if only 1 million, or 7 percent of the total families,
> thought well of the idea, it would, at the figure mentioned, mean
> a gross business of about $75 million.[15]

Almost in passing, Sarnoff broached the idea of an industry that did not yet exist, one that would be called "broadcasting." It is a feat of innovative thinking, delivered in an offhand manner.

But he was addressing men who came from the world of telegraphs and telephones. They viewed radio as an extension of these technologies, limited to sending and receiving messages, point to point, individual to individual. "Streaming" music and news – to use an Internet catchphrase – to a large audience seemed a bizarre concept to them. Yet that's exactly what Sarnoff's memo presupposed.

It didn't stop there. Characteristically, Sarnoff also analyzed the scheme's business potential. His projected revenues of $75 million ($1.6 billion in 2011 dollars) would represent a fabulous windfall for American Marconi. When the plan was finally implemented in

---

[15] Sarnoff, *Looking ahead*, pp. 31–33. Some historians have argued that the memo was actually written in 1916.

a somewhat different form, his figures proved remarkably accurate. That wouldn't happen for several years. Marconi officials had no confidence in his project, and the memo was shelved.

THE US NAVY MANDATES A MONOPOLY

Meanwhile Europe was fast in the grip of World War I. Allies on both sides of the conflict were finding strategic uses for electronic communications technologies, while trying to sabotage those of their enemies. With communications cables especially vulnerable to attack, wireless began to assume greater importance as a medium for exchanging military and diplomatic messages.

Even before the US officially entered the war, the government recognized the strategic significance of radio and took steps to protect its interest. In 1914 the US Navy, whose need for ship-to-shore communications made it especially interested in wireless, teamed with AT&T, the government-sanctioned telephone monopoly, to expand its capabilities.

In 1916 the Navy assumed control of all radio patents. When the US declared war on Germany, the Navy was in command of most transatlantic wireless stations and equipment in the country as a matter of national security.[16] The shockwaves from this action produced a radical change in the structure of the nascent US radio industry in the United States, and shaped the development of all electronic mass media for years to come.

With the Navy Radio Bureau controlling wireless communications, American Marconi, as a preferred supplier, remained in a dominant position. But everything changed once the war was over. Public sentiment against foreign domination of radio in the US had been building for years. The war only reinforced these feelings. Radio had

---

[16] In 1916 Congress considered a bill authorizing the Navy to operate radio stations in competition with private industry even in peacetime. Later bills to similar effect were proposed in 1918 and 1919. Sarnoff, as Secretary of the Institute of Radio Engineers, testified before Congress in opposition to this legislation – his introduction to dealing with government initiatives. See D. Sarnoff, *Looking ahead,* pp. 10–13, for his testimony.

proven valuable in combat and diplomacy, and Washington decided that it was intolerable to have such a crucial national resource in foreign – that is, British – hands.

Government involvement: Creating RCA

British Marconi managed to fan the flames in 1919 by offering to buy up General Electric's total output of the Alexanderson alternator, a key transmitting device. The Navy feared that by cornering the market on the alternators, Marconi would effectively control US radio for years to come. Navy chiefs met with GE officials to express their strong opposition to the sale. They proposed instead that government and business collaborate to establish an American-owned company that would wrest control of the country's airwaves from foreign interests.

Under this mandate GE officials met with Marconi officials in London and negotiated the purchase of American Marconi, with GE holding a controlling interest. On December 1, 1919, the patriotically named Radio Corporation of America was formed. Its board included a Navy admiral along with executives from GE and officials from the former American Marconi.

The firm's incorporation documents specified that the new corporation had to remain in American hands. David Sarnoff, only twenty-eight years old but already recognized as a savvy judge of technology and an aggressive businessman, was its commercial manager.

The rise of IP pools

It was one thing to found an American radio company. Ensuring its survival was another. RCA, as it came to be known, faced a structural problem in the industry. Unlike Edison's light bulb, the invention of radio had been a group effort, and several individuals had developed and patented key technologies. To be successful, RCA needed access to any intellectual property (IP) that could help it establish a fast, reliable radio system.

This IP was scattered among various interests. For example, Westinghouse owned the rights to Fessenden's patents. And when RCA didn't act on Sarnoff's recommendation that it buy the rights to Armstrong's regenerative circuit for broadcasting and reception, and the rights to his even more advanced superheterodyne receiver, Westinghouse acquired them instead. It paid $335,000, plus a $200,000 contingency (totaling nearly $7 million in 2011 dollars) should Armstrong lose his then-pending patent infringement suit.[17] In addition, AT&T owned the rights to De Forest's audion tube, and claimed a monopoly over the idea of sending voices through the air.

Pooling IP from several sources to create complex new products is commonplace in today's high-technology world. Standards committees regularly put together specifications that include technology from various companies, each of which collects royalties for its use. But in 1919 this was a new concept. It is not too much to claim that radio set the pattern for every technology that followed.

RCA had powerful help in negotiating the licensing of the IP it needed. The Navy pressured patent holders, especially AT&T, to cooperate. In return for their roughly 2,000 patents, the original IP holders would get large blocks of shares of the new company. Soon RCA had four owners: GE, AT&T, Westinghouse, and (rather oddly) the United Fruit Company. The latter not only licensed patents it held on loop antennas, it agreed to purchase stock in lieu of paying the new company for Marconi transmitters that it had found unsatisfactory. All four companies assented to a cross-licensing agreement so that RCA could develop practical trans-oceanic and ship-borne wireless communications without fear of litigation. Sarnoff would soon use this agreement to pursue his broadcasting vision.

Viewed from a twenty-first-century perspective, the birth of RCA stands out in two ways. First, if you substitute "venture capital

[17] See T. Lewis, *Empire of the air: The men who made radio* (New York: HarperCollins, 1991), pp. 150–55, for a summary of the patent situation surrounding RCA. This chapter draws heavily on Dreher and Lewis for its history of RCA's early years.

firms" for "corporate owners," the deal is strikingly similar to the way entrepreneurial companies have been established over the last thirty years. Decades before the birth of the modern venture capital industry, GE, AT&T, Westinghouse, and United Fruit acted like venture capitalists, exchanging value (money, IP, or both) for major ownership shares in the new entity.

Second, the action of the US government in creating RCA bears comparison to how other countries, from that era right up to the present day, have taken an active role in developing telecommunications in particular and industrial growth in general. Other countries defined telecommunications as a national interest and created state-owned monopolies aligned with their postal systems. In its determination to create an American wireless company, the US government created monopolies in radio hardware (GE and Westinghouse) as well as telephones (AT&T). And today's mercantilist countries, such as China, are using state-controlled companies to build their industrial bases.

At the outset, of course, RCA was essentially a radio services company, focused on receiver sales and marine communications, and beholden to its owners. But things were about to change. David Sarnoff, acting as behind-the-scenes advisor to the new company's executives, took on the role of entrepreneur in promoting the company's entry into a totally new industry. Ultimately this would transform RCA, and elevate Sarnoff to the executive suite.

THE BIRTH OF COMMERCIAL RADIO

Although RCA had limited autonomy, it gave Sarnoff the entrepreneurial platform he needed. His vision for achieving commercial success for radio was to turn it into a household necessity by broadcasting voice and music, and he immediately started promoting that agenda.

His first move was to preserve RCA's ability to produce technical innovations on its own. In 1919 GE had proposed to take over all of the company's research and engineering activities. Without its engineers, RCA would be no more than a service and marketing organization. Sarnoff lobbied against the idea on the grounds that the young company needed its own development team, one that wouldn't be distracted by the larger corporate priorities at GE. He won his point.

That done, in 1920 he resurrected his "Radio Music Box" idea. In a twenty-eight-page memo to Owen D. Young, the GE executive who sat as chairman of RCA's board, he expanded his original 1915 proposal with a three-year plan for achieving sales of a million sets. Young was impressed enough to authorize construction of a prototype receiver. All that was needed now to commercialize the new communications medium was an audience – and a business model.

Finding an audience

Audience-building was a crucial task if radio was to be a commercial success. It was especially urgent for Sarnoff because, to borrow twenty-first-century parlance, his radio music box idea had gone viral, and competition was heating up. By 1920 a small but lively community of amateur radio buffs was experimenting with broadcasts of news, comment, and music over their own amateur stations. One of them, Frank Conrad, a Westinghouse engineer based in Pittsburgh, was broadcasting programs that a local department store used to promote sales of receivers.

It didn't take long for Westinghouse to recognize broadcasting's business potential. It quickly founded KDKA, still a major radio and TV broadcaster, thus elevating Conrad's intermittent broadcasts to the status of a daily occurrence. Soon it was setting up stations on the roofs of its manufacturing plants in Newark, NJ, East Springfield, MA, and Chicago, IL (all of which are broadcasting to this day). Westinghouse also began manufacturing tube and crystal receivers for sale to the listening public.

Meanwhile RCA was playing catch-up. Plans for mass production of its own broadcast receivers were in process, but it needed the Westinghouse patents to make them marketable. By the end of

1920 the two companies were negotiating, and in March of 1921 the IP-for-stock swap described above was complete.

Events were moving fast. On April 29 Sarnoff was made general manager of RCA, giving him the power to push forward his broadcasting concept. He decided to stimulate interest in radio among the general public, and at the same time establish RCA as a force in broadcasting, by staging a spectacular broadcasting event that would attract an audience beyond any previous program.

He chose the biggest audience draw of the time: the heavyweight championship boxing match between Jack Dempsey and the French champion Georges Carpentier on July 2, 1921, in Jersey City, New Jersey. "In less than three months, he and a group of engineers assembled from RCA received permission from the federal government to establish a station, appropriated a transmitter that General Electric had built for the Navy, strung broadcasting aerials from towers at the Lackawanna Railroad yards, and publicized the broadcast through newspaper articles."[18]

Few people owned radio receivers at the time, so RCA devised a plan to let a significant number of non-owners listen to the event. It partnered with the National Amateur Wireless Association to arrange for the installation of loudspeakers in nearly 100 theaters and other public places between Pennsylvania and Massachusetts. Then, in an effort to use postwar patriotic sentiment to boost attendance, Sarnoff announced that a portion of the proceeds would go to two charities: the Navy Club and a fund for rebuilding France.

The announcer for the broadcast, Major J. Andrew White, the editor of RCA's magazine *Wireless Age*, later recalled that few people thought the event would be a success. "This experiment, frowned upon as 'just plain crazy' by financiers, had been built on the enthusiastic dream of young David Sarnoff. To pull it off, Sarnoff and I had scrounged $1,500 from a special account of the then new Radio Corporation of America."[19]

[18] Lewis, *Empire of the air*, p. 158.
[19] Reprinted from *Reader's Digest*, December 1955, in Sarnoff, *Looking ahead*, p. 34.

Sarnoff's risky promotion paid off. Perhaps 300,000 people paid to hear the broadcast of the prizefight, and another 100,000 listened for free through loudspeakers attached to the *New York Times* building. The event jump-started the age of mass media: "That night the scale and potential of the medium were transformed. Suddenly the size of an audience was no longer constrained by floor space or seating capacity; it became almost limitless."[20]

Dempsey knocked out Carpentier in the fourth round, fortunately for RCA, because the transmitter melted down minutes later. It had done its job. Sarnoff's entrepreneurial vision of a new medium and a new industry had been validated. Radio was on the map as a growth industry.

Ads and networks: New models for a developing business

Two years later hundreds of stations were on the air across America. They were established by banks, churches, police departments, schools, corporations, small businesses, newspapers, and other organizations.

Over 400,000 households had bought radios, so there was a sizeable audience for broadcasts. Broadcasting was a playground for self-expression and self-promotion, much as the early Internet was, when personal websites were popular. Also like the early Internet, radio did not have a fully developed business model. Even visionaries like Sarnoff saw broadcasting as a public service, not a business, conceiving its principal function as "entertaining, informing, and educating the nation and ... therefore ... a public service."[21]

Set makers, with RCA the largest of all, saw it as a service that would promote the sale of their radio receivers, not as a business in itself. Sarnoff had proposed this model in his 1915 memo. In 1921 RCA founded its own station, WJY in New York, to fulfill this

---

[20] E. Robinson, "Mass mediums: They channeled the modern age (and made it pay)," *Fortune*, September 6, 1999; accessed August 23, 2011 at http://money.cnn.com/magazines/fortune/fortune_archive/1999/09/06/265282/index.htm

[21] Sarnoff, *Looking ahead*, p. 41.

purpose. It later acquired WJZ, the Westinghouse station in Newark, which it moved to New York. The twinned stations began broadcasting on May 16, 1923.

Sarnoff clung to this flawed model for broadcasting until a major corporate crisis prompted him to consider another, more entrepreneurial one. RCA's New York stations were in direct competition with WEAF, AT&T's New York outlet, just when tensions were rising between the telephone giant and RCA's two other big shareholders.

Their dispute grew out of the terms of the company's incorporation agreement, which had set up a loosely defined division of labor for the four companies. GE and Westinghouse would manufacture receivers on a 60/40 split for RCA to sell. AT&T took on the manufacture of transmitters. In return it granted RCA rights to build and maintain one-way wireless transmitting stations, whose purpose was not clearly identified as broadcasting.

By 1922 GE and Westinghouse were making money on radio, but AT&T was not, an intolerable situation for its new young president, Walter Sherman Gifford. Gifford also saw broadcasting as an unwarranted expansion of RCA's business model, and moved to correct the situation. At his direction

- AT&T sold its 200,000 shares of RCA stock and gave up its two board seats;
- his company's laboratory began to design a radio receiver that skirted RCA's patents;
- RCA was not allowed to lease telephone lines for broadcast purposes; and
- WEAF would sell commercial time (he called the concept "toll broadcasting").

It was a challenge to the new company's very existence. Without high-quality leased lines RCA would not only have a hard time doing remote broadcasts, it would be unable to link its stations into a network. And "toll broadcasting" changed the rules of the business.

Network radio as a service

Sarnoff has been credited with inventing the network concept for electronic media. In fact, AT&T's two stations in New York and

Washington, DC were the first to be networked, and the telephone giant used its lines to tie in other, non-AT&T stations as well. "By early 1926, the 'WEAF Chain' had expanded to nineteen cities in the Northeast and Midwest, as it slowly spread from its base in New York City."[22]

But Sarnoff was certainly the architect of networks as a commercial enterprise. On June 17, 1922, with RCA still in its infancy and his voice-and-music broadcasting concept just beginning to gain traction, he had proposed that RCA "organize a separate and distinct company ... to acquire the existing broadcasting stations of [Westinghouse, GE, and RCA]." The aim was to build broadcasting "along national rather than local lines."[23]

This network was realized four years later with the formation of the National Broadcasting Company (NBC). At the time of his proposal, however, Sarnoff was still tied to the concept of broadcasting as a "public service." He proposed that it be supported by subsidies from radio manufacturers and their distributors and dealers, and even through philanthropic donations (a foreshadowing of the support mechanism for today's public radio and TV stations).

By 1926, when NBC was formed, he had reversed his opinion, as any savvy entrepreneur must when market conditions and financial realities demand it. Meanwhile a government action set the table for the establishment of the network.

Government involvement: Antitrust action
By labeling ads as "toll broadcasting" AT&T put RCA in a bind. Its nomenclature tied radio to the telephone concept of a "toll call," an area where the telephone company had the right to do business and presumably, under the terms of its incorporation, RCA did not. In August 1922 WEAF carried its first commercial, or "toll broadcast," making it the first national company to do so.

---

[22] http://earlyradiohistory.us/sec019.htm (April 16, 1912).
[23] Letter to E. W. Rice, honorary chairman of GE, reproduced in D. Sarnoff, *Looking ahead*, pp. 41–43.

When negotiations over their dispute failed, all of the companies involved finally agreed to binding arbitration, which Sarnoff had been recommending all along. Matters quickly got more complicated when the government's Federal Trade Commission (FTC) dropped a bombshell in early 1924, charging all five companies – AT&T, GE, Westinghouse, United Fruit, and RCA – with conspiring to restrain trade and create a monopoly in every aspect of radio device manufacture and sales. RCA was under siege from inside and outside.

Before the FTC's charge was acted on, the results of the arbitration were announced. They went RCA's way on every substantial point, including the right to collect "tolls" for broadcasts. AT&T countered by pointing out that if the cross-licensing agreement of 1921 stood, it was proof of the government's claim of a conspiracy to restrain trade. RCA's patent structure was in danger – and so was AT&T's.

Sarnoff's entrepreneurial skills came to the fore. In negotiations sanctioned by RCA's Young and AT&T's Gifford, he proposed a business-based solution: get AT&T out of broadcasting, with RCA buying WEAF and taking over its Washington outlet, in return for AT&T providing nationwide landline and microwave linkages for RCA's proposed network. AT&T got an upfront payment and a handsome continuing revenue stream, while RCA got control over its patent pool and the freedom to seek its destiny.

This was not the last assault by the government on RCA's patent policies, but for the moment the point was moot. Sarnoff turned his attention to finalizing the NBC network, which was announced in late 1926. He had also come to the realization that broadcasting had to develop a source of revenues, and advertising was the obvious way to do it. A new era had begun.

In those days the pioneers were figuring out the rules as they went along, with the government looking over their shoulders. It is not surprising, then, that RCA unwittingly structured NBC in a way that eventually invited government oversight. A few months after NBC's launch it divided the stations into the more commercial "Red" network built around WEAF, and a "Blue" network that emphasized news and cultural programs, with WJZ as its flagship. Twelve years later the government would decide that this looked like a monopoly, too.

Sarnoff continued his entrepreneurial activities through the rest of the decade. In 1928 he joined forces with Joseph Kennedy, the Boston financier, diplomat, and scion of the Kennedy political dynasty, to build a movie studio around RCA's sound system for motion pictures. Radio Keith Orpheum (RKO) produced mostly B pictures, but was moderately successful.

His most daring business innovation of the 1920s, after RCA and NBC, was the acquisition of the Victor Talking Machine Company of Camden, New Jersey. Victor needed radio chassis for combination radio/phonograph sets if it was to survive the onslaught of the radio craze. It had been buying them from RCA since 1925, but sales continued to decline. In 1928 it agreed to negotiate with RCA to be acquired. For RCA the deal was a strategic masterstroke. Victor's manufacturing facility promised to free the company from its dependence on GE and Westinghouse, and Victor's recording business allowed it to earn profits from content as well as broadcasting.

Initially the terms of the contract, negotiated while Sarnoff was in Europe on a diplomatic mission, were unsatisfactory. The new entity was set up as a separate manufacturing company, and GE and Westinghouse had the same 60/40 split of this manufacturing firm as they did in making receivers for RCA. Sarnoff renegotiated the terms so that RCA owned 50 percent of the new company. The deal was ratified in December 1929. It put considerable strain on the company's finances, as upgrading Victor's facilities proved costly, but Sarnoff – and RCA – was now the dominant force in electronic media and technology.

Television: Intrapreneurial beginnings
On January 3, 1930, David Sarnoff became President of RCA. He had arrived in America as a nine-year-old boy in a desperately poor immigrant family just thirty years before. Now he was at the top of a burgeoning industry he had helped to create. Between 1919 and 1929

RCA's revenues had grown from $2 million to $182 million ($2.3 billion in 2011 dollars).

From this point on he sought to consolidate and grow the corporate empire he had been instrumental in building. But he did not abandon his entrepreneurial approach. Instead he became an intrapreneur, constantly pushing RCA to create the next big technological breakthrough.

As an entrepreneur Sarnoff's history goes right to the heart of the major topic of this book. He is an outstanding example of how innovators can work within or around externally imposed constraints to build companies – or whole industries – that create significant economic value. As an intrapreneur he continued this work, indeed enlarged on it, but this period of his life is less central to our theme. Nevertheless it deserves to be summarized, not just in homage to a giant of innovation, but to demonstrate how even established companies have to concern themselves with the opinions and actions of government.

ADDING SIGHT TO SOUND

RCA was successful beyond its founders' wildest imaginings, thanks to its move into broadcast radio equipment, stations, and networks. Yet Sarnoff saw bigger things ahead. As early as 1923, when radio was still in its infancy, he advised the RCA Board of Directors that

> television, which is the technical name for seeing instead of hearing, will come to pass in due course ... Thus, it may well be expected that radio development will provide a situation whereby we shall be able actually to see as well as read in New York, within an hour or so, the event taking place in London, Buenos Aires, or Tokyo.
>
> I also believe that transmission and reception of motion pictures by radio will be worked out within the next decade.[24]

[24] Sarnoff, *Looking ahead*, p. 88.

Sarnoff was not a prophet, at least not in the sense of seeing things that did not yet exist. Television experimentation had begun in 1873, a half-century before his memo. Speculation about the future of television had begun to appear in newspapers and in hobbyist magazines such as *Wireless World and Radio Review* in England and *Radio Times* in the US.

In the early 1920s there had been some successful experiments by British inventor John Logie Baird and American Charles F. Jenkins at sending moving pictures over a wire. They used crude electromechanical apparatus to capture the images. In 1927 General Electric succeeded in broadcasting a moving picture from such an electromechanical system. Its inventor, Ernst Alexanderson, who had developed the Alexanderson alternator, predicted that every American home would have a TV set within ten years.[25]

While Sarnoff was not a prophet, he was a visionary. Although he publicly supported Alexanderson's efforts as part of the GE team, privately he was not convinced by what he saw, and even less certain that Alexanderson's system was practical.[26] In January 1929, a year before he became RCA's president, he met with the engineer who would help him realize his vision: Vladimir K. Zworykin, a Russian émigré then working at Westinghouse.

Zworykin had taken out patents on what he dubbed an "iconoscope," an early vacuum tube-based TV camera. He had also adopted a promising approach to displays from French inventor Edouard Belin. Westinghouse was not interested – but Sarnoff was. An electronic camera and display opened the door to all-electronic television. An electronic system promised better pictures and less cumbersome receivers. That was something Sarnoff could sell to the public.

---

[25] For a thorough and balanced history of the development of TV, see A. B. Magoun, *Television: The life story of a technology* (Baltimore, MD: The Johns Hopkins University Press, 2007). It is the source for many of the facts and dates in this section.

[26] D. Stashower, *The boy genius and the mogul: The untold story of television* (New York: Broadway Books, 2002), pp. 122–23.

Over the next quarter-century David Sarnoff focused a large portion of RCA's resources on the development and commercialization of television. Throughout the same period he found himself dealing with repeated attempts by the US government to control RCA's expansion and curb its business practices. He also faced the task of assuring that the government would set the standards for TV signals, so that any receiver could capture transmissions.

We will briefly survey RCA's progress in developing the technology and the IP portfolio for television. Then we will look at the accommodations the company had to make to satisfy government demands.

Television decade

At his meeting with Zworykin Sarnoff famously asked how much it would cost to realize the electronic system he was proposing. Zworykin estimated it would require $100,000 and two years of work. Equally famously, Sarnoff later claimed the project ultimately cost RCA ten years and $50 million.

The actual figure over that first decade seems to have been closer to $10 million, but Sarnoff may have been referring to the investment up to 1950, when RCA made its first profit on television. Whatever the amount, it was a lot of money. Most of it was spent on RCA's own research, but the company (contrary to myth) also acquired IP from other inventors, as it had during the development of radio.

One holder of IP, however, proved difficult: Philo Farnsworth, a brilliant if erratic inventor and a loner to the core. In 1922, at the age of fifteen, he had developed the concept of "creating an image from a photoelectric surface and scan[ning] it back and forth, before a single aperture that led to the amplifier and transmitter."[27] He didn't have the money to patent this "image dissector," but four years later his

---

[27] Magoun, *Television*, pp. 23–24.

ideas for a working electronic television system convinced an angel investor and eventually a bank. His initial estimate of the cost to build a system around this invention was $5,000. It was about as accurate as Zworykin's.

In 1927 Farnsworth filed a patent for his electronic television system. In 1929 he built the first all-electronic TV system in the world. Although the system was far from being ready for manufacture, his patents later threatened to derail RCA's whole television endeavor. The patents on the image dissector camera were to prove especially troublesome. Zworykin had filed patents for the iconoscope earlier than Farnsworth did for his camera, but Zworykin's filings were flawed. A contest ensued over whose patents had priority. In 1935 a patent examiner held that Farnsworth's image dissector patents were valid and vacated many of Zworykin's claims.

Ironically, it was the iconoscope, not Farnsworth's invention, that served as the basis for all early TV cameras. The image dissector ultimately proved impractical. It had no way to store electrons, resulting in a light sensitivity so low that it could not generate a usable image except under bright direct sunlight or powerful (and hot) studio lamps. Instead of abandoning his design, Farnsworth tried to remedy the flaw through improvements in the circuitry that followed the imager. In the process he produced valuable work (and patents) in other areas of TV, but his dissector was a commercial failure.

However, its design included some fundamental imaging technology. During the 1930s "it became clear to RCA's technical staff [that they] would have to draw on Farnsworth's electronic image and low-velocity scanning"[28] to improve their own cameras. In 1939 RCA finally agreed to license Farnsworth's patents for a million dollars plus royalties.

---

[28] *Ibid.*, p. 62. See the following pages of this book for a more detailed account of the progress of television during the decade summarized here.

Throughout the 1930s, Sarnoff made sure that corporate funding was available to support the television research and development effort at RCA despite the Great Depression. The company's engineers responded by discovering that VHF frequencies (40 to 80 MHz) were adequate for broadcasting; that a frame rate of 30 frames per second (fps) would avoid flicker on brighter displays; and that a resolution of 400 lines was needed to give viewers the equivalent of a home-movie experience. They also developed a system of interlacing that showed two half-images at 60 fps.

Other companies pursuing the dream of future home television sales, including Farnsworth, Philco, Zenith, DuMont, and GE, were concerned that RCA would dominate the market. RCA tried to allay their fears by partnering with all of them but DuMont and Farnsworth. It shared its research, tested their equipment, consulted with them on design issues, and more.

Starting an industry

By 1938 Sarnoff felt the technology was ready. He decided to force the hand of the Federal Communications Commission (FCC) to finalize broadcasting standards so he and his competitors could begin selling receivers and other equipment that were compatible with each other.

As he did with the Dempsey-Carpentier broadcast that launched radio, he chose a big event to dramatize the new technology. Ten days before the opening of the 1939 New York World's Fair in Queens, New York, he stood in front of the RCA pavilion and read his now-famous announcement of the birth of television. An NBC camera captured the moment for viewers at the RCA Building in New York City.

> On April 30th, the National Broadcasting Company will
> begin the first regular public television-program service in
> the history of our country; and television receiving sets will
> be in the hands of merchants in the New York area for public

purchase. A new art and a new industry, which eventually will provide entertainment and information for millions and new employment for large numbers of men and women, are here ... And now we add radio sight to sound.[29]

Twice during the speech he stressed the economic benefits of the new industry. As a chief executive he knew this argument would serve him well in disputes with the government, which were sure to come. He also arranged it so that when Franklin Delano Roosevelt opened the Fair, FDR became the first president ever to appear on television. Thousands of fair-goers saw RCA's live demonstration of television at its pavilion.

There was still no television standard. With the television roll-out in jeopardy, Sarnoff bore the brunt of ridicule from the media and attacks by RCA's competitors Zenith, Philco, and DuMont. When the FCC met in January 1940 under new chairman James Fly it declined to set a standard, and in a caution obviously targeted at RCA warned industry members against trying to set a de facto standard.

Soon the media changed their minds and accused the FCC of obstructing progress and interfering with business. Sarnoff and Fly were called in to testify before the Interstate Commerce Committee. Even FDR got involved, asking Sarnoff to have lunch with Fly to resolve their dispute. Finally Fly turned to an industry expert to form the National Television Systems Committee (NTSC) to resolve the impasse. After much testing of systems and arguments over different approaches, in May 1941 the NTSC recommended a standard of 525 lines at 30 fps interlaced, in most respects similar to the RCA system.

Television was a reality at last. Sarnoff's vision was achieved. But commercialization would have to wait. On December 7, 1941, the day of the attack on Pearl Harbor, David Sarnoff sent FDR a telegram saying, "All our facilities are ready and at your instant service.

[29] Sarnoff, *Looking ahead,* pp. 100–101.

We await your commands." TV manufacturing was put on hold for the duration of World War II.

Postwar television boom

It wasn't until September 1946 that RCA began building TV sets again. During the war RCA had put its research and manufacturing resources to work for Allied military efforts. David Sarnoff, always a proud patriot, had attained the rank of brigadier general through his personal involvement in military communications and media management. His biggest achievement was setting up the communications structure for D-Day and later, under personal orders from General (later President) Eisenhower.

During the war engineers at RCA Laboratories in Princeton (founded in 1941 to centralize the company's research activities) and at RCA Victor had made significant advances in cameras and receivers, for use in guided bombs and aerial reconnaissance. They now adapted this new technology to commercial products.

But the market for receivers in particular promised to be so large that RCA would not be able to meet the demand on its own. To promote the manufacture of TV sets, in 1947 RCA invited its patent licensees to tour the RCA Victor factory in Camden and consult with its engineers. Its technical bulletins helped competitors build versions of RCA's flagship television set for sale under their own names.

On the transmission side, Sarnoff urged affiliates of the NBC radio network to take out television licenses, and threatened to cancel their affiliation if they didn't. NBC began programming a heavy schedule of sports to attract viewers, and Milton Berle's weekly comedy show was TV's first hit program. Pooled coverage of the Democratic and Republican national conventions by the NBC, CBS, ABC, and DuMont networks in 1948 created even more buzz around the new medium.

It was a comprehensive strategy to promote commercial TV, and it was a huge success. According to Carl Dreher, there were

175,000 receivers in use by the end of 1947, and seven million in 1950. "About half of this bonanza accrued to RCA. Sarnoff soon had his $50 million back, and then some."[30]

Adding color to black-and-white

Instead of accepting the "bonanza" and shifting his focus to maximizing profits, Sarnoff followed his entrepreneurial instincts, much to the dismay of Wall Street. He poured even more money into a new R&D project: the development of an all-electronic color television. His motivation came from his vision of the future of TV – and the threat of competition from CBS, his chief rival.

This drama played out as a repeat of the debate over electromechanical vs. electronic systems from the early days of TV. CBS engineer Peter Goldmark, who was convinced that monochrome television was a blind alley, had campaigned for a delay in the FCC's 1941 march toward a television standard until color was feasible. He wanted to hold out for a color system, and was exploring electromechanical systems to realize color broadcasting and reception.

Having failed to block implementation of the NTSC standard in 1945 and again in 1946, he proposed a color system he had developed for CBS as the next television standard. It drew on color experiments from the 1920s, and used spinning color wheels at the camera and the receiver to capture and reproduce color information. CBS conducted hundreds of demonstrations of its system for advertisers and the public.

Sarnoff was just as interested in color. In 1930 he had foreseen a day when television would advance "to the stage when color as well as shadow would be faithfully transmitted."[31] But he and his engineers, who experimented with color and 3D television using color wheels and drums as late as 1945, rejected the electromechanical approach

---

[30] Dreher, *Sarnoff*, p. 162.

[31] Sarnoff, *Looking ahead*, p. 130. The quote comes from an article in *The New York Times*, July 1, 1930.

as too limited and too complex. Instead they raced to develop an all-electronic system, which they announced and demonstrated in 1946.

The story of RCA's battle with CBS for FCC approval of its color television system has become a legend in the annals of corporate/government interaction. In 1947 Wayne Coy became the chairperson of the FCC. Coy "became a partisan supporter of the CBS color system. He disliked RCA's monopolistic position in broadcast technologies."[32] In July 1949 he called for proposals for color television systems that would be compatible with the booming NTSC monochrome system. The deck was stacked against RCA.

By the time of the first hearings in September, CBS had a single-tube electromechanical system that worked, but required three inches of spinning color wheel for every inch of screen size. A 17-inch screen would require a 51-inch spinning wheel. RCA had a bulky electronic system with three picture tubes projecting onto a screen that failed more than it worked. Electronic color TV needed a single-tube display.

RCA's Princeton laboratory actually delivered that tube, the world's first integrated color video display, only six months later in March 1950. It worked, and it was monochrome-compatible, but it produced an unrefined picture with inaccurate colors. In spite of these faults the NTSC, in its second incarnation, began to support the early-stage RCA system. By then, however, it was too late. At the FCC hearings in May, Sarnoff said the choice was, "Shall American television move forward or backward?"[33] In spite of his testimony the FCC declared the CBS system as the US standard for color TV.

It was a disaster for television – and for CBS. The network's manufacturing partner was never able to produce receivers in volume with adequate quality. CBS was forced to subsidize each of the

---

[32] Magoun, *Television*, p. 98.
[33] Sarnoff, *Looking ahead*, pp. 135–41 reproduces the relevant sections of his testimony.

sets it sold. When the Korean War started, and parts became hard to obtain, the network had an excuse to cease production.

Meanwhile RCA and NBC had been steadily improving their electronic system. On December 17, 1953, Coy and other FCC members having stepped down, the commission approved it as the new standard.

RCA did not reap the fruits of its victory quickly. Color TV cost the company $130 million over ten years,[34] and it only began to show a profit in 1962, eight years after commercialization, when Sarnoff ordered NBC to broadcast all its prime time shows in color. Eventually, however, sales of color sets and license fees from its patents in the field provided the company with another bonanza. It had been well worth the intrapreneurial risk.

LOOKING BACK

David Sarnoff proved to be an uncommonly gifted corporate executive, and maintained an intrapreneurial drive that pushed his organization to continue its innovations. There are valuable lessons to be learned from analyzing his strategies. The short summary:

- owning and controlling intellectual property is a key to long-term success in dynamic technology industries;
- having internal innovation resources is vital to continued success;
- the government can be both friend and foe – the trick is to manage relationships; and
- the wisdom to know when to do battle and when to concede can determine the future of a business in the public eye.

In the present era, Qualcomm, under the direction of its founder Irwin Jacobs, is a close analog to RCA and Sarnoff. Both companies pioneered advanced wireless technologies, both built business strategies around IP, and both faced charges of monopolistic practices. The astute reader will be able to come up with other examples of contemporary leaders and their companies that compare to these two.

[34] Dreher, *Looking ahead*, p. 215.

Sarnoff's career was not without controversy, of course. Critics have bemoaned his aggressive business tactics, his later treatment of his old friend Edwin Armstrong, and some of the hawkish political stances he took in the 1950s and 1960s. But on balance he did more for his industry – and the American economy – than any other business leader of his time.

He would not have succeeded without his remarkable ability to manage intellectual property and, especially, his company's relationship with the government. In spite of his influence with Washington politicians, his policies at RCA led to battles with the FCC and other governmental agencies that can stand as cautionary tales for entrepreneurs of our time. It is an unfortunate fact of life that creators of new industries often find themselves painted as monopolists. Google and Microsoft are recent examples.

Here are some of the major challenges that Sarnoff faced and managed to survive.

1930: Electronics monopoly action. Five months after Sarnoff became president of RCA, the company was hit with an antitrust action over the patent pool among itself and GE, Westinghouse, and AT&T, its major shareholders. Sarnoff had helped establish a royalty structure with high licensing fees, a requirement that radio set makers use RCA vacuum tubes, and other constraints, and the set makers complained. The government charged that the patent pool and the ownership structure under which RCA was operating were monopolistic and illegal – even though the government had helped create that structure.

Outcome. After two years of negotiations, the Department of Justice approved a consent decree in which Sarnoff got most of what he wanted: total independence and the unification of RCA. GE and Westinghouse left RCA's board, distributed their RCA stock among their shareholders, and agreed not to compete with the newly independent company for two years. This also solved the patent pool question, as all parties were free to compete with each other. The company also lowered its royalty terms to silence set-maker complaints.

1939: FCC radio network action. Networks made radio commercially viable, but the FCC was concerned about their monopolistic effects. Commission chairman Fly "championed increased regulation of the networks and used his power to force the National Broadcasting Company to divest itself of the blue network."[35] His grounds were that the Red and Blue networks used their wholly owned stations to dominate audiences, affiliates, and advertising.

Outcome. NBC divided the networks into two companies in case RCA's appeal of the decision failed. In 1943, after the Supreme Court ruled against RCA, the company sold the Blue Network and its stations for $8 million. In 1945 it was renamed the American Broadcasting Company (ABC). This spinoff ultimately became the third major US radio and TV network after NBC and CBS, and branched out into music and other media as well. Acquired by the Walt Disney Company in 1996, it is a major player in broadcast and cable television, with a particular strength in sports thanks to cable sports network ESPN, its corporate partner. Although Sarnoff was forced to divest ABC, it should still be taken into account when calculating the economic value that resulted from his business innovations.

1954: Package licensing antitrust suit. RCA's patent licensing policies came under scrutiny again nearly a quarter-century after the patent pool action. In 1946 Zenith Radio had stopped paying royalties on patents licensed by RCA and brought triple-damage suits against RCA, GE, and Westinghouse, starting "a jungle growth of litigation"[36] among licensees and codefendants. The Justice Department joined in with a civil antitrust complaint in 1954.

Outcome. The core of the complaints was the practice of "packaging" patents for license, which forced licensees to pay royalties on several patents even if they only needed one. RCA defended its policies by saying it granted "patent licenses to competitors and others

---

[35] Lewis, *Empire of the air*, p. 302.
[36] E. Lyons, *David Sarnoff: A biography* (New York: Harper & Row, 1966), p. 287.

on reasonable and non-discriminatory terms and without restriction."[37] RCA lost the suit in what was then the largest antitrust recovery in history, and had to modify its licensing structure. In 1957 RCA signed a consent decree on patent licensing, granting free licenses on all broadcast technology to US companies, finally putting to rest an issue that had been pursued by the FCC, the Federal Trade Commission, and the Department of Justice since 1925.

Sarnoff and RCA's example demonstrate that entrepreneurs and corporations may be the darlings of the government in some areas while serving as the target of its displeasure in others. RCA was a government creation, and Sarnoff was influential in the halls and committee rooms of Washington. But he was also operating in a highly charged antitrust environment, and the government could and did step in to block operations that appeared to challenge that stance.

As RCA's encounters with crusading agencies show, it is possible to turn government actions to your advantage, but you must be willing to compromise. And you must also accept the fact that there are times you will have to accept a negative result. Here are a few additional lessons that today's entrepreneur or would-be corporate executive can draw from David Sarnoff's career.

Growth comes with continued innovation. Sarnoff understood better than his peers that technology businesses must innovate to thrive. Indeed, he took a personal interest in new technologies. Every year RCA Laboratories prepared new inventions, "Christmas presents," as he liked to call them, in anticipation of his visits. He had the vision to create RCA Labs, where I spent many years, which became one of the foremost electronics research laboratories in the world. RCA Labs developed and commercialized innovative products and services for as long as Sarnoff was in charge, in fields as diverse as electronic materials and devices, electron microscopes, and microwave drying of penicillin.

---

[37] "RCA asks court to dismiss government anti-trust suit," *Radio Age*, vol. 14, no. 2, April, 1955, p. 12.

IP builds businesses and markets. RCA acquired IP through its own aggressive R&D effort and by licensing crucial patents from others. Its massive patent portfolio allowed the company to build innovative products before anyone else, and to dominate markets. But it also recognized that by licensing IP to others, even competitors, it not only generated cash flow, it helped grow the markets it dominated. The patent licensing strategy of RCA was managed by a dedicated licensing organization with the mission to maximize revenues from this source, consistent with the product strategies of the company. Some patents were off limits to licensing because they were too closely linked to current products. This strategy was so successful that the revenues paid for the operations of RCA Laboratories. In effect, the company got its innovations at no cost.

You can't commercialize an innovation overnight. Sarnoff was the undisputed boss of RCA and was able to continue product investments for many years – even if their prospects were unclear to others. None of the world-changing products developed by the company came fast. Radio took over a decade to find its market, and voice-and-music broadcasting took another half-decade to achieve commercial success. Electronic television was under development for fifteen years, and after World War II took another five years to become a major industry. Color TV didn't produce a profit for eight years after commercial introduction. In some cases such things take much less time today – products and services can build their markets in as little as three years – but you still need patience and resources to wait for the results.

In these and many other ways David Sarnoff's extraordinary career is a touchstone for all entrepreneurs. We now turn to more contemporary figures whose successes and failures mirror, extend, or counter his example.

4 Global problem, golden opportunity: Ron Stanton profits from market disruption

> I suppose I could have worked for someone else, but that wouldn't have been fun.

Ron Stanton

Unlike the other entrepreneurs and innovative companies in this book, Ronald Stanton and Transammonia Inc. are not involved in a high-technology industry. While David Sarnoff, for example, built his electronics empire by envisioning markets that did not yet exist for technology still under development, Stanton achieved success by setting up an innovative but non-technical service company in a commodity industry.

Without doubt his business innovation has had a huge impact. Stanton started Transammonia, a company that trades in anhydrous ammonia, in 1965 with only $2,000 of equity capital. In 2008 it became the twenty-eighth largest private corporation in the US, with over $11 billion in revenues. It is the world leader in its sector, and has branched out into other commodity chemicals and liquid natural gas.

That is a remarkable achievement. But why do we include a commodity trading business in our study of global entrepreneurship when all our other cases focus on the high-technology electronics, computer, and communications companies that seem to define our age? In a word, the reason is clarity. It is easy to be distracted by the glamour of the latest technology from appreciating the fundamentals of building an innovative business that creates lasting economic value. With Transammonia, there is no danger of that. Its history and well-defined business model embody the essentials of innovation and entrepreneurship.

Indeed, the story of Transammonia reinforces a basic fact about entrepreneurship: it is mostly about finding a dislocation in the market and building a business to address it. It does not matter whether the dislocation is created by disruptive technology, new government regulations, or an unexpected demand for services. It is the vision of the entrepreneur in finding a solution that makes the difference.

In Transammonia's case the market disruption was precipitated by an industry changeover to a troubled technology for producing ammonia. Stanton realized that this crisis grew out of a logistics problem, not a technical one. The temporary technical glitch had simply exposed the fundamental shortcoming in the commodities market. His response was to introduce a business model that addressed the underlying cause.

Instead of patentable inventions and a portfolio of valuable IP, Transammonia was built on an idea for a new kind of business. Success did not come easily, and the early years were not always "fun." But Stanton exhibited one of the defining traits of the entrepreneur: tenacity. In May 2009, talking about the startup years of his business, he told me: "In the early days I alternated between exhilaration and dejection. It was very tough … I know from experience that no matter how secure you think you might be, complacency is dangerous. Everything you own, everything you've worked for or ever cared about, can vanish in an instant."

As we shall see, his success was not solely a result of his business acumen. It grew in large part from his courage in maintaining the highest level of business integrity, even in the face of possible financial ruin.

In order to understand the challenges he faced, we will begin by looking at the nature of his business and how it diverged from standard industry practice.

TRADING IN REAL COMMODITIES

Stanton's business is specialty commodity trading. Mention commodity trading to most people and they immediately think of financial speculation, which bets on the future prices of commodities such as oil, copper, wheat, or corn.

In normal practice traders in commodity futures never handle the physical materials. They make their profit by correctly anticipating price movements, the way that stock traders make money by buying company stocks low and selling them high.

Transammonia is different. It actually trades and transfers the physical products. It started by trading ammonia, which is one of the most important chemicals in the world, but is also very difficult to handle because of its unpleasant chemical properties.

The entry wedge exploited by Stanton was transitory, but he seized on it to build an enduring company. Stanton understood from the start that key operating factors such as geopolitics, communications, logistics, weather patterns, agricultural policies, and financial strategies were all closely interwoven with the success of the commodity trading business. His mastery of these difficult interrelationships allowed Transammonia to thrive in an intensely competitive market.

Ammonia's importance in a modern economy

Ammonia, which consists of nitrogen and hydrogen (NH_3) molecules, is the second most important chemical in the world economy after sulfuric acid. It is an indispensable feed stock used to make fertilizers, pharmaceuticals, explosives, and other industrial products, including cleaning solutions. Its impact on agriculture is enormous: 85 percent of all ammonia is used to make fertilizers.

About 120 million tons of ammonia are produced globally every year. The process for making it is so energy-intensive that ammonia production consumes 2 percent of the man-made energy generated in the world.

It has a curious history. Most of the nitrogen needed to produce ammonia was originally derived from bird droppings, which had accumulated as a nitrate-rich organic material called guano. Guano deposits, found mainly in Peru and Chile, are the result of millennia of droppings. At the end of the nineteenth century, with easily accessible guano deposits rapidly being exhausted, the world was facing a potential deficiency in low-cost nitrates. This would have been disastrous for agriculture.

Fortunately, science and technology soon supplied an alternative to guano. In 1913 the commercialization of the Haber-Bosch process for ammonia production freed the world's fertilizer industry from its reliance on a diminishing natural resource. The novelty of the process is that nitrogen for ammonia production is extracted from the air. It is then combined with hydrogen under high pressure (as high as 1,000 atmospheres) and high temperature (between 450 and 600 degrees C) in the presence of a catalyst.[1]

While the Haber-Bosch process solved the raw materials problem, producers and users still had to deal with ammonia's chemical properties. Unlike other widely traded commodities such as oil, copper, and wheat, ammonia is a difficult material to ship and store. The form that has the most commercial value is anhydrous (water-free) ammonia, which is used in fertilizer production. This is a liquid that must be kept either at high pressure or low temperature because of its low boiling point.

Given the problem of shipping such an unstable compound, it is not surprising that ammonia is commonly produced and used by vertically integrated companies that need it for the end products they also make. As a result, only about 10 percent of the world's ammonia production is traded on the open market.

Ammonia plants are complex, requiring the highest level of mechanical and chemical engineering for reliable operation. New

---

[1] Fritz Haber invented the basic technology, while Carl Bosch developed the commercial production process. Both received a Nobel prize for their contributions, Haber in 1918 and Bosch in 1931. An unanticipated side-effect of their technology is that it allowed Germany to produce explosives (and fertilizers) during World War I (1914–1918) despite a British naval blockade which blocked the importation of guano. If Germany had not possessed its own source of ammonia, it might not have entered the war in the first place, averting World War I and its many consequences.

plants come on stream periodically when innovations in technology promise lower production costs. The 1960s was a time when the introduction of better technology spurred the construction of many new plants, creating turmoil in the market. Stanton was perfectly prepared to take advantage of it.

Learning the peculiarities of international trading

Dealing with change came naturally to Ronald Stanton. He arrived in New York City from Germany with his mother in 1937, at the age of eleven. Just over a decade later, in 1948, he had adapted so well to his new environment that he was able to earn a degree in economics from the City College of New York.

His education in the so-called "dismal science" had not given him any skills that were marketable in the job market of the day. This actually worked to his advantage. He wound up taking part-time sales jobs, and found the idea of trading commodities appealing. A friend of the family, who owned a small commodity trading company called Interore (International Ore and Fertilizer Corporation), hired Stanton as a trainee.

One of the commodities traded by Interore was fertilizers, and Stanton eventually became an international fertilizer trading specialist. In this role he developed two skills that were to prove crucial to his future success: a mastery of low-cost logistics for transporting the actual commodities, and an understanding of international trade.

Stanton's education in international commodity trading started in the 1960s, when he was learning the fertilizer business. With Korea as his major customer, he quickly saw how government pressure can work to the advantage or disadvantage of a business.

At that time the US government had established the USAID program to provide developing Asian countries with economic assistance. USAID had a policy of favoring American suppliers for export, leaving Japanese fertilizer vendors to complain of unfair competition from American suppliers. Stanton found himself facing a difficult situation.

Under pressure from the Japanese, eventually USAID decided to make the tenders to South Korea 50 percent competitive (i.e. non-US) and 50 percent non-competitive. Now I had already bought the product and loaded all these ships.

In a panic, I went to Washington and started walking into the offices of US Senators and Congressmen and meeting with their staff members, complaining that making life easier for Japan went against the campaign to Buy American. I raised hell that the stupid bureaucrats are buying from Japan that was until recently our bitter enemy.

USAID was forced to reverse their policy because I went to Congress and USAID was dependent on Congress for allocations. I swung Congress my way. We sold the product and made a healthy profit.[2]

His skill in dealing with government officials would later prove just as valuable as his commodities expertise and international outlook.

FROM OIL TO AMMONIA

Stanton was not destined to remain a company man all his life, but it took a push to get him to start his own company. In 1963 Interore was sold to Occidental Petroleum, one of the world's largest oil and gas exploration companies. Occidental was headed by Armand Hammer, a flamboyant CEO who loved the spotlight and had a decidedly high opinion of himself.

This was not a happy event for Stanton. Because he owned no equity in Interore, he derived no financial benefit from its sale. More worrisome was the fact that, besides being a notorious character, Hammer was a terrible boss. But with no other job options and a family to support, Stanton decided to stay with Occidental Petroleum. He didn't last long.

---

[2] R. P. Stanton, *Recollections and reflections: A trader's life* (Privately published, New York, 2009), p. 71.

After years of trading fertilizers, Stanton thought he had identified a highly attractive opportunity in trading ammonia, a related commodity, very little of which was openly traded at the time. When he approached Hammer with this idea he was rewarded with a verbal explosion. Hammer took pains to tell him that this was a stupid idea that would bankrupt the company.

After this rebuff, Stanton knew that his days at Occidental Petroleum were over. And anyway, he was tired of answering to bosses. So in 1965, at the age of thirty-nine, he decided to open his own business. He got a commitment for the aforementioned $2000 equity capital from a small investment banking firm. His ownership stake was only 24 percent, but, with no money of his own to invest, that was the best he could do.

If you talk with Stanton for any length of time you realize that this is a man who is averse to taking any risks that are not absolutely essential. Starting a company was thus a big step for him. But while he was uncertain of the outcome of his venture, he had one consoling thought. He told himself that, if his venture failed, he could always get a job working as a trader in a big company.

Now he laughs at the idea, saying, "Little did I know that once you have your own business you never want to work for someone else again." So despite a difficult first few years, he never looked back.

When he told Hammer that he was leaving, he was offered the equivalent of eighteen months' salary on condition that he agree not to compete with Occidental in trading any commodity *except* ammonia. He immediately accepted. Ammonia trading was going to be his focus. He remained convinced that he had spotted a new opportunity that would let a newcomer with little capital build an enormously lucrative business.

Leveraging change

As mentioned earlier, a huge wave of new ammonia plants had come on stream in the 1960s. They were built to take advantage of innovations in production technology that cut ammonia costs by 50 percent compared to existing processes. But there was a catch: the new plants proved unreliable. They were built around newly designed compressors, which kept breaking down.

With the old plants shuttered and the new plants underperforming, the world supply of ammonia became unpredictable. Many users found themselves unable to get ammonia supplies from normal sources because their plants were not producing. This caused major disruptions in the production of fertilizers and other vital products.

Stanton believed that a third party could smooth out the market dislocations and make a profit by matching producers with users and managing the supply chain. His idea was to use the global relationships he had formed while trading in fertilizers to establish his new company, Transammonia, as the preferred supply hub in the ammonia market. The key to success was twofold. He had to know the producers and the state of their plants. He also had to understand the requirements of the users.

Stanton positioned Transammonia as a trusted intermediary between producers and users, offering guaranteed delivery at agreed-upon prices. Transammonia handled the logistics of shipping the product, and assumed the financial risk that the market price might change as the product moved from ammonia sellers to buyers.

The company's profit came from the fees it charged for logistics services, and from leveraging price movements when the company took inventory risks. Fixed costs were minimized by leasing transport and storage facilities. Bank financing was the key to the operations of the company, and Stanton became very skilled at managing his banking relationships.

The cost of integrity

It was quite a change from trading in stable, predictable products on someone else's behalf, and all did not go smoothly. Early in the life of the company, in the late 1960s, Stanton faced his first major crisis, one that tested his financial solvency and personal integrity. It ended up determining the future of the company.

He had negotiated a deal with Imperial Chemical Industries (ICI), then one of the world's biggest chemical companies, to deliver a million tons of ammonia at a fixed price. This opportunity came about because ICI had built three new ammonia plants, none of which had proven reliable. The company was in desperate need of ammonia.

Stanton signed a multiyear contract based on his knowledge of ammonia sources and their prices. He was certain the terms of the contract would produce a profit for him. Unfortunately, he bet on the wrong suppliers. Just when deliveries were due, their plants broke down too, leaving Stanton with a massive problem. Unable to deliver the contracted amount to ICI from his planned sources, he was forced to turn to other suppliers. Their prices were so much higher that he would incur a huge loss if he honored the terms of his contract.

Stanton had three choices, all equally unattractive: walk away from the contract; offer to deliver at a higher price; or ship at the agreed time and price and absorb a $1.8 million loss. He did not have the capital to absorb such a loss without finding a new source of money outside of the banks. He chose to honor his contract, take the loss, and find creative ways to finance the deficit. "Doing otherwise would have doomed Transammonia. I needed to build a business with 100 percent integrity," he says. "My word was my only asset in developing the trust of sellers and buyers and growing my company."

This is a story with a happy ending. It not only solidified Transammonia's reputation in the industry – it consolidated Stanton's ownership of the company. When his investors saw how much his decision had cost the company in trading losses, they wanted out. He took the opportunity to negotiate a very favorable leveraged buyout scheme with them.

Their despair, it turned out, was ill-timed, because the business turned profitable in the 1970s. Meanwhile, in 1971, five years after starting Transammonia, Ronald Stanton acquired all of the outstanding stock and became the sole owner of the company. He was now truly his own boss.

Eventually the reliability of the new ammonia plants improved. By then his niche ammonia trading strategy had evolved into a more consistently profitable mainstream operation. Stanton had built the infrastructure for a global ammonia trading system, and it continued to be a valuable platform for smoothing out world demand. Its opportunities continued to grow as rapid agricultural expansion in Asia and Eastern Europe created huge global demand for ammonia.

Today Transammonia continues to model itself as a supply chain manager dealing in commodities, but it is also equipped to take advantage of special opportunities. It has evolved a set of capabilities that combine trading, storage, and shipping. To manage its logistics economically, the company owns or leases its own marine terminals. It also charters specialized cargo ships and has rail cars built to its specifications on long-term leases.

Transammonia is now the largest independent ammonia trader in the world, and it has expanded into fertilizers, potash, sulfuric acid, and olefins. It is also the largest importer of LPG (liquid petroleum gas) in the northeastern US. Ronald Stanton has become an expert in building partnerships in various markets to ensure favorable pricing and low logistics costs.

INTERNATIONAL PRESENCE

Transammonia's development as an international trader serves as a model for entrepreneurs with global ambitions. International trading is the reason for Transammonia's existence, and Stanton is always focused on new market opportunities around the world.

While China and India have both become important markets, the opening of the former Soviet Union provided the most opportunities for high drama. In the course of developing the post-Soviet market, Stanton learned that bringing a little capitalism to former communist states is far from straightforward. For Transammonia, it meant engaging in activities far beyond its normal scope of business.

- The company had to finance a railroad link in Grodno (Belarus) to allow the shipment of fertilizer from a local plant to the nearest port facility.
- It assumed partial, though temporary, ownership of a fertilizer plant in a town called Nevinnomysk. That investment ended badly when the local Russian manager ran afoul of corrupt local authorities who were in cahoots with gangsters.
- There was the huge problem of trading with various entities and factories whose ownership was in dispute. Settling who really owned assets involved less than fair legal maneuvers.

Ultimately the company's adventures ended well anyway. By dint of enormous persistence, Transammonia got its money back without hurting its trading opportunities in Russia and the former Soviet republics.

Part of the reason, of course, was Ronald Stanton's hard-won savvy in international commerce and its pitfalls. Way back in the 1960s, when he was trading fertilizer to South Korea, Stanton had figured out that the officials of foreign states and local entities would be working with operating principles very different from those used in the US. He had to take these differences into account as the owner of an international business. Since fertilizers – and ammonia, of course – were considered essential commodities, they would be subject to rules and regulations that varied from country to country.

In many of those countries people in authority were inclined to treat essential commodities as cash cows for the benefit of themselves and their friends. Making money in such environments called for ingenuity, patience, and building the right local relationships. One popular way to establish business relationships was the joint venture, and Transammonia became a master of that business format. It has put in place over 127 different companies and joint ventures over the years, in practically every significant country in the world.

The running of a profitable business under alien conditions also requires unusually talented people, and Stanton has a knack for recruiting them. He provides them with the financial incentives to do their jobs well, and gives them enough independence to permit them to succeed on the local level. When it comes to any major decision, however, he has final say. This requires him to have an extraordinary understanding of his business and its market. To make this possible he restricts his trading to a few commodities in which the company has a mastery of the market and supply chain.

There is also a broader advantage to be gained from Transammonia's specialization. It allows the company to compete effectively with larger but more diversified firms, which do not have its detailed knowledge of commodity trading and international relationships.

Stanton's company has been consistently profitable since 1971, despite the periodic business cycles that afflict all commodities markets. Its success is based on low operating costs, smart management of the financial risks associated with pricing moves, and control of key physical assets. Transammonia has competitors, but none of them match its full scale of service capabilities. That's what makes it a unique business.

Because of the way it manages its physical asset requirements, the company operates with only about 380 employees. This is a remarkably small staff for a business that operates in thirty locations around the globe. I asked Stanton how he managed with so few people.

"It's simple," he said. "We can't afford to spend more in this thin-margin business and still make good money. We sell the same products as others do, so our competitive edge lies in inventory management, pricing risk control, efficiency, integrity, and outstanding customer service. We do these things better than others and this is why we continue to thrive."

LOOKING BACK

When I asked Stanton why he thought he has been so successful for so long in a notoriously risky business, he dwelt on the flawless execution of a narrowly defined, well-focused business model.

As a matter of strategy we don't make anything within the company, although I confess I was occasionally tempted to go into the production business on a long-term basis. So we buy the same products with the same specifications as everybody else and somehow we have to add enough value to make a profit.

How do you add value? We do it by adding financing, adding logistics, adding knowledge and a feel for what is happening in the market. Our internal communications are a key to our success. Our traders know they are in the middle of a fast-moving international market and they talk to each other before any significant deal is done. This ensures that we bring the best knowledge and judgment to bear on every decision.

Finally, we always ask ourselves how we can do better. This is a complex, worldwide business and timing is critical. We really pay attention to every detail and in the long run it pays off in success and profitability.

Stanton's answer spells out a business approach that every entrepreneur would do well to emulate. It is all too easy to be caught up in the excitement of a new opportunity and neglect the basic principles of running a disciplined, responsive company.

But his explanation of his success does not account for the origins of the business. Where did the opportunity come from? How was he able to recognize it? How did his approach match the conditions at hand? A review of Transammonia's history reveals several factors crucial to the establishment and long-term success of a new business.

Other people's pain can be a business opportunity. The creation of Transammonia is a classic example of an entrepreneur perceiving an opportunity created by a market dislocation. Why did he perceive this opportunity? Call it a prepared mind – Stanton had traded fertilizer for over ten years on a global scale. He recognized that an erratic supply of ammonia was causing a market dislocation in fertilizers. He knew the business opportunity did not lie in solving the problems with the new production technology that had caused the dislocation. It lay in addressing the market problem.

Market dislocations get fixed. What follows? A wedge into the market is a start, but nothing more. This must be followed with a more enduring business model. In commodities a business is not built around product differentiation, but on service and cost. Once it pioneered the market in ammonia, Transammonia's success was based on a creative supply chain solution. The company built a network of producers and users, and exploited its unmatched capabilities in storage and transportation. Because of its scale, focus, and proprietary market information, Transammonia became a leader in its commodity trading markets.

Understand your business focus. In order to expand businesses rapidly, entrepreneurs are often tempted to diversify beyond the areas where they have adequate talent or business judgment. I asked Stanton whether he ever considered entering into the manufacturing of any commodity that he understood well, such as fertilizers or even ammonia. "We understand how to trade commodities and the associated logistics, and are undisputed masters at it," he answered. "Manufacturing is an entirely different discipline and I never felt the need to diversify in that direction." However, he did enter into long-term partnerships with manufacturers, focusing on the distribution of their products in order to ensure a more secure supply chain for his business.

There is no substitute for business integrity. This may be the most important lesson of all. Stanton's willingness to honor a contract in the face of serious losses helped establish his reputation. In his words: "We don't have a proprietary advantage. So why do people want to work with us? We stick to our word. If a deal turns sour, we don't run away. We've built a reputation for integrity and reliability, doing what we say we're going to do." Integrity is the key ingredient in any business, not just commodity trading. It is an attitude that starts at the top. Commodity trading has more than its fair share of shady operators. Transammonia under Stanton always stressed that his employees act in a manner that is fair and honorable in order to build the reputation of the company as a valuable partner.

Learn to operate seamlessly around the globe. When asked how his company manages to operate successfully in so many countries while dealing with a wide range of organizations (private and public), his answer was simple: "We are worldly chameleons who learn to integrate into the environment as needed to conduct our business. Folks need our products and we need them as customers."

Entrepreneurial businesses come in all types, sizes, and areas of specialization, but the fundamentals of success are similar for every one of them. Transammonia's history stands as a monument to the basics. In the next chapter we'll encounter a company that operates in the hyperspeed world of high technology and built its success on innovative microprocessor technology.

Nothing could be further removed from commodity trading. Yet RMI, our next subject, also reached its goals by following many of the basic principles of global business so clearly demonstrated by Transammonia.

5 Speeding voice and data traffic worldwide: Network microprocessors from RMI

The network will truly be the computer.[1]

If you happen to make a wireless phone call to China, it may be routed through a microprocessor chip produced by Raza Microelectronics Inc. Although RMI (later merged with NetLogic Microsystems) only began supplying integrated circuits in mid-2005, its microprocessors now power some of the most advanced communications network equipment in the world, and it counts the leading Chinese equipment suppliers among its customers. It has become the acknowledged technology leader in its chosen market.

How a Silicon Valley startup developed the world's most sophisticated network microprocessor is a remarkable story. It is also especially relevant to our theme of global entrepreneurship, because RMI's success hinged as much on its understanding of international markets as on its technical expertise.

RMI's management realized early on that overseas markets were more open to network chip innovations from a startup than the domestic US equipment manufacturers, who had well-established chip suppliers with long-standing reputations. So the company decided that its primary sales target should be China, the world's fastest-growing network equipment maker.

This may seem like an odd choice. China has become the world's factory. Its trade surplus with the US has risen from $202 billion in 2005 ($243 billion in exports vs. $41 billion in imports) to

[1] http://googlesystemblogspot.com/2006/11/network-will-truly-be-compter.html, accessed November 4, 2011.

$273 billion in 2010 ($365 billion vs. $92 billion).[2] American businesspeople and government officials routinely complain that, while China floods the US with manufactured goods, the Chinese market is closed to American products. But RMI's success in China proves that its market is very open to innovative products no matter where they originate.

RMI also embodies another common characteristic of the successful technology startups surveyed in this book: it was built by immigrants. Its founder and first CEO, Atiq Raza, was born in Pakistan, while his successor, Behrooz Abdi, is a native of Iran. The drive to succeed, tolerance for risk, and comfort with international dealings that marks the educated immigrant community must be counted as an important element in the company's growth and success.

However, while global perspective and immigrant origins certainly help, they aren't the whole story. Ultimately every successful startup enterprise is built on the same foundation: recognizing and filling an unmet market need. In RMI's case, it was an urgent demand for ever-higher speeds in network communications. This is the story of how the company met that need through technical breakthroughs, business savvy, and the flexibility to adapt to changes in the business environment.

INFORMATION AUTOBAHN

The demand for more speed in communications networks has been building for decades, and shows no sign of abating. It really started to ramp up about thirty years ago, when the Internet was just getting started. At that time only large corporations could afford digital network connections, and they ran over dedicated lines that were closed to everyone else.

Smaller organizations and individuals had to make do with analog telephone lines, using devices called modems (for

---

[2] www.census.gov/foreign-trade/balance/c5700.html#2010, accessed September 9, 2011.

modulation/*dem*odulation) to convert digital data to and from analog transport modes. Early modems could handle a maximum of 300
bps (bits per second) of data. Eventually modems reached top speeds
of 56 kbps (thousands of bits per second). This was the equivalent of
about three typewritten pages per second.[3]

Today's data networks are end-to-end digital. Comparing analog modem speeds to what can be achieved in the digital realm is
like matching a slow stroll on a suburban sidewalk to a Grand Prix
race car on the autobahn. Broadband wired Internet connections
can deliver data at up to 100 Mbps (millions of bits per second) –
or 120 copies of the complete works of Shakespeare every minute.
Wireless is slower, but even the latest cell phones are capable of up
to 10 Mbps.

Digital data networks emerged on a global scale in the 1990s,
fueled by the rise of the Internet and its enormous data-handling and
security requirements. As people demanded ever more data-inten-
sive digital applications on their personal computers and wireless
handsets, the pressure to provide faster transmission speeds showed
no sign of lessening.

RMI was founded precisely to meet this demand for faster data
traffic. But providing higher data speeds isn't as simple as stepping on
an accelerator. In order to appreciate the magnitude of the achievement, it is necessary to understand the basics of modern networks
and the hardware that runs them.

Routing bits and packets

The speed, flexibility, and reliability of digital communications,
from the simplest text email to video on the Web, are a direct outcome of their "packetized" network structure.

Analog networks carry a continuous stream of information
that must be kept intact from origin to end-point. Digital networks

---

[3] See www2.sims.berkeley.edu/research/projects/how-much-info/datapowers.html
(accessed September 9, 2011) for a handy table by Roy Williams that matches
various quantities of digital data with everyday forms of information.

are built on the radical concept that you can break up information into smaller units, called *packets*, and send them as separate components, to be reassembled into a single communication at their destination.

This structure has two main benefits: the network can carry many individual communications at the same time; and individual portions of each message (the packets) can travel different routes to their destination without destroying message integrity.

It may take millions of packets to contain the content of a single data transmission. Each packet has two parts: the *payload*, or data that has to delivered, and a *header* that identifies the packet's origin, contents, and destination.

The header is the crucial part of the message from the network's point of view – the payload is not so important. In fact, header instructions can account for as much as half of a packet's total bits.

Headers contain more than simple routing information – much more. They identify the order in which packets are to be reassembled, and ensure the packets are treated properly as they travel to their destination. When the message includes voice and video, for example, headers tell the network to treat the packets in such a way that the contents play back smoothly at their destination.

When packets in a single transmission travel along different routes to their destination, they may arrive out of sequence. This is because the computers that direct the data traffic along the way, appropriately called *routers*, are independent engines, giving the network built-in redundancy. If one segment goes down, or a router is busy, packets can be rerouted to their destination through alternate paths.

At the end of the journey, a router must reassemble the message in the proper sequence. Since data travels over an optical fiber cable at the speed of light, the biggest limiting factor in network speed is clearly the routers that analyze headers and move the packets to their destination. In order to speed up the network, faster routers must be created.

Microprocessors: Breaking the router bottleneck

That's where RMI's focus on faster microprocessors comes into play. A router is simply a special-purpose computer, and microprocessor chips are the brains of computing systems. To make routers work faster, the speed of their microprocessors must be increased.

Anyone familiar with electronic products tends to talk about microprocessors as if they always existed. In fact, it was only in the 1970s that a single microprocessor began to replace the cluster of integrated circuit chips on a circuit board that formed the central processing units (CPUs) of previous computers.

The concept of a single chip designed to perform the core computing operations originated at Intel. Its first commercial microprocessor chip, dubbed the 4004, was introduced in 1971. The 4004 contained only 2100 transistors, but it had the same computing power as the ENIAC computer of World War II vintage, which weighed 30 tons, occupied 3,000 cubic feet and used 18,000 vacuum tubes.[4] (Of course, this was before the invention of transistors.)

Gordon Moore, co-founder of Intel, saw the microprocessor as an alternative to building custom chips for each computing system. He described the device as "a broadly applicable, complex integrated logic circuit that can be produced in huge volume, and hence [at] low cost, and that utilizes the technology advantageously."[5]

Moore's idea was that all computing could be handled by software running on a general-purpose microprocessor. Instead of having custom hardware (chips) for each application, the microprocessor would carry out all basic computational operations, with software supplying application-specific functions. This would result in computing systems that were both faster and cheaper, because these versatile chips would be mass produced.

[4] M. White, "25th anniversary for microprocessor," *Toronto Star*, November 17, 1996.
[5] G. E. Moore, "Microprocessors and integrated electronics technology," *Proceedings of the IEEE*, vol.64 (1976), pp. 837–841.

Moore's vision of huge production volumes has been fulfilled beyond anything he could have predicted. Today microprocessors are everywhere, at all levels of performance. There are hundreds at work for each human being in the world. As the speed and performance of microprocessors have improved, and their cost has dropped, they have found their way into everything from toys to washing machines to large computers and communications systems.

In his famous "Moore's Law," the Intel founder also predicted that the processing power of chips would double every two years with no increase in price. This was based on the rate at which transistors were being shrunk in size, permitting more logic gates (and higher performance) on each chip. Making transistors smaller thus meant getting more speed for less money. But gate dimensions could shrink only so far before they began to bump up against physical constraints on performance. In particular, the power dissipated by very-high-performance chips became excessive, and cooling them increased the size and cost of the systems.

Fortunately, another path forward had emerged: multiple processors on a single chip working in parallel to process data. In these configurations each processor core has its own resources, but shares access to centralized control functions, including instructions and data storage. Since the individual processors have significant autonomy in the execution of instructions, this arrangement achieves much higher processing speeds even if the speeds of the individual cores do not increase.

Parallel processing is not a new idea. It was the architecture of choice in powerful mainframe computers that combined many discrete processor chips. Designing a microprocessor chip containing a group of suitably interconnected processor cores, however, is new. To make such a device work called for not only extraordinary engineering skills but also the invention of new technology.

Multicore processors were just beginning to appear in the market in 2002, the year RMI was founded. It was the challenge of designing such devices to greatly speed up data networks that attracted the company's founding engineers. Their idea was to create a whole new family of multicore microprocessors that would dramatically increase the capacity of networks to meet the ever-growing demand for higher-speed communications.

To do so, they had to design chips that processed the routing information in packet headers in parallel rather than in the serial manner of then-current single-core processors. This required the invention of a novel chip architecture where multiple individual processors were synchronized and shared timely access to information needed to complete a computing task. This rapid access to common information would enable a remarkable increase in packet processing speed, eliminating the major bottleneck in data network operation.

Designing the new chips was only the beginning. RMI's customers, the companies that built the routers, would have to learn how to program the chips to meet their equipment objectives. For this reason the microprocessors would have to be designed for versatile programming. This opened the way for RMI's customers to write software that differentiated their network products by lower cost, improved performance, and a superior ability to incorporate security control. RMI's founders were uniquely qualified to achieve these goals.

READY FOR INNOVATION

Atiq Raza, the Pakistan-born founder of RMI, earned his degree in physics and philosophy at the University of the Punjab, and then moved to the US. He founded his first startup, NexGen, in 1988, where he developed a general-purpose microprocessor designed to compete with Intel's top-of-the-line products. It was the first company to challenge Intel in the high-end microprocessor market.

Developing such a highly sophisticated product involved extraordinary effort. NexGen had to avoid infringing Intel patents or copyrights, yet deliver products that were interoperable with Intel chips. It took until 1995 for the company to develop a marketable product.

At the same time AMD, a big chip manufacturer with a license to serve as a second source for Intel processors, was also committed to breaking the Intel monopoly. It attempted to design its own microprocessors, but failed to come up with a competitive product.

For AMD the obvious next move was to acquire NexGen. AMD paid $850 million in AMD stock for the company, laying the foundation for AMD to launch a series of successful chips to compete with Intel. Raza joined AMD where, as president and chief operating officer, he led the microprocessor product line as it established itself against Intel.

But not for long: always looking for the next challenge, Raza left AMD in 1999 to become a venture capital investor. His idea was to incubate new technology companies, and manage their growth to the point where they would become attractive acquisition candidates. Raza launched a number of companies but, when financing startups proved difficult after the public market crash of 2000–2001, he decided to refocus his efforts on building a single company targeting specially designed microprocessor chips to improve data traffic on networks. With the explosive growth of Internet traffic, the amount of data carried was believed to be doubling every three months, so better equipment, powered by faster microprocessors, was urgently needed.

Raza founded RMI in 2002 specifically to launch a new generation of microprocessors that were designed to deliver a dramatic increase in data network performance. This was clearly a growing market that would be targeted by others, so RMI was off to a race to be first with the best. In a first for the industry, these new products would incorporate eight powerful, closely linked processor cores on the same chip.

In addition to novel ideas, his competitive edge in starting the company was a team of exceptional managers who had worked with him before. These included Waqar Shah (head of operations), Dr. Nazar Zaidi (head of product development), Dave Hass (product architect), and Dr. Kai-Yeung (Sunny) Siu (head of sales and marketing for Asia).

Silicon Valley is the kind of place where talented engineers are always willing to leave big companies to join a promising startup. Raza's reputation in Silicon Valley constituted a very high level of promise. Everybody knew he had led the only successful challenge to Intel's monopoly in high-end microprocessors.

In a remarkably short period of time he assembled sixty of the best microprocessor design engineers in the world. Their mission was to produce the industry's best single-chip data network microprocessor. That's the kind of challenge that gets the juices flowing in that part of California. All that remained to be done was raising enough venture capital to get to the finish line.

This is where Warburg Pincus came in. Our team was introduced to Raza and his startup in 2002. Whether the proposed product would find a ready market was not at issue. It was evident that the rapidly increasing demand for data network traffic was spurring a corresponding need for equipment to meet the demand.

What was startling was the ambition of the plan. There was no precedent for the proposed product family in terms of performance and value. Only a world-class talent had a hope of succeeding. What convinced us to help fund the company (along with Benchmark Capital) was Raza's reputation and the quality of the team that he had assembled. If any group could succeed, we concluded, it was this one.

RMI had talent in the realms of both software and chip design. It created and refined a set of specifications for the new product in the process of consulting with potential customers. Production of the actual chips was contracted to TSMC in Taiwan, the world's leading contract chip manufacturer.

This class of semiconductor products is not sold simply as a chip but as part of a total solution, including the software needed to integrate the processor into network equipment. Therefore, RMI started a software development organization in India under the leadership of an Indian engineering manager who had returned home after a ten-year career in the US.

RMI was an international company from the start. In 2009, out of about 300 employees, about 40 percent were in India and Asia. The core chip development team stayed in the US, but a large number of the managers and engineers in the US were born outside the country.

Furthermore, recognizing that China was likely to be an important market, RMI had Dr. Sunny Siu build a customer engineering support organization in China. Born in China, Dr. Siu had earned a Ph.D. from Stanford University in electrical engineering and had served as assistant professor at MIT – another example of the phenomenon of Chinese-born technologists moving back to China and serving as "bridges" between US companies and Chinese customers.

So, before actually having products to ship in volume, RMI had prepared the ground to deal with Asian customers to smooth the sales process.

PRODUCT LAUNCH

The first of RMI's new generation of multi-core microprocessors was completed for customer sampling in 2004, and released for production in 2005. It took three years from start to finish. Given the complexity and novelty of the technology, this is record time for getting a product to market.

Its reception was outstanding. "A new MIPS powerhouse arrives," was the headline of the lead article in *Microprocessor Design*, the respected industry newsletter, on May 17, 2005. The article detailed how RMI's product had outclassed the competition and was opening new markets. To start with, it delivered a tenfold increase in packet processing speed compared to other devices doing the same job. The article quoted Raza as saying, "The XLR processor design is my greatest accomplishment to date. It is the first architecture in my experience that met every architectural goal set for it. Today, this is the highest throughput machine on the planet."[6]

Once RMI's new product was available, there were some interesting market developments around it. You would have thought that the first serious customers would be in the US. In fact, they were in China and Israel. Why? After the failure of a number of US chip startups in the period following the 2000 market crash, US network equipment manufacturers became apprehensive of committing new generations of their equipment to products from private companies with uncertain economic futures.

At the time RMI was not yet profitable. As a result, although Juniper in the US and a small network equipment company in Israel designed the RMI microprocessor into their products, the company's success was built on its overseas customers. Sales outside of the US grew rapidly because new equipment manufacturers in emerging economies were willing to take a chance on buying from a startup. The advanced performance of RMI's new microprocessor gave them a competitive edge against the dominant vendors in the market, such as Alcatel and Cisco Systems.

China was home to the most important early customers. These included Huawei and ZTE, the fast-growing national telecommunications equipment vendors that dominated the Chinese market. RMI benefited from the explosive growth not only of Internet traffic but also of wireless traffic, as shown in Figure 5.1. In addition, both Huawei and ZTE were developing overseas markets for their products. The number of wireless subscribers in China was booming and local service providers needed equipment to keep up with service demand. RMI's microprocessor became the technological underpinning of a new generation of equipment for the local Chinese carriers such as China Mobile.

As a result of its early focus on Asian customers, RMI had the right organization on the ground to take advantage of the opportunities

---

[6] K. Krewell, "A new MIPS powerhouse arrives," *Microprocessor Design*, May 17, 2005, pp. 1–7.

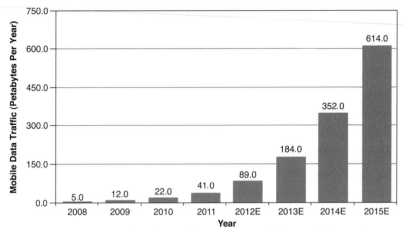

FIGURE 5.1 Wireless data traffic volume growth by year (figures for 2012 and later are projected).
Source: From IBS, private communications, 2011.

created by the booming Asian telecommunications market. In 2007 sales in the Asia-Pacific region were $52 million. Sales in the US were $8 million, and in the rest of the world only $4.6 million.

Transition

In mid-2007 Atiq Raza resigned from the company he had created and guided to success to return to venture capital management. He was replaced as CEO by Behrooz Abdi.

Though born in Iran, Abdi received his B.S. degree from Montana State University and an M.S. degree in electrical engineering from the Georgia Institute of Technology. He joined RMI from Qualcomm Inc., where he had been Senior Vice President and General Manager of the chip division. Prior to Qualcomm he had been at Motorola, where he headed the Radio Products Division.

Abdi joined RMI at just the right time to take it to the next level as a market leader. His experience with wireless technology at Qualcomm and Motorola was an enormous asset in this effort because wireless networks were exactly the market where RMI had the most to gain. In choosing Abdi, RMI had positioned itself to adapt to new market realities.

With over 100 patents either issued or pending, the company had an impressive portfolio of intellectual property to support expansion into new markets. But it faced a challenge common to all startup enterprises: the need for more revenue to solidify and extend its early success. Although its first generation of products had been launched to great acclaim, RMI had to gain widespread customer acceptance and build revenues rapidly if it wanted to head off the competitive pressures it would inevitably face from later entrants into its market segment.

Abdi's approach to this challenge was to turn the complex nature of RMI's network products into a competitive advantage by helping its customers design their equipment. In effect, RMI set out to deliver not only chips but also the software to integrate them into its customers' extremely complex communications equipment. This was particularly important for new Asian equipment builders, who lacked some of the established engineering skills that US companies such as Cisco, Juniper, or Lucent had accumulated over the years.

As a result, RMI found itself increasingly in the position of a system enabler. In addition to expanding its internal chip design and support organizations, it had to develop a cadre of collaborative software vendors if it was to win new customers. It needed these industry partners to provide the enabling software for its customers.

Drawing on his extensive background in communications systems, Abdi built an ecosystem of over one hundred corporate partners. These organizations developed and sold complementary chips and software that allowed the company's customers to build their products in record time around RMI chips.

By 2008 RMI had over 200 customers and revenues of $79 million, an increase of 25 percent from the prior year. It had proven that it understood the network equipment market, had the technology to meet its needs, and could work in a global environment. It was in a good position for future growth – but it needed an infusion of new capital to fund its expansion. Though successful, it was not yet profitable due to its heavy investment in product development.

Under normal circumstances, the right place to raise this capital would be the public market. Accordingly Goldman Sachs was selected to underwrite an IPO on NASDAQ in mid-2008 – just before the US mortgage crisis triggered a stock market debacle and the deepest recession since 1929.

After the 2008 market crash an IPO was clearly impossible. The company's board of directors was faced with the task of planning a different future for RMI.

Weighing options

Deprived of the ability to raise capital in the public markets, RMI's directors had two strategic choices.

- Keep the company independent; reduce product development costs to maintain profitability.
- Merge RMI with a public company with complementary products and a similar customer base, in the expectation that the combined companies would have enough resources to continue their growth.

Staying independent posed the bigger risk. If RMI chose that course, it would have to cut back on new product development, possibly mortgaging its future. In a highly competitive industry like microprocessors, inadequate investment in product development could be fatal. There were already a number of bigger competitors racing to overtake RMI's lead.

If, on the other hand, the company chose the merger route, it would obviously have to find the right partner. As it happened, in the course of building RMI's industry ecosystem, Behrooz Abdi had run across a compatible company.

RMI MERGES WITH NETLOGIC

NetLogic Microsystems was the world leader in a specialized category of semiconductor chips called knowledge-based processors (KBP). These chips incorporate massive parallel signal processing with content-addressable memories (CAM), which store the data needed to move data packets to their destinations. Such specialized memories can greatly increase a router's processing speed.

We have already seen that the headers on data packets carry information to identify packet contents, origin, and ultimate destination. When the microprocessor in a router analyzes each packet's header to determine its destination, it must then look up information in its own routing tables to decide how to send the packet on the next leg of its journey through the network.

CAMs are specially designed to increase the efficiency of the process of matching a packet's address information with its destination path, while meeting network security requirements at the same time. You can think of the operation as similar to the mail-sorting procedure in an old-fashioned post office, where the routing information for each letter is stored within easy reach of the sorting clerk.

After extensive meetings between the investors and the managements of RMI and NetLogic, we mutually concluded that by combining the two companies we would produce a technology leader with a market position superior to what either company could achieve on its own.

One avenue of potential growth opened up by this merger, for example, was the combined company's ability to develop products that more closely integrated packet processing with NetLogic's chips. This would allow customers to increase network performance while reducing chip costs. In addition, the merger would realize substantial financial benefits by combining two sales, marketing, and product development organizations into one, thus reducing administrative overhead.

We agreed that RMI would exchange its shares for new NetLogic shares so that shareholders in both companies could benefit from the new value created by the merger. The merger was completed in October 2009. RMI's shareholders ended up with about 20 percent of the shares of the combined company.

Behrooz Abdi joined NetLogic as executive vice-president and general manager. In 2010 NetLogic introduced a new family of microprocessors that had been in development at RMI. These products extended the market leadership of RMI's previous offerings, delivering over four times the processing power at the same price as its nearest competitors, including entries by Intel. Needless to say, they were very well received.[7]

They also required a heavy investment in engineering expertise. You get an idea of the engineering requirements for this kind of company from its manpower: out of a total staff of 650 at the end of 2010, over 60 percent were engineers.

Despite this technology investment, NetLogic's financial performance after the merger did not disappoint its shareholders. Revenues in 2010 reached $382 million (38 percent in China). Its market capitalization was about $3 billion in March 2011. This meant that the shareholders of RMI were credited with a value of about $600 million for their part of the ownership.

LOOKING BACK

RMI successfully challenged the biggest companies in its business with products that required a unique set of skills. In fact, when the company was started in 2002, there were only two companies in the world with the technical skills to design such products. One was Intel, the industry pioneer and leader in microprocessors. The other was AMD, whose ability to compete in the market was largely the result of the initiatives of Atiq Raza, the founder of RMI. However, neither of these big companies addressed the market that RMI identified.

But there is a sobering message in this story. Despite having performed an extraordinary feat of product engineering, its ultimate destiny as a business was not as a standalone company. The reason is that an enterprise committed to RMI's class of highly sophisticated products requires an enormous investment of resources for continued

---

[7] T. R. Halfhill, "NetLogic broadens XLP family," *Microprocessor Design*, July 2010, pp. 1–11.

success in the international market. Most startups simply don't have the resources to sustain that level of investment unless they have access to the kind of capital available from public markets.

Still, the story of pre-merger RMI is valuable for what it tells us about the way entrepreneurs and investors have to think in a global market. Here are some of the most important points to consider.

Management changes can be healthy. A large part of RMI's success must be credited to two outstanding entrepreneurs: Atiq Raza and Behrooz Abdi. Raza was the visionary leader who got the breakthrough product designed and launched. Abdi took the company to the next stage, launching the second-generation product family while ensuring revenues from the first. His work in building an ecosystem of complementary software and hardware products to win customer acceptance was critical to the company's growth strategy.

There is no substitute for access to international talent. RMI attracted outstanding talent from around the world right from the start. Engineers from India, Pakistan, and China were prominent both in the Silicon Valley location and in the overseas location. Their geographical dispersion and their understanding of different markets, to say nothing of their talent, played a large role in the penetration of the Asian market.

Startups are often viewed with suspicion by big customers in the developed economies. The more strategic the component, the more difficult it is to convince big customers to bet their new product lines on an offering from a startup. This was the case with big companies whose concern about the financial stability of RMI precluded their purchase of its microprocessors.

A global outlook can lead to willing buyers. RMI's ability to address the needs of Asian customers saved the company. Equipment manufacturers in Asia were more focused on using the most advanced chips than on the financial viability of their vendors. They wisely concluded that companies with winning products get financed, and that their support would make that happen. The company's ultimate success in selling in China and the Asia-Pacific region, however, was no accident. Right from the start RMI had outstanding marketing and customer support management located there, and it actively engaged with potential customers while the products were being designed. It takes years of effort and very talented people on the ground to gain the respect of new customers. RMI was prepared.

Industry consolidation is a fact of life. The best products in the world are no substitute for business scale. This is especially true for technology companies, which require costly and ongoing investments in product development. Despite high gross profit margins of 60 percent, RMI was never profitable as an independent company. It was constantly pouring money into new products, a necessity in an industry where products are obsolete in less than three years. Under these circumstances any company with the ambition to remain independent needs access to large amounts of capital at attractive valuations.

In the 1990s public markets were very open to financing companies such as RMI. The crashes of 2000 and 2008, however, made the timing of IPOs problematic. The investors' decision to merge RMI with NetLogic recognized that the combined companies would create more value for their shareholders than if they were independent. This turned out to be the case – NetLogic remained profitable after the RMI merger and was valued as a very high performance growth company – over six times annual revenues. It also spends nearly 40 percent of its revenues on product development. This is what it takes to stay a winner in the microprocessor game. NetLogic was in turn acquired by Broadcom in 2012.

In the next chapter we'll look at a very different approach to a similar situation: a company that leveraged IP and partnerships, instead of mergers, to reach a scale where it could remain independent.

6   A world leader emerges: SanDisk and flash memories

> Technologies emerge from the coming together of existing technologies into wholes that are greater than the sum of their parts.[1]

Imagine having to re-program your smartphone, digital camera, music player, tablet computer, e-book reader, or similar device with phone numbers, photos, songs, or other crucial information every time you turned it on. Or think how much bigger its battery would be, and how often you would have to recharge it, if you decided to keep it powered up all the time so it would remember that data.

Fortunately, that's one dilemma we don't have to face. Our electronic devices keep all our information in memory, ready for use, even when we turn them off. They store the data in semiconductor chips called "flash memory," either in the devices or on handy, removable memory cards and USB thumb drives. Their convenience and functionality are owing in large part to the flash memory innovations of Dr. Eli Harari.

Dr. Harari did not invent flash memory. Credit for that goes to Toshiba, the giant Japanese electrical and electronics company, which developed the semiconductor chips in the mid-1980s. But he did find ways to improve their reliability. Even more important, he developed flash memory *systems*. He developed and commercialized these systems through SanDisk, an amazingly successful startup, which he founded in 1988 in Silicon Valley.

Today SanDisk is the world's leading producer of flash memory cards. In 2011 the company had revenues of $4.8 billion, net income

---

[1] M. Ridley, *The rational optimist: How prosperity evolves* (New York: HarperCollins, 2010), p. 271.

of $1.3 billion, and a NASDAQ-traded enterprise value of $12 billion. It produced over 50 percent of the flash memory cards used in the world.

How a Silicon Valley startup in one of the most competitive industries in the world reached these lofty heights is a remarkable example of global entrepreneurship. SanDisk achieved its success through a combination of cutting-edge innovation, leadership in establishing industry standards, marketing flexibility, and the construction of a unique international manufacturing relationship.

None of this would have been possible, of course, without an entrepreneurial instinct for market needs. When asked why his company succeeded, Harari, who was CEO until his retirement in 2010, answered "Total focus. Over the years our tactics changed, but never our objective." That objective was to allow people to store and move their personal data from device to device, for convenient sharing of information with friends and relatives.

For a better understanding of SanDisk's story, we'll start with some background on pre-existing solutions for storing and sharing information on PCs, and indicate why flash memory cards displaced them.

MEMORY AND DISKS GET FLASHED

Flash memory is relatively new. In the 1980s, when work on the technology was just getting under way and PCs were in their infancy, the dominant memory type in computers was (and still is) random-access memory, or RAM.

The only competition for RAM was read-only memory (ROM), the predecessor of flash memory, and it was no contest. While ROM also retains information while in an unpowered state, it cannot be easily erased or rewritten. As a result ROM was relegated to storing firmware or other permanent data.

By contrast, RAM can be erased and rewritten countless times at very high speeds. This makes it the memory of choice for storing working data. Every digital device, from the mainframe computer to the wireless handset or the humble pocket calculator, uses RAM chips to store digital data for recall or processing.

Unfortunately, RAM only stores information when it is connected to a source of electrical power. If you turn off your computer, or run down the batteries in your portable device to zero, all of that information will vanish. Most computer users can tell stories of power outages that wiped out work they hadn't "saved" to a more permanent storage medium.

Mechanical solutions
Permanent storage for digital information has long been the province of the spinning magnetic disk. Most computers today use hard disk drives for this purpose. These are rigid platters coated with magnetic material, spinning in hermetically sealed enclosures to prevent dust from ruining their surfaces. They allow easy erasure and rewriting of information, and they retain data indefinitely even when disconnected from power.

They also boast huge capacities and by far the lowest cost per byte of storage of any non-volatile memory device. In 2011 a two-*terabyte* hard drive for a desktop computer cost around $100.

Of course hard disks have their drawbacks. They draw substantial power when reading and writing information. Since they are electromechanical devices, they are orders of magnitude bulkier and heavier than semiconductor memory. They are subject to damage from physical shock, especially during operation. And their access time is much slower than that of semiconductor memories.

Clearly the hard disk was not designed as a portable data storage device. For many years that role was filled, however inadequately, by the now-obsolete "floppy" disk. This was a disk of magnetically coated film, 3.5 to 8 inches (89 to 200 mm) in diameter, packaged in a protective plastic sleeve or rigid case, and with limited data capacity. In its most popular form it held only 1.44 megabytes of data.

Floppy disks were also easily damaged. Although the disks were readily portable, the devices required to access their data were not. Floppy drives were similar in size, weight, and power requirements to hard drives.

Toward flash memory

Getting rid of mechanical disks in favor of all-electronic systems was an attractive concept. It would make devices much more portable, reduce their power requirements, and increase their ruggedness and reliability. It would also make information exchange a lot easier.

When electrically erasable programmable ROMs (EEPROMs) appeared in 1980, people began talking of them as replacements for rotating disks. While it was not difficult to imagine the potential of these memories, there were enormous technological hurdles to be overcome. They had limited data capacity, and their cost was high. Reliability was an issue too – the early programmable transistors on the chips would fail after a few cycles.[2]

The term "flash" came into vogue in the late 1980s, when EEPROMs appeared that could be programmed and erased at much higher speeds than previously achieved. It took more than fifteen years for flash memories to realize their potential, but their ultimate impact has been enormous, enabling whole new generations of consumer products.

Figure 6.1 shows the spectacular growth of the flash memory market between 1995 and 2011. The $27 billion in global revenues in 2011 represents over 43 percent of all semiconductor memories produced.[3]

The latest flash memories offer enormous data capacities. Up to 64 GB of storage is readily available on a single SD card, with the

[2] W. S. Johnson, G. Perlegos, A. Renninger, G. Kuhn, and T. Ranganath, "A 16kbit electrically erasable nonvolatile memory," *ISSCC, Technical Digest*, 1980, p. 152. For a detailed discussion of memory technology, see B. Prince, *Semiconductor memories* (New York: John Wiley & Sons, 1991), pp. 529–605.

[3] T. Luke, "Semiconductor handbook 2010," Barclays capital equity research (June 10, 2010), pp. 302–303.

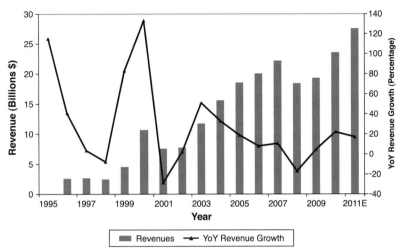

FIGURE 6.1 Global flash memory revenues and their year-over-year revenue growth.
Source: Based on data from SIA and Barclays Capital (ref. 3).

potential for 2 TB.[4] The chip that provides this level of storage packs billions of transistors into an area the size of your thumbnail.

Flash memories are now inexpensive, fast, and reliable. They enable portable devices including digital cameras, USB "thumb" drives, MP3 players, and cell phones. Even GPS navigation devices use flash memories for non-volatile storage.

In the computer arena, flash memory-based thumb drives long ago consigned floppy disks to oblivion. They are now replacing hard disks in PCs, especially portable units, where their inherent ruggedness, light weight, superior speed, and lower demand for battery power outweigh their somewhat higher cost and significantly lower capacities.

Given the course of their development, it is not hard to imagine that eventually they may surpass hard disks in capacity and undercut them in price. Whether or not that happens, the success of flash memories thus far owes a great deal to SanDisk's initiatives and Harari's inventions.

---

[4] Capacity information comes from www.sdcard.org/consumers/cards, accessed July 13, 2011.

According to Harari himself, however, a large part of his achievement should be credited to lessons he learned from his first startup, Wafer Scale Integration (WSI). He kept making this point when we discussed the history of SanDisk and flash memories.

TOWARD SANDISK: WAFER SCALE INTEGRATION

As it happened, my own interest in what became flash memory began in 1980. While at RCA Labs I became intrigued by the potential of non-volatile semiconductor memories, and started a program to develop a commercial product based on this technology. Investing in a company that developed new products exploiting this promising technology became one of my objectives when I joined Warburg Pincus in 1983.

The opportunity to help build such a company came in 1984. I was introduced to Dr. Harari, who had earned a Ph.D. in Solid State Sciences from Princeton University and had held management positions at Intel, Honeywell, and Hughes Aircraft Microelectronics.

He and his colleagues were planning the start of a new company, Wafer Scale Integration (WSI), to commercialize novel non-volatile memories. Impressed with his ideas and the technology roadmap, Warburg Pincus financed the start of the company along with several other investors. It was headed by Harari.

From the beginning, everyone involved recognized that cost-effective manufacturing was going to be essential to the success of the company. WSI would use new process technology to manufacture its chips. This posed a problem, even though the technology shared many elements with the generic CMOS process then gaining ground in the industry. Whatever the manufacturing process, it was certain that it would have to constantly evolve over time to reduce chip cost and improve functionality.

Implementing manufacturing innovations requires a focused engineering production staff working closely with development engineers. Ideally, WSI would have liked to build its own factory, but this required an investment in excess of $100 million. A capital commitment that large was beyond the means of venture capital investors of that period. Nor were investors inclined to bet such huge sums (at the time) on a risky new venture.

So the WSI team proposed the next best thing: contract with a semiconductor company willing to accommodate "guest" products on its production line. Harari convinced the Sharp Corporation in Japan to share the use of one of its production plants in return for a license to the WSI technology.

Manufacturing impacts competitiveness

The company's first products were called programmable system devices (PSDs). These provided non-volatile memory for microprocessors from Intel, Motorola, and others. The products found customers, but the market was limited.

WSI's high production costs proved to be its Achilles heel. While the semiconductor industry as a whole was reducing its costs by producing ever-denser chips, WSI did not follow suit. It could not implement similar process improvements fast enough. Since developing more complex devices would require significant production changes, that route to lower cost was closed to it as well.

In the final analysis, the basic reason for WSI's limited success was not lack of innovation, but the difficulty of actually implementing change. Sharp's management was reluctant to allow WSI to alter their facility's production process for fear of affecting Sharp's own products. As a result, WSI's new products reached the market too slowly, and carried too high a price.

Limited to a narrow market niche, the company did not grow beyond annual revenues of $40 million. In 2000 it was acquired by ST Microelectronics, which saw value in its memory technology.

WSI had entered the new non-volatile memory field in its early stages. But without the right kind of production facility it was impossible to take advantage of the many opportunities created as applications proliferated and the basic technology matured.

It has become fashionable to believe that owning production plants is a bad idea for a corporation. Why burden a company with the capital costs of manufacturing plants if better alternatives exist, such as outsourcing?

It is too easy to ignore the fact that control of its own manufacturing process can give a company an edge in responding to market changes, or that manufacturing can be a great source of competitive innovation in certain markets. Better alternatives do exist, as SanDisk eventually showed when it created a very successful manufacturing partnership with Toshiba. But no matter which path is chosen, you must control your own destiny.

SANDISK PIONEERS FLASH MEMORY SYSTEMS

Unhappy with the progress of WSI, Harari left the company in 1988, to found a new company, SunDisk. He was joined by Sanjay Mehrotra and Jack Yuan as co-founders. The company was later renamed SanDisk.

Their business plan was extremely ambitious. Its strategy was very different from that of WSI and other companies in the market. Instead of component memory *chips*, SunDisk was going to offer self-contained flash memory *systems* for auxiliary (removable) computer data storage.

Harari's vision was to deliver a convenient memory system that would enable data portability between computers. This would make it simple for consumers to transfer their personal data. The easiest way of visualizing such a product is as a less cumbersome replacement for floppy disks, with the ability to carry much larger amounts of data.[5]

Since computers were designed to work with magnetic disk memories, these new flash memory systems had to emulate the operation of disk drives if they were to work properly. They had to

[5] Eli Harari, "2008 Analyst Day" (Transcription). Available on SanDisk website.

be reliable, cheap enough to attract consumers, and with sufficient capacity to store meaningful amounts of data. And they had to meet industrial interface standards to allow interoperability among computers made by different manufacturers.

Devices like this did not yet exist. Harari and his colleagues had to invent them, and SanDisk's future was based on turning Harari's inventions into successful products. Starting with US patent 5,095,344, "Highly compact EPROM and flash EEPROM devices," filed June 8, 1988, Harari described a series of inventions that addressed key technological hurdles:

- a new and superior chip architecture, allowing much denser transistor arrays;
- new ways to manufacture such chips; and
- novel algorithms for programming and erasing the information stored on the transistors, which increased their reliability.

His algorithms made it possible for flash memories to emulate disk storage operations.

The SanDisk system products that eventually emerged consisted of two parts – flash memory chips and a proprietary controller. The flash memory chip stored the bits, while the controller chip contained the "secret sauce," providing system-level management of the stored data when interfaced with its host computer.

SanDisk's system developers also faced the problem of partial failures. In the course of use, some of the memory chip's data storage transistors could "wear out." To make flash memory systems practical, they had to find a way around the failed components, analogous to the process of taking areas on a hard disk that generate errors out of use.

To solve that problem, SanDisk's controller software detects the presence of failed storage elements and reroutes the data flow around these failed elements to allow unimpeded operation. The controller also executes software that emulates the operation of a floppy disk, so that the computer sees the flash memory chips as a normal magnetic disk.

From startup to the big leagues

It took three years for the company to complete its first products. SanDisk did not become profitable until 1995, seven years after its start. Its revenues that year were $62 million, with a net income of $9 million. IBM and Hewlett-Packard were the major customers, selling the flash memory systems as removable accessories for their personal computer lines.

Capital to keep the company going was a constant problem while it was building its revenues. The company had raised capital from various equity sources. These included Seagate, a leading magnetic disk manufacturer clearly interested in a potentially competitive technology.

As the company progressed, it became possible to raise money in the public market. To take advantage of a hot public market, SanDisk launched its IPO on NASDAQ on November 7, 1995, raising $37 million at a valuation of $210 million.

The company has come a long way since its IPO. Figures 6.2a and 6.2b show its revenues and net income from 1995 to 2010. Revenues passed $1 billion in 2003 and $4.5 billion in 2010. The company has been consistently profitable with the exception of 2008, when inventory write-off and other asset revaluations led to a loss.

You will note in Figures 6.2a and 6.2b that revenues are broken into two parts: product revenues and license income from patents. We will discuss the reason for this later.

Success factors

As we noted earlier, after a slow start SanDisk became a very successful company. Why did that happen when so many other companies failed to succeed in this market? There are several significant reasons.

- SanDisk leveraged its record of seminal inventions into both profitable products and licensing income.
- It led the way in establishing industry standards for interfacing memory systems to devices; without such standards its products could not be sold into large markets.

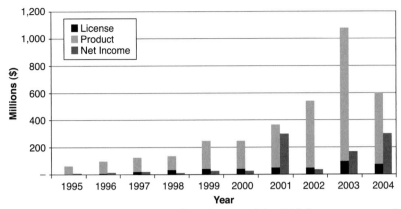

FIGURE 6.2A Revenues and net income of SanDisk between 1995 and 2004.

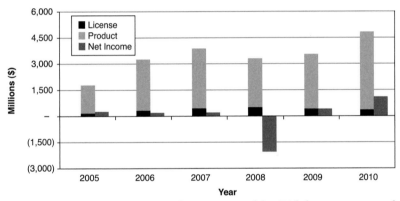

FIGURE 6.2B Revenues and net income of SanDisk between 2005 and 2010. (*Note:* Year 2008 loss was owing to inventory write-off and other asset revaluations.)

- The company benefited from serendipity: generations of battery-driven consumer products that emerged in the 1990s were enabled by flash memories.
- It was able to offer leading-edge products while dramatically reducing costs over a period of years because of manufacturing joint ventures with Toshiba.
- SanDisk succeeded in building a consumer brand around its peripheral memories – a rare feat for a chip company.

We will examine these elements of SanDisk's success in turn.

Patents and a clever licensing strategy

Inventions were crucial to the company's success. Over the years, Harari himself authored or co-authored 119 patents. In 2010, the company had over 1,500 patents and was filing new ones at the rate of 300 a year.

Protecting all this intellectual property was a daily battle. The growth and profitability of the flash market was no secret, and lots of companies were infringing key SanDisk patents to get a share of the profits. The company's annual public filings contain extensive lists of legal battles with companies big and small over its IP.

These legal processes are part of a larger strategy. They show that SanDisk will defend its IP in the courts when necessary. But knowing that legal fights in and of themselves are not productive, in 1997 the company started to cross-license its patents with competitors.

This sounds counter-intuitive, but actually proved to be a very wise policy. The reality was that the flash industry was growing very rapidly and patent infringement was rife. While SanDisk's patents were basic to creating a new market, without more entrants it was unlikely that the industry would adopt the new standards essential for flash memory's widespread acceptance. By licensing its patents the company helped expand the flash system market.

The decision to license its patents brought SanDisk a number of other benefits.

- Because SanDisk led the industry in innovation, it collected substantial royalty fees from licensing, amounting to between 10 and 20 percent of total revenues depending on the year (see Figures 6.2a and 6.2b).
- Through the trading of suitable IP, it gained access to patents from other companies that were essential for its own products.
- Cross-licensing made it easier to establish industry standards, under which participants made their patents available in return for royalty payments.

From a financial perspective the strategy was a boon to the company's bottom line. In 2008, for example, licensing income amounted to $508 million. It is interesting to note that Samsung, SanDisk's major competitor with a 40 percent share of the flash memory market, is also its biggest source of license fees.

In essence, SanDisk's licensing strategy allowed it to fund a great deal of its product development with money from its competitors. It is an updated version of the approach David Sarnoff used to underwrite R&D at RCA.

Leadership in setting industry standards

Flash memory systems were originally designed as computer peripherals, not as built-in data storage like RAM. Their purpose was to transfer data from one machine to another. If they could not be easily moved from computer to computer, regardless of maker, there would be no market for them.

Clearly the concept of transferrable storage products would work only if the electronics industry adopted standards to enable interoperability among equipment sold by all vendors. This would take the form of a standard interface that would allow flash memories (and other peripherals) to plug into any PC. So right from the start, SanDisk focused on creating and leading industry standards-setting bodies.

PCMCIA standard. SanDisk was a founding member of the Personal Computer Memory Card International Association (PCMCIA) in 1989. Just one year later, in 1990, this organization set the first international standard for removable peripheral cards, covering memory storage, network communications, and other functions.

The PCMCIA standard benefited both computer and peripheral makers. It made computing equipment more versatile by providing a seamless interface to peripherals that added capacity and functionality. Peripheral manufacturers who adhered to the PCMCIA standard could make cards with the assurance that they would work with any computer regardless of maker.

With PCMCIA in place, SanDisk's data storage cards could transfer information among all computers, and even among different types of devices, as long as they adhered to the standard. For example, the PCMCIA standard allowed the transfer of photos from a digital camera to a computer.

SanDisk's main product at the time was the FlashDisk, a card designed to replace floppy disks in handheld wireless terminals, personal computers, and audio recorders. It weighed only half an ounce (14g), used very little power to operate, and was the size of a matchbox. As the technology improved FlashDisk peripherals got smaller and thinner while providing more storage capacity.

Hewlett-Packard used the product in the 1990s to provide outboard storage for its small 200LX personal computer. IBM, which was still in the personal computer business, was also a major customer for a similar application, as were makers of hand-held computers.

Though a big step forward in portability, the PCMCIA card (later PC card) was still fairly large. It measured 3.37 × 2.125 inches (85.6 × 54 mm), exactly the size of a credit card, and had a thickness of between 0.13 and 0.4 inches (3.3 and 10.5 mm), depending on its type. Its primary market was owners of laptop computers, who wanted to add storage capacity or additional functions to their somewhat limited portable machines.

USB standard. PCMCIA cards were later superseded by the smaller, faster, more versatile Universal Serial Bus (USB), which is now routinely built into desktop and laptop computers, smartphones, digital cameras, and many other electronic devices. Right from the beginning the USB standard defined the requirements for the now ubiquitous USB flash memory drives.

First offered by IBM for their PCs in 2000, flash drives (called drives because they could replace both floppy disks and their drives) are small and inexpensive, yet hold massive amounts of data. A typical flash drive in 2011 weighed less than an ounce (30 g) and stored as much as 16 gigabytes at a cost of about $5 per gigabyte.

Smaller-capacity USB drives are now so inexpensive that many companies give them away as advertising premiums. They are also extremely reliable. Some allow one million write/erase cycles and have a ten-year retention cycle.

With the introduction of its USB flash drive SanDisk found itself with a true consumer product. While PCMCIA cards were sold mostly through computer specialty stores, flash drives quickly found their way into general merchandise outlets, from office supply stores to Walmart. Yet the company's biggest market success was yet to come.

Flash card standard. As the capacity of flash memory chips increased, it became possible to consider even smaller form factors for memory cards. In 1999 SanDisk, working with Matsushita and Toshiba, led the standard-setting initiative for the Secure Digital (SD) memory card, which is still in use at this time of writing.

These thin (0.08 inch, 2.1 mm) flash cards immediately found a ready market as removable storage for digital cameras. The three companies cross-licensed their patents, but competitors have to pay license fees to the group members to make cards according to the standard.

SanDisk then worked with manufacturers of wireless handsets to develop standards for much smaller memory cards, called miniSD, to bring removable storage to top-quality cell phones. By allowing transfer of data between phones and personal computers, miniSD cards made it possible to use the handsets as multi-purpose devices. For example, users can move pictures taken with the phone's built-in camera directly to a PC for viewing and editing, or load the card with music from the PC and use the phone as a music player.

Standardization was a necessity for SanDisk's survival, as it helped grow the market for flash memory past critical mass. Its downside is that it commoditized the company's core technology. But by helping to set the standards for popular products and being an owner of the associated technology, SanDisk was in a position to collect huge royalties, which continue to fund its technology development.

New portable consumer electronic devices hit the market
Throughout the 1990s one new generation of battery-powered consumer products after another emerged, all of which were built around flash memory storage. SanDisk reaped the benefits of the growing demand for its memory devices.

Why did these products emerge and why did flash memories become essential? It was partly serendipity.

- As computing chip performance doubled every two years (following Moore's law), and chips shrunk in size, cost, and power requirements, it became possible to design tiny portable consumer products such as audio and video players along with ever smaller personal computers.
- Makers of these devices relied on flash memory to store information because magnetic disk storage was too large, too prone to failure, and required too much power.
- Digital cameras were completely impractical without flash memory cards. To help people understand why they needed the cards, one maker branded its products "digital film." Consumers needed an easy way to add storage and transfer photos to PCs or printers for editing and viewing.
- Cellular phone service became affordable for an ever-expanding portion of the population worldwide. Handsets grew in sophistication while shrinking in size; flash memories were essential for non-volatile data storage.

The fact is, however, that SanDisk created a lot of its own luck. Management kept up with the advances in semiconductor technology that made these devices possible, and had a clear understanding of the place of flash memories in the big picture. They drove the market as much as followed it.

As the flash memory market grew, so did competition. Capital-rich companies with excellent manufacturing technology, such as Samsung and Toshiba, increased their production efficiency and drove costs – and prices – down. For SanDisk the moment of truth had arrived. Its manufacturing had to stay competitive in order to survive. As a result of an innovative and prescient manufacturing strategy, it was ready.

SANDISK'S JOINT MANUFACTURING ENGINE

To get some idea of the pressure SanDisk was facing, consider the fact that over the life of the company production costs per bit for flash memory declined by the astounding factor of 25,000. Single chips with 64 GB of memory capacity were in volume production in 2011 at prices that mass market consumers could easily afford.

The pace of development in the technology is unrelenting. Storage capacity on a given size of chip doubles every twelve months, because new ways of increasing the density keep getting invented. As a result, flash chip costs are declining at a rate of better than 50 percent a year, producing cheaper consumer prices, a growing market, and headaches for companies trying to keep up. It took quite a few years for the company to develop the capabilities it needed to compete in this environment.

SanDisk's biggest challenge, as it had been for Harari's first company, WSI, was where to manufacture its products. SanDisk's venture capital investors, like WSI's, could not finance a factory. So early on, in the absence of other alternatives, the new company adopted the same strategy as the old one: sign contracts with manufacturing companies for access to their plants. The outcome was just as unsatisfactory.

Its first major manufacturing site, at a Matsushita plant, was in use between 1990 and 1996. But that relationship left much to be desired, as did agreements it signed with four other companies during that time. Delays in ramping up new processes were common. Yields were not predictable, either, because of the continuous tuning of processes to increase chip performance.

For manufacturing changes to be implemented as rapidly as possible, the plant had to be more responsive to SanDisk's constant need for process improvements. Only a dedicated facility would meet these requirements.

Building one was out of the question. It would have cost SanDisk over $1 billion and involved significant risk, to say nothing of the time needed to make it functional. So rather than go it alone, the company decided to partner with Toshiba, the third largest chip manufacturer in the world.

Joint venture with Toshiba

The Japanese electronics giant seemed a highly unlikely choice to deal with a Silicon Valley startup on an equal footing. But deal it did, because it was also committed to the flash memory market, and SanDisk had unusual technological assets that it needed to succeed in the business.

In June 2000 SanDisk and Toshiba signed a deal to create a flash memory manufacturing partnership named FlashVision. SanDisk initially committed about $400 million of the capital cost for joint ownership of a new facility in the US dedicated to flash memory production. SanDisk also committed itself to buying, at cost, 50 percent of the plant output, and to paying its share of the operating costs. This is how SanDisk gained access to a factory where its technology could be implemented and controlled.

Manufacturing was eventually consolidated in Toshiba's Yokkaichi chip factory complex in Japan. Each company continued to fund its own product development. In effect, SanDisk and Toshiba became production partners but market competitors. Further partnership deals were signed in 2004 to fund expanded production requirements, committing SanDisk to further capital funding.

Teaming up with a competitor to create a manufacturing facility for your respective products sounds just as counterintuitive as licensing your technology to companies who are trying to beat you in the marketplace. But like SanDisk's licensing strategy, this manufacturing partnership paid big dividends, even ignoring what it saved by not building its own factory.

First, by sharing technology with Toshiba, SanDisk was rapidly able to increase its production capabilities. The production line was located in Toshiba's first-class manufacturing complex and benefited from its excellent infrastructure. Toshiba also contributed technology of its own to the joint venture, which complemented that of SanDisk.

Second, with a high-volume facility dedicated to manufacturing one product, there were bound to be reductions in production costs over time.

Third, by owning their facility the partners were in a better position to protect proprietary process technologies. For example, SanDisk implemented a proprietary technology that stores three bits instead of only one in a transistor cell. Multilevel bit storage enabled SanDisk (and Toshiba) to sell much denser memory chips than their competitors at a lower cost per bit stored.

Of course, these advantages came with a price tag. Through 2010 SanDisk borrowed about $7 billion to finance its part of the partnership. However, considering the cost savings reaped by sharing infrastructure and technology with Toshiba, this was undoubtedly less than what SanDisk would have had to invest if it attempted to build its own factory.

This deal made sense for Toshiba too, because they not only gained a partner who paid its fair share of the plant cost, they got access to the most innovative flash memory skills in the world. Their partnership allowed Toshiba to remain a leading flash chip vendor. Most other manufacturers had to exit the business because they could not muster the technology to compete. In 2011, the joint Toshiba-SanDisk factories produce about 30 percent of the world's flash products.

It is true that the partnership calls for an unusual level of cooperation between companies that are basically competitors once the chips leave the factory. It also requires that SanDisk engineers work closely with Toshiba engineers in the manufacturing plants. This is not something that is easy for a big company jealous of its technology and management control. There were issues and misunderstandings, but amazingly enough, this unique partnership has worked very well. It has been renewed a number of times since 2000.

SanDisk builds a consumer brand

Finally, after twenty-five years of development, flash drives are low enough in price to allow their substitution for magnetic memory disks as permanent storage in small personal computers. The emergence of tablet computers is accelerating the rate at which flash memories are finding their way into personal computing devices. Consumers love small computing devices and only flash memories make these practical.

As we have seen in Figure 6.1, global flash product shipments increased from $2 billion in 1995 to $27 billion in 2011. With memory densities increasing and costs dropping at a rate of 50–60 percent a year, the flash memory industry has become mainstream. Product prices declined from $19 per gigabyte in 2006 to $1.2 per gigabyte in 2011.

As its manufacturing capabilities and cost structure became competitive, SanDisk was faced with strategic issues. How could it build unique market value in a business that was increasingly commoditized by big producers? Should it remain a supplier of chips to original equipment manufacturers (OEMs) to package in their own branded products? Or should the company build its own consumer brand in some consumer categories?

SanDisk decided to build a consumer brand. This strategy was designed to overcome the commoditization process, which inevitably follows when industry standards are open to all comers for the price of a license fee.

It was a bold choice: no chip company had ever developed a successful consumer brand for itself. Even Intel, with its famous "Intel inside" ad campaign, was not trying to sell branded computers. It was establishing a preference for PCs, which Intel did not build, that used Intel microprocessors.

It is tempting for a company to go up the product chain and sell a complete product rather than the component that enables it. SanDisk succumbed to the temptation and introduced a consumer product, an MP3 music player called the Sansa, which ended up as a very distant second to Apple's iPod in the market.

"You can't out-iPod the iPod," Harari concluded in 2009. It is not obvious that this product idea produced any long-term value to SanDisk, except to reinforce the need to focus on areas of expertise. That area of expertise was, of course, peripheral memory products.[6] Over the past decade or so, SanDisk has succeeded in building consumer preference for its branded memory peripherals for digital cameras, personal computers, and wireless handsets.

USB flash drives and SD cards are the two auxiliary storage products that consumers see most often with a SanDisk brand. Neither of these is a unique product. SanDisk's competitive advantage comes from better reliability and higher capacity storage on a given chip. Its premium brand reputation results in a higher retail price and better profit margins.

Overall the company sells 50 percent of its chips to OEMs, with the other half used in its own consumer products, sold in retail stores under the SanDisk brand. SanDisk is now the world's leading producer of flash cards with an estimated 50 percent of the global market. It makes 1 million cards a day and is the dominant brand in tens of thousands of retail outlets, including Best Buy, the largest consumer electronics store chain in the world.

LOOKING BACK

The story of SanDisk holds a number of valuable lessons for the ambitious entrepreneur who is targeting opportunities in the big, international electronics market. Chief among them: in a market likely to attract major international competitors, ambitious plans require meticulous execution on many fronts. Invention is not enough.

I cannot think of another example of an entrepreneur succeeding in the semiconductor business against greater odds than Eli Harari. He is the source of seminal inventions that helped to launch flash storage systems. He also built a great company that competes on an equal footing with the largest corporations in the world.

---

[6] Quoted on www.CNNMoney.com, June 3, 2009.

But his inventions were always a means to an end. From the very start he had the vision to realize that non-volatile semiconductor technology would make the storage and exchange of information so easy that consumers would make it an integral part of their lives. But he didn't stop with vision. He developed a strategy that turned his vision into reality. Today SanDisk branded flash cards and USB flash drives are ubiquitous in popular consumer products.

The methods he and his team used to achieve their success show that entrepreneurs can get ahead by combining a flexible approach to business, a global mindset, and unwavering focus on their target market. The most interesting lessons from the SanDisk story are that working with selected competitors for mutual advantage is an avenue worth exploring, and that creative answers to the manufacturing innovation process are an imperative.

We will review the most important factors in SanDisk's success.

International standards are important in promoting a new technology. While the inventions of Harari and other technologists on his team removed the key roadblocks to realizing useful flash products, it was their pioneering work in setting industry standards that made it possible for these products to reach their intended markets.

For an emerging company, industry standards pose challenges and dilemmas. Promoting industry standards for removable flash memories opened the market to competitors. But SanDisk had no other choice, because without standards computer manufacturers had no incentive to build products accepting interchangeable memories.

Licensing patents can be very productive. SanDisk's strategy of leadership in standard setting was the right way to go, but only if the company continued to lead the industry in innovation. Its licensing of patents, paradoxically, helped in this effort. The licensing fees were high enough to generate considerable revenue. This revenue, in essence pure profit, allowed SanDisk to continue to invest heavily in innovations that kept it ahead of the pack.

There is no place to hide when your production costs are too high. Harari's most challenging business issue came down to controlling costs. In the semiconductor memory industry a manufacturer's success hinges on its ability to reduce aggressively the cost of its products over time. To do this it must produce memory chips in high volume in its own factories. Those factories require huge capital investments.

To avoid head-on competition in this market, Harari focused his startup on building a new market around removable storage systems enabled by his controller invention. This allowed SanDisk to compete on its own terms. But ultimately it could not hope to stay in the business by relying on contract manufacturing.

Harari's innovative solution was to create SanDisk's manufacturing partnership with Toshiba. This lowered the cost barrier to building a chip plant and gave it control of its manufacturing, without which the company would not have survived to benefit from its vision.

When moving to branded products, pick the right ones. SanDisk's experience in building its consumer brand has implications for every component vendor hoping to move up the food chain. While the attempt to compete with Apple in a consumer music player failed, it was never a fair contest. Apple's success with the iPod was not based solely on its technical merits but on the remarkable infrastructure it built to make attractive music content available to its customers. This was not an arena in which SanDisk, a chip company, could compete.

On the other hand, SanDisk's marketing of branded peripheral memory products did succeed, precisely because the end products leveraged its technical and cost leadership in chips. Once the distribution infrastructure was built, allowing it to capitalize on having the lowest cost structure in the industry, the company was positioned for success.

7 Implementing information technology across the globe

Technology companies and global investors are beating a path to Israel and finding unique combinations of audacity, creativity and drive everywhere they look.[1]

If you mention a successful startup called Ness Technologies, there is a good chance that a US listener will assume it is one of those high-technology Silicon Valley companies. That listener would be mistaken. Ness Technologies is a multinational information technology (IT) services corporation, created in Israel in 1999. It is also the first company in this book that does not have its headquarters in the US.

This chapter will examine how the Israeli entrepreneurs who founded Ness dealt with the challenges of a global marketplace. Within five years of its founding, this Israeli startup became a leading company in its field with operations in Asia, Europe, and the Americas. Its rapid rise to prominence has fully justified its name, which means "miracle" in Hebrew. It did so by melding subsidiaries in countries with cultures as diverse as Bulgaria and Thailand into a global corporate culture, with a common set of goals and expectations that was held across national boundaries.

DEMAND FOR IT SERVICES RESHAPES THE WORLD

Ness Technologies is a provider of IT services to other companies. As such it didn't "invent" any basic technology. Like Ronald Stanton's Transammonia, its innovations took the form of a new

---

[1] D. Senor and S. Singer, *Start-up nation: The story of Israel's economic miracle* (New York: Twelve, Hachette Book Group, 2009), p. 11. This book contains a wealth of information about the Israeli environment for new business building.

business model and new approaches to international service. Unlike Transammonia, however, Ness operated in an industry characterized by the most rapidly advancing technology in history. Even those who lived through the rise of the computer can hardly believe how quickly and profoundly digital data processing has changed the way the world does business.

In just twenty years, between 1980 and 2000, corporations replaced the river of paper that had carried business forward for centuries with a stream of digital information flowing through wires. Computers and associated software flooded into offices to handle all aspects of business, including payrolls, supply management, customer billing, and everything in between. This transformation, from a paper-trail business model to a digitally wired one, required enormous investments in successive generations of hardware. Processors evolved from big, centrally located machines, accessed with "dumb" terminals, to networked business computers. When low-cost PCs became available most employees got their own.

As computers proliferated in every aspect of business, enterprises faced an urgent need to implement and manage their software and communications infrastructure. To satisfy this need companies began hiring IT specialists to configure and operate their systems. They soon faced a classic supply-and-demand problem. Because of the rapid growth in demand, skilled IT engineers were suddenly in short supply. Predictably, a proliferation of enterprising startups quickly emerged, offering contracted IT services to help companies meet the needs of their computer users.

Corporate IT infrastructures continued to grow in complexity as the technology advanced. Companies found they needed specialists to write software, install security systems to control access to data, and install and configure data networks, to name just a few areas of expertise. The arrival of the Internet in the mid-1990s greatly increased the demand for highly skilled IT specialists.

IBM was certainly the giant in the IT services industry throughout this period, but it was not alone. Many other companies, both large and small, provided expertise to enterprises that lacked the internal skills to design, build, or maintain their IT infrastructure. Yet demand for IT specialists kept rising – as did the amount of concern about their cost.

Companies went looking for other sources of supply. They came to the realization that it was possible to have enterprise software developed and configured at lower cost by skilled engineers in countries with lower wages, such as India. Thus was born the offshore IT service model, with India at its center. Of course, the outsourcing of jobs from countries like the US and Britain to what used to be thought of as "third-world" countries attracted a lot of negative attention. But India's ascendancy as a nexus of outsourced IT services revealed a striking new truth about the developing world: countries that were once considered economic and technological backwaters were rapidly catching up to Europe and the US, especially where IT was concerned. They too had IT infrastructure problems that needed solutions – and they had skilled engineers who could provide those solutions. In fact, in every part of the world where demand existed, an army of startups was emerging to provide IT services. Most of them were satisfied to remain small regional companies focused on industry sectors important in their geographies.

Some Indian startups, however, built technical teams in India and sales organizations in the US and Europe to solicit business. A few startups there and elsewhere ultimately emerged as large multinational companies. Ness Technologies was one of these.

Israel: Technology company incubator

Ness, of course, was different. It was an Israeli company, which prompts the question, why start such an ambitious venture in Israel? Israel is a small country with a population to match: only 7.5 million people in 2011. That is quite a contrast to India, which has a population of 1.2 billion. And it is a relatively new player in technology. Not so long ago oranges and flowers were key Israeli exports, not software or medical products. Today the country can boast a remarkable record of technical innovation and entrepreneurship. It was ranked fourteenth out of 125 countries in the 2011 Global Innovation Index, published by INSEAD.[2] Its economic clout extends far beyond what its small size would predict. In 2009 Israel exported goods and services valued at 35 percent of GDP, ranking it above Germany (34 percent), China (24 percent), and India (13 percent).

Israel developed as a technology powerhouse largely due to the need to ensure its national survival. It took a sudden French boycott of defense sales during the 1967 war, after years of close collaboration with French industry, to wake the country up to its vulnerability. Because of the boycott, the government decided that it could no longer rely on the importation of strategic defense products. It launched a massive program to foster internal industrial development and build a technology-based economy.

Trained engineers and scientists are the basis for any technology sector, and Israel was fortunate in having the resources to develop engineering talent.

- There are several outstanding universities, plus many private colleges.
- The country has benefited from the immigration of many engineers and scientists, particularly from the former Soviet Union.
- Young engineers can gain practical experience in technical organizations run by the Israel Defense Forces, which employ young people during their mandatory military service.

It is worth expanding on this last point. Israel Defense Forces draftees take rigorous tests for the opportunity to work on defense-related product development. When those who are selected leave the service they are well qualified for an industrial career. Many either start companies of their own or join existing startups.

Israel's focus on education and training has produced an unusually talented and experienced pool of software and hardware engineers. Their presence has attracted many major foreign

---

[2] www.globalinnovationindex.org/gii/main/analysis/rankings.cfm, accessed September 16, 2011.

corporations to open engineering centers and product development facilities in Israel, among them, Intel, Motorola, and Siemens.

In addition to its support of technical education and training, the government has taken an active role in encouraging the creation of innovative new companies. The Office of the Chief Scientist of Israel provides modest amounts of seed capital to technology start-ups that are deemed to be promising. Companies that survive the seed stage then seek funding from venture capital funds or large corporations. There is a healthy venture capital industry in Israel. In 2009 Israel ranked first in venture capital investment as a percentage of GDP at 0.43 percent. This compares, for example, to 0.08 percent in China and 0.2 percent in the US.[3]

Most Israeli startups eventually get acquired, but some remain independent and become publicly traded companies. Over 100 Israeli-originated firms are listed on US stock exchanges, the largest number of any foreign country. Many others are listed on the Tel Aviv exchange.

With a deep pool of engineering talent, an abundance of entrepreneurial spirit, a solid legal system, and a history of intellectual property protection, Israel is a good place to build innovative businesses or develop products for the global marketplace. So when Warburg Pincus encountered an opportunity to invest in an Israeli company, we paid attention.

HOW NESS TECHNOLOGIES BEGAN

Our opportunity to invest in Ness Technologies came through Morris Wolfson, an experienced American investor in Israeli businesses, who had acquired a small Israeli IT services company in 1997. He realized that he needed an experienced, professional investing partner to build it into a major company. We were introduced to Wolfson through a mutual friend, and began to discuss the idea of

---

[3] Data from NVCA and EVCA, quoted in C. Dickson and O. Shenkar, *The great deleveraging: Economic growth and investing strategies for the future* (Saddle River, NJ: FT Press, 2011), p. 181.

acquiring several IT services companies in Israel and merging them to create the foundation for a global business. We had been investing extensively in IT businesses in a number of countries. Given what we had heard of the business climate in Israel, we thought this was an idea worth exploring. So we went on a fact-finding trip there.

Our first step was to meet Raviv Zoller. A former officer in the Israeli Navy, Zoller was a certified public accountant and the founder of an investment bank focused on technology businesses. He was familiar with the IT industry and was working with Wolfson. He would be the driving entrepreneur of the new venture, morphing from investment banker to CFO of Ness and finally to its CEO. Zoller had identified five companies with outstanding technology and established market positions, one of which had already been acquired. He believed that these firms, consolidated under a unified management, would provide the core of a leading IT services company in Israel. Once a solid local base was established, international expansion would be a real possibility.

We visited each of the candidate companies, met their managements, and reviewed their projects, capabilities, and finances. Their combined revenues in 1999 were $94 million with a profit of $7.5 million. They were selected because, taken together, they covered many of the most important and valuable IT services, including enterprise networks, custom software development for defense systems, and IT system integration for banks, telecommunications carriers, hospitals, and utilities. Table 7.1 summarizes their size and areas of practice.

We then talked to their major customers, who confirmed our favorable impression of the quality of their work and the productivity of their engineering staffs. We were sufficiently impressed that we decided to participate in funding Ness Technologies.

Assembling a senior management team was the first step. Over a period of six months we recruited three senior-level executives to launch the company. Aaron Fogel, former Director General of the Israel Ministry of Finance, became the chairman of the board. Yaron

Table 7.1 *Israeli acquisitions that started Ness Technologies*

Year acquired	Company name	Business type	No. of employees
1999	Gilad	Software development and system integration	340
1999	Conthal	Information technology services	310
1999	Advanced Technology	Software development and system integration	650
1999	IPEX	System integration	350
1999	IPEX ISI	Software development	40

Polak, a seasoned and highly respected executive who had built a software company that had gone public on NASDAQ, became CEO. Raviv Zoller became CFO and Chief Operating Officer.

Putting the pieces together

Merging companies is never easy, but merging five entrepreneurial companies at one time is best qualified as "Mission: Impossible." The fact that it was done successfully is a tribute to the skills of the management team we had recruited.

We felt it was essential to establish a common culture for the new company. That would be difficult to do with employees scattered among five facilities. Hence, the initial step in the integration process was to move most of the 1,690 employees to a single location. Fortunately, attractive office space became available in a new Tel Aviv industrial park, and everybody moved to that facility practically overnight.

Moving to nice new quarters was the easy part of integration. It was much harder to decide which managers to retain so we could create a coherent business organization to unify the original companies. As central functions such as finance, personnel, and marketing were staffed and business units were defined, some managers lost their jobs, while others were promoted to greater levels of responsibility. Making such wrenching personnel decisions is always difficult and disheartening. Israeli culture made it more stressful than usual.

Israel is a close-knit society. As people's jobs were either threatened or eliminated, their friends and relatives anxiously sought to talk to me about the situation. They waited for me in the hotel lobby during my frequent visits to Israel. They told me that the people losing their jobs were actually the best people there, and that Ness was starting down a ruinous path. Would I not reverse management's decision and keep those talented folks in the company?

Of course I could do no such thing. The process of integration would work only if the company's investors backed its management's decisions. The subsequent progress of the company suggests that they picked the right people. It took just over a year to complete the major consolidation process, after which Yaron Polak left Ness to become a venture capitalist.

Raviv Zoller became CEO in mid-2001, just in time to tackle the next phase of the project: leveraging the assembled resources to grow the company's market share in Israel, in preparation for international expansion. Zoller put new service initiatives in place, built relationships with the biggest potential customers in Israel, and built the Ness brand – all while making the company profitable.

Ness had a roster of established customers, but it needed to acquire new ones. It faced fierce competition not just from small companies, but from big multinationals such as IBM and Accenture. It won business on the basis of both quality and price against these formidable opponents, rapidly earning a reputation as a quality vendor. Soon it had emerged as the leader in the domestic market.

Zoller also demonstrated considerable promotional talent. He picked former US president Bill Clinton to be the featured speaker at the Ness annual customer meeting, which he had instituted as a brand-building opportunity. Clinton was very popular in Israel, and this event won Ness a great deal of national press coverage.

By 2002 Ness could count many leading Israeli banking, industrial, and defense firms among its customers for IT software and solutions. It had annual revenues of $167 million and a 13 percent market share in Israel, slightly ahead of IBM. It was time to look overseas for growth opportunities.

INTERNATIONAL EXPANSION

Ness Technologies was conceived from the start as a global company. Now it had to execute on that vision. Its strategy was to develop an innovative business model for international expansion, particularly into India, that maintained the integrity of regional operations, yet integrated them into a worldwide resource for IT services.

There were several ways to penetrate foreign markets. One approach was to establish sales offices in various countries, have them solicit projects locally, and execute the work in Israel. This strategy was rejected. It would take too long for an unknown newcomer like Ness to gain credibility in a new country. Instead, we decided that Ness's expansion strategy had to be based on the acquisition of well-established IT service companies in our geographies of interest. As known quantities, these companies would make initial market entry easier. We would then enhance their competitive position with technology transferred from Israel.

All business is local

Given this approach, it was clear that retaining senior management in each of these companies was the key to successful mergers. We knew that acquisition by Ness could hurt a company's relationships with local industry, utilities, and government agencies. These customers would be concerned about contracting mission-critical IT services to a foreign provider.

Therefore, the operating paradigm for the acquired companies was to continue to "look local" while offering, wherever appropriate, Israeli technology as a competitive edge. Each company would continue to have local management, and we would keep the folks who had relationships with customers in place on sales and service teams. Since these local companies would be Ness Technologies business units, however, we would standardize operating practices across all of them as much as possible. This included, among other things, training and technology implementation. In addition, each local Ness unit would be able to access resources at other locations to meet customer needs.

In short, the success of Ness Technologies was to be built on a network of companies that offered the consistent business practices and technical resources of a multinational, yet maintained a local presence with local management in the countries where they operated. These basic principles drove the company's later spectacular growth. Its biggest innovations, however, came about when putting its principles into practice.

Ness goes global

When the word got out through investment bankers that Ness was looking to expand beyond Israel, a large number of companies in various countries around the world quickly identified themselves as candidates for acquisition. The entrepreneurs who had started these small companies realized that they were too small to compete against larger rivals over the long term. At this point the only issue was selecting appropriate acquisitions. Ness narrowed the field by looking at GDP growth in the countries under consideration to assess the economic opportunities there.

One of the regions that appeared attractive was Eastern Europe. This region had developed a number of rapidly growing economies after the fall of the Iron Curtain. Having analyzed local competition, the nature of the potential customer base, and the availability of native talent, Ness focused on APP Group, a company in the Czech Republic. A startup with 180 employees, APP had received Warburg Pincus funding when it started in 1990. In the interim it had established itself as a quality provider of IT services to the local utilities, government agencies, and manufacturing enterprises. It was a perfect fit. Through its relationship with Warburg Pincus, Ness kicked off its expansion program by acquiring the APP Group in September 2002.

In line with the overall Ness strategy, APP's senior management continued to run the business after the acquisition. APP provided Ness an entry into the whole East European region. It eventually grew to nearly 1,000 engineers providing IT services in Slovakia and Romania as well as the Czech Republic.

Off-shore challenges

By 2003 the IT services industry was facing the acceleration of the trend noted above: using engineers from countries with lower wages, such as India, to reduce IT support costs. With the cost of local engineers on the rise, thanks to a growing demand for IT talent in the developed economies, this had obvious appeal.

At Ness Technologies, responding to increasing customer demand for cost control became a subject of strategic discussion. Its opportunity to develop an innovative solution to the problem came about through another major acquisition, this time of Apar Holdings in India, another Warburg Pincus investment. Apar was started by Indian entrepreneurs in 1998. Its business model was quite different from that of Ness. Instead of having intellectual property of its own, Apar sold IT engineering services to enterprises on a daily or annual contract basis. Indian engineers worked for its customers either in India or on location in the US, Singapore, and the UK. The company had 1,200 engineers, with a core group of 300 located in India. The others were deployed in other countries and moved to meet customer demand.

A merger with Apar represented a change from the existing Ness business model, but added management and engineering talent in India, and promised access to new customers. We decided that combining the companies was appropriate, and completed the merger of Ness and Apar in 2003.

At the time of the merger we recognized that Apar's business model had to change. It suffered from a basic problem: when Apar engineers were involved in software development, customers had no assurance of the continuity of staff assigned to their projects. And since there were a lot of comings and goings of engineers on the assigned projects, there was little assurance that intellectual property would be protected either.

Shashank Samant, a software engineer trained in India but with extensive international experience, joined Ness as a manager during the Apar acquisition. He came up with an idea for a totally different business model: the "managed laboratory." His idea was to offer corporate customers their own "managed laboratories" for software development, consisting of a team of engineers contracted on a long-term basis, all located in India. Working together in a dedicated facility, they would function as part of the customer's IT organization, even though they were actually Ness employees. The customer would define the software projects, and the head of the managed lab would report to the customer's IT department head. Ness was responsible for training, recruiting, and all employee personal matters. Customers would get the continuity they needed, and with a dedicated team reporting directly to the customer's IT group there would be more control over IP.

Ness embraced this idea. Samant became head of the managed lab business, splitting his time among India, the US, and Israel. He molded the organization and developed the management structure that made the business successful. The managed lab model proved attractive to medium-sized software companies in the US and Europe who wanted the benefit of low-cost software engineering but could not afford to build their own facilities in India. Ness provided them with a dedicated staff that operated as part of their organization in terms of project oversight. To make the service more attractive to companies who might be interested in eventually operating their own facilities, Ness also offered an option under which it would transfer its managed lab staff to the customer.

This model offered clear benefits to Ness, too. First, the customer paid staff costs plus a fee for the service, assuring profitability.

Second, the contractual nature of the IT services made the business more predictable. Instead of hiring engineers in anticipation of potential future projects, the company could plan manpower utilization consistent with its current billings.

As a clear "win-win" situation for buyer and seller, the managed lab model was quickly embraced by customers across the US and in Europe. Ness's first managed lab customer contracted for 200 engineers in 2003. By 2006 Ness was operating fifty such facilities, employing a total of 3,000 people and generating $120 million of profitable revenues annually.

Although the first managed lab was in India, the concept worked wherever wages for engineers were lower than those in the developed countries. Ness also used engineers in Eastern Europe to provide this service to clients in Western Europe.

Cultural considerations

Building the India operation was a lesson in cultural adaptation. As our Israeli management team did not have an easy time managing the rapidly growing Indian operation; management talent had to be recruited locally. It became evident that the key to success was having Indian senior management with prior experience in the US, an appreciation of the local culture, and an understanding of modern IT technology.

Staffing problems posed another serious challenge. Local competition for talent was (and is) intense. At Ness and similar companies, turnover of engineers in Bangalore, the technology capital of India, was between 20 percent and 30 percent annually, compared to less than 10 percent in Israel or Eastern Europe. Such turnover rates put great stress on the efficiency of an engineering organization and make training an ongoing headache. In fact, recruiting qualified engineers, even in an increasingly competitive Indian market, was the easy part. It was much harder to retain the talented ones in a market where wages were rising at a rate of about 10 percent a year (much faster than elsewhere) and employers were beginning to compete on the basis of fringe benefits, the offer of exciting projects, and opportunities for personal development. Once good engineers were on staff, their enthusiasm had to be kept high to retain them by offering opportunities for professional growth.

The staff stayed young, and increasingly included women with young children, so special provisions had to be made for them. Ness became used to providing benefits such as meals, transportation, and even visits by doctors to the Ness facilities to discuss family medical needs and provide access to treatment as needed.

GOING PUBLIC AND AFTER

After APP and Apar, Ness made a number of smaller acquisitions to increase its global footprint. International sales and marketing for all these units was conducted by a staff of 200 professionals. The strategy of leveraging technology skills globally was showing results. For example, Ness developed and delivered a novel IT system to a pharmaceutical company in Switzerland using engineering teams from Europe and Israel. Similarly, a global delivery service for an international law firm was implemented by teams from Israel, the UK, and India. The service was made possible by a proprietary information management system, developed by Ness engineers, that allowed users around the world to share information and work collaboratively on projects.

At the end of 2003, Ness had a total staff of 4,300 employees serving over 500 customers, including Lockheed Martin, Coca Cola, Citibank, AT&T, Israel Aircraft Industries, the Israel Defense Forces, Pfizer, American Express, and Czech Telecom. No single customer represented more than 5 percent of revenues. There was a high level of customer satisfaction, indicated by the fact that, at the end of the year, 80 percent of the following year's business was with the same customer base as the prior year. Clearly the company's management was doing a lot of things right, and it was on a solid footing to continue its global success.

By the end of 2003 the company had accomplished a great deal of what we had hoped to see. Revenues had grown 23 percent annually since inception, to $226 million. The company was profitable and doing business in fourteen countries. It was time to consider an IPO. In September of the following year, the company had its IPO on NASDAQ, selling $140 million of its shares.

At the end of 2006, Raviv Zoller decided to leave the company to resume an investment banking career. He was replaced by Sachi Gerlitz, an executive with extensive international business experience. By then the company had 8,900 employees and was on a clear growth path. It was ranked among the top thirty IT service companies globally by the Brown-Wilson Group, a respected industry consulting firm. Its revenues had increased from $474 million in 2006 to $563 million in 2007. Israeli revenues accounted for 48 percent of the total.

A business of this type is affected by business cycles. As a result of the global recession of 2008, revenues declined in 2009, stabilized in 2010, and resumed growth in 2011 to $620 million. In 2011, the company was taken private by the private equity group of Citigroup Inc.

LOOKING BACK

Building a successful multinational services company is perhaps the most difficult management task entrepreneurs can face – especially starting from a small country. Such a business succeeds only if it learns how to share resources globally while maintaining a common internal culture and uniform operating principles. It must also adapt to the cultures of the places it does business without compromising common corporate goals. Internal regional politics also pose a threat if management interests are not aligned. Without a common operating methodology, each region can easily become a fiefdom that optimizes its business results at the expense of the company as a whole. An employee reward system must be put in place across the entire organization that encourages collaboration among disciplines and geographies.

How the management at Ness was able to avoid the pitfalls and build a successful organization will reward consideration by any entrepreneur with global ambitions. Their approach can be summed up as follows.

- Careful selection of acquisitions to meet strategic objectives: adding desired geographical coverage and skills to the company.
- Retention of the most talented senior managers in acquired firms to help build the local business. There was no attempt to import Israeli management into overseas locations.
- Immediate installation of financial management and control systems in acquired companies, to integrate them into the corporation and allow timely and accurate reporting of business activity.
- Frequent, prolonged visits by senior Ness management in the various regions to work with the local staff. In a remarkably short time this interaction developed a common culture in which international collaboration was accepted as the best means of generating business. This effort was greatly helped by an annual meeting where the fifty top company managers met to review the annual plan. The location changed each year – Bangkok, London, New York, Bangalore, Prague – so that local employees had the opportunity to meet company managers from various countries. Such meetings are a valuable venue for building personal relationships – over twenty nationalities were typically represented among the managers.
- Leveraging the company's diverse skills to serve the needs of international customers in different locations. To further this effort the company developed proprietary information-sharing technology that allowed resources throughout the company's operating regions to address customer needs.
- Rigorous enforcement of a code of conduct – a necessity when operating in some countries where bribery is a common method of acquiring business.

Ness Technologies blazed a new path from its very beginning because its founders designed the company from the ground up to be an international enterprise. They used acquisitions to give it a global reach, and created an innovative business model to attract customers. The strategy for leveraging Indian talent is particularly noteworthy in this regard. They also developed approaches to unifying the company's operations, creating a common corporate culture, and leveraging its worldwide resources to serve major corporations.

In the next chapter we will look at how three Chinese telecommunications startups, operating only in China, dealt with entirely different problems.

8 Three startups in China: Entrepreneurs in a controlled economy

> China's entrepreneurs provide valuable lessons in managing effectively in an unpredictable context ... Besides the usual challenges, Chinese companies face extremely high levels of uncertainty across multiple dimensions ... Executives in China must anticipate and react quickly to a constantly changing environment.[1]

China's influence on the global economy has been a recurring topic of discussion in this book – and in the world at large. How could it be otherwise? It is literally changing the balance of economic and political power among nations.

Just thirty-five years ago this would have seemed impossible. The country was in social and economic turmoil following Mao Zedong's Great Proletariat Cultural Revolution. In a resolution issued on June 30, 1981 the Chinese Communist Party said that this initiative, "which lasted from May 1966 to October 1976, was responsible for the most severe setback and heaviest losses suffered by the party, the state and the people since the founding of the People's Republic."[2]

Today China has recovered from this low point to become the world's second largest economy. Its factories churn out consumer goods and industrial products for export to every part of the globe. Its balance-of-trade surplus is the envy and despair of its trading partners. The Chinese people are increasingly affluent, buying modern conveniences and luxury goods that many never dared to dream of possessing.

---

[1] D. N. Sull with Y. Wang, *Made in China: What Western managers can learn from trailblazing Chinese entrepreneurs* (Boston, MA: Harvard Business School Press, 2005), p. 3.

[2] J. P. Sterba, "Peking assessment asserts Mao made errors as leader," *The New York Times*, July 1, 1981, pp. A1 and A12.

Despite this astonishing progress, the country's potential for development remains enormous. In 2010 about half of its 1.3 billion people were still in the agricultural sector. Millions of them move to cities every year, and state planners talk of building fifty new cities to accommodate them. It is hard to think of a product or service familiar to people in the developed countries that would not find a growing market in China as it continues to evolve.

It is no wonder that China has been a magnet for foreign corporate investment since the 1980s. Big companies from overseas have funded local production plants to gain access to local markets and low-cost labor. In addition to creating local jobs, these transplanted factories have helped to fuel China's export boom. According to government figures, $112.5 billion of China's $170.4 billion trade surplus in the first eleven months of 2010 came from foreign-funded enterprises.[3]

Another reason Chinese authorities have encouraged controlled investment by foreign corporations is to attract sources of leading-edge industrial technology in addition to capital. Attracting foreign investors is still a priority. Li Keqiang, deputy premier, "promised to 'enlarge [the country's] openness' to foreign investment in an attempt to keep Western companies committed to China and complete its industrialization by 2020."[4] Few doubt that this ambitious goal will be achieved. China really has little choice but to try. It must greatly expand its industrial base just to satisfy the projected growth in local demand, to say nothing of increasing its exports.

China is not relying solely on Western money and technology to build its economy. Several of its state-owned or controlled companies have emerged as fierce challengers to the leadership of established multinational corporations, not just in commodity products,

[3] "Chinese manufacturers increase trade figures, but multinationals enjoy most margins," *China Daily*, updated March 1, 2011, www.chinadaily.com.cn/bizchina/2011–01/03/content_11787895.htm, accessed July 19, 2011.

[4] G. Wiesmann and V. Mallet, "Li vows China will become more open to investors," *Financial Times*, January 7, 2011, p. 2.

but in such high-technology areas as communications equipment, mobile phones, and personal computers.

Yet there is more to the Chinese economic miracle than foreign corporate investments, mercantilist methods, and state control of industry. We will look at three entrepreneurial startups, all in telecommunications – arguably the most competitive technology industry in the Chinese economy.

OPPORTUNITY AND CONSTRAINTS

One would not think that a state-controlled economy like China's would have room for classic entrepreneurs funded by private capital. But it does. While major sectors of the economy are controlled by big state-owned or state-controlled corporations, in certain areas an increasing number of privately funded businesses manage to thrive.[5] Recently the scale of foreign private equity investments has been growing – about $50 billion was invested between 2007 and 2010.

Common magnets for private investment are companies providing consumer products or services over the Internet, such as retail stores, housing, and information services. Private equity has also gone into minority investments in companies controlled by the state, which also controls their senior management appointments. Here the private investor expects to realize his profit by either the ultimate sale of the business with state blessing, or by an initial public offering, in which the state sells all or part of its holdings.

Remarkably, more companies originating in China had public offerings in 2010 than those of any other country, including the US.[6] In 2010, forty-three Chinese companies have had IPOs in mainland

---

[5] Lenovo is one of the successful private companies worth noting. It acquired IBM's personal computer business. See Sull with Wang, *Made in China*, pp. 75–83.

[6] *Source:* Dialogic as quoted in L. Cowan, "IPOs, the recovery: Starring China," *The Wall Street Journal*, January 3, 2011, p. R6.

China (Shenzhen and Shanghai) and Hong Kong. Another nineteen were listed in the US.[7]

Concerns for private equity

Private equity investors from the West, realizing they cannot ignore what is now the second largest economy in the world, have joined the wave of China investment. This can be a challenging environment for investors used to US or Western business practices. The questions asked by private equity investors looking to put money to work in China can be summarized as follows.

- How does state control affect independent entrepreneurial companies?
- How difficult is it to recruit experienced management people?
- Are Chinese technology companies that are not state-controlled and are focused on the local market somehow protected from foreign competition?
- How important are state-provided financial incentives such as loans and tax reductions?
- Western companies rely on patents for protecting intellectual property. How relevant is that situation for companies operating in China?
- How do investors and entrepreneurs realize a return from their investment?

Directly or indirectly, state authorities and their regulations are everywhere in China, so knowing the rules (which can change in unpredictable ways) matters a great deal. At the end of the day, what investors really want to know is whether the risk of funding companies will be rewarded in a manner comparable to that in the US and other developed countries.

Three companies, different approaches

To help the reader gain a broader appreciation of what investing in high-technology Chinese startups is like, we have chosen examples that illustrate the impact of local conditions across three

---

[7] H. Sender, "US private equity favors China," *Financial Times*, December 17, 2010, p. 16.

very different business contexts. The first company, AsiaInfo, was launched in close collaboration with a government ministry. The second, Harbour Networks, entered a market where it ended up in direct competition with big local and foreign companies. The third, RDA Microelectronics, was a neutral player that benefited from the proliferation of new wireless handset manufacturing companies interested in buying from a local company instead of dealing with imported products.

Although they targeted different sectors of the telecommunications industry, all three primarily addressed the Chinese market. That did not make matters easy for them. China is far from being a backwater – if a local company's technology lags behind world standards, even state-controlled companies have no compunction about buying foreign.

The companies were all funded between 1996 and 2004 with the participation of Warburg Pincus. These investments were arranged by Warburg Pincus partners responsible for Asian investments, headed by Sun Q. Chang. Julian Cheng led the investment in RDA Microelectronics. Other Warburg Pincus partners participated in assisting these investments at appropriate times.

Telecommunications in China

Our three entrepreneurial companies found their business opportunities in the fastest-growing communications market in the world. State investment in telecommunications services dramatically increased from the 1980s, and continues to this day. Fiber optic network construction, begun in the late 1990s, enabled high data rate services on a national basis. The market for equipment and associated software and services grew 30 percent a year, making China a desirable destination for equipment vendors from all over the world.

When Warburg Pincus started to invest in this sector in China in 2000, there were seven nationwide licensed carriers serving 160 million telephone subscribers. State authorities later decided to consolidate these entities into three giant state-controlled carriers covering the whole country: China Telecom, China Mobile, and China Unicom. China Mobile and China Unicom are wireless service providers, while China Telecom provides wireline service. Adding national cellular wireless service became a high priority and spectacular growth in wireless later proved the wisdom of this initiative. The number of wireless subscribers grew from 180,000 in 1992 to 7 million in 1996 and 950 million in 2011, giving China the world's largest population of wireless users.

Many local manufacturers emerged to supply handsets to the ballooning numbers of subscribers, offering lower-cost products to compete with phones from the likes of Motorola and Nokia. In 2010, 551 million handsets were produced in China, of which 421 million were exported. One of the startups that we will discuss, RDA Microelectronics, provides key semiconductor chips for wireless handsets.

Equipment for the country's telecommunications infrastructure was initially provided by foreign companies, but state planners had a strategy to develop a domestic state-owned industry capable of building world-class equipment. Huawei Technologies emerged as the national champion, along with a smaller company, ZTE. A number of privately funded companies also entered the market, including Harbour Networks.

In addition to equipment, telecommunications systems require operation support services, billing software, and experts to manage system integration. AsiaInfo provided such software and services.

ASIAINFO: ENABLING CHINA'S INTERNET

AsiaInfo was founded in 1993 in Dallas, Texas, by Edward Tian and James Ding, two entrepreneurs in their thirties. Tian was born in China, and earned a master's degree from the graduate school of the Chinese Academy of Sciences and a Ph.D. from Texas Tech University. Ding, also born in China, earned a bachelor's degree from Beijing University and a master's degree from UCLA. Their business provided online information about China to Western news agencies. It was not a very exciting niche, so the founders looked for other opportunities. They found them across the Pacific.

New location, new model

Having tracked developments in their birthplace, Tian and Ding saw the growing telecommunications industry and the rise of the Internet as opportunities to be exploited.

So in 1995 the founders, exemplifying the flexibility of true entrepreneurs, decided to move their business to Beijing and totally change their business model. It was at that point that they were introduced to the Warburg Pincus investing team and we provided some of the funding to launch their Chinese venture.

Thanks to their familiarity with local business customs and conditions, they knew that a newcomer trying to serve a growing industry owned or controlled by the government would need the right local relationships. At that time the key governmental agency was the Ministry of Post and Telecommunications (MPT), which regulated the telecommunications industry and was also a near-monopoly wireline service operator. (The MPT was a predecessor to the Ministry of Information Industries, which now oversees tele-communications services.) AsiaInfo's founders were able to estab-lish two joint ventures with a subsidiary of the MPT. One focused on selling telecommunications and Internet infrastructure software; the other sold system integration services. AsiaInfo came on the scene just as the Internet emerged as a serious service in China. Its timing was perfect.

The numbers tell the story. In 1993 China had only 2,000 Internet subscribers. There were 330,000 in 1996 when the com-pany started doing business. Just five years later, in 2011, the num-ber of Internet subscribers in China exceeded 500 million. AsiaInfo became the first and largest Chinese information technology com-pany to provide infrastructure software and services for the Internet and related fields.

- It established de facto standards for Internet infrastructure in China in collaboration with the MPT.
- In its first year of operation, the company gained a 70 percent market share of Internet integration services.
- AsiaInfo built the infrastructure for ChinaNet, the first national commercial Internet backbone company, covering the 31 capital cities of all the provinces of mainland China.

The company became profitable in 1997, one year after full operations began, generating $19 million in revenues and a profit of $6 million.

As Internet technology evolved, the requirements of the Chinese telecommunications infrastructure grew more sophisticated. To meet this need and maintain its market position, the company licensed foreign products for sale in China and developed its own proprietary products. It also turned to acquisition activities. By that time small software companies had begun to emerge – some started by Chinese technologists returning from the US. Following a pattern familiar from Silicon Valley, AsiaInfo acquired some of these startups for their advanced technology. Between 1998 and 2002, AsiaInfo absorbed three local companies to bolster its portfolio of software products for the wireless industry, which had emerged as the fastest-growing sector of telecommunications. It acquired other companies later.

AsiaInfo's growth was impressive. Revenues grew from $60 million in 1999 to $176 million in 2000. It was time to consider an IPO in the US – something very new at the time for a China-based company.

Going public across the Pacific

Internet companies were the darlings of the public markets in 2000, and China was seen as a great growth market. AsiaInfo's NASDAQ offering was very successful, selling shares that valued the company at a very rich $800 million.

The company's stock price has fluctuated in the years since, along with its growth rate and profitability. To this day, all of the customers of the company are either state owned or directly or indirectly state controlled. When a company is dependent on a small customer base its revenues will be tied to the ups and downs of capital investment cycles. Yet throughout these vagaries AsiaInfo has remained a dominant vendor of software products to the three telecommunications carriers in China. This complex software, which now enables service to hundreds of millions of subscribers, was developed in China. Experts consider these products to be of outstanding quality.

The company merged with Linkage, another telecommunications software company, in 2010. The combined company is called AsiaInfo-Linkage. The merger consolidated the company as the leader in its field in China. In 2010, its revenues were $350 million and its market value on NASDAQ reached $1.3 billion.

HARBOUR NETWORKS: AGAINST THE TIDE

"Harbour Networks is quite capable of designing and developing switch-routers to compete with the same level of products offered by US vendors today ... at a much lower cost." So wrote a well-known consultant after visiting the new company in Beijing in 2001, shortly after Yinan Li founded it with $4 million of seed capital from local investors.

Yinan Li combines a strong technology background with industry knowledge and senior management experience – just the sort of résumé that one values in entrepreneurs in a dynamic industry. He had been vice-chairman of Huawei Technologies, where he ranked among the three top leaders of the largest telecommunications equipment company in China. Huawei was very successful. Starting from scratch, it developed a growing portfolio of products to compete with various imported equipment. Huawei's revenues grew to reach $2 billion in 2000, only seven years after it was founded. Of course, Huawei also enjoyed advantages over the foreign firms. It had access to state-targeted bank funding, plus a strong vendor position when selling to the big carriers that came to dominate the Chinese service market.

Leaving a major company to found a competing firm is a daring move for a senior executive, regardless of country. Departing from a national champion like Huawei carries an even higher level of risk. It does not compare with leaving Intel or HP in California, where Yinan Li would have been viewed as a bold entrepreneur. In China's business culture he might have been regarded as disloyal, to both the organization and his mentors. Yinan Li was well aware of the other risks a new company such as Harbour Networks faced. It was entering a highly competitive international business where big buyers, which dominate the service industry, liked the safety of the big, established vendors. It faced formidable, well-managed foreign competitors such as Cisco Systems, Alcatel, Lucent, and Ericsson. And Huawei was a growing force in the market.

Yet he believed Harbour Networks could build a competitive edge with early offerings of leading-edge products. Switches and routers derive a great deal of their performance capabilities from proprietary chips, and he intended to build a very strong chip design team. Once he had a competitive product, his status as a domestic vendor would enable him to win sales by adapting his offerings to local needs, including time-to-market, price, and service. This was clearly an ambitious program, but investors familiar with similar startups in the US knew that highly successful equipment companies were often launched by outstanding managers even in very competitive markets. Yinan Li certainly qualified on that score.

In 2001, on the strength of his vision and reputation and the quality of his team, Harbour Networks was funded by three sources: Warburg Pincus; a venture capital group sponsored by the Shanghai city government; and another Chinese private venture capital group. To gain marketing experience while developing its own products, the company started by reselling Huawei equipment. But this was only a temporary effort because it was developing its own competitive products.

Harbour Networks made remarkable progress in completing its own products. The company's pool of skilled chip designers completed custom chip designs in about two-thirds of the time I would estimate to be needed by US-based companies. But just as the company began to offer its own products, it came face-to-face with the twin realities of today's telecommunications equipment market: the rapid pace of innovation required, and its crushing capital requirements. Designing a clever chip was no longer enough to vault a company over the competition. To continue to grow and compete with the big vendors, Harbour had to offer ever more complex state-of-the art equipment to the major carriers. This required growth capital – lots of it. The company was innovative. Its engineers filed over 100 patents to protect the intellectual property they were developing. But Harbour's profit margins were too thin to support the expanded product development needed to become a major provider of equipment in a league with the big established companies.

One way to raise equity capital was to do what similar US equipment companies had done in the past – sell shares through a public offering in the US. But the public market for telecommunications equipment companies in the US was still suffering with a hangover from the bursting of the "dot-com and telecom" bubble in 2000–2001.

Then, in 2005, Huawei, impressed with the quality of the company's technology, offered to buy Harbour Networks. Its bid was accepted. As it turned out, this was a timely move. The telecommunications equipment market continued to consolidate, and resources required to compete soon grew even more enormous. Huawei certainly has those resources. In 2010 it employed over 50,000 engineers and had more than 49,000 patents filed or issued around the world. It also has the capital to match its global ambitions. Its $30 billion in revenues was second only to Ericsson in the industry, and it had access to $30 billion in funding from the China Development Bank.[8]

---

[8] M. Dalton, "EU finds China banks aid Huawei and ZTE," *The Wall Street Journal*, February 3, 2011, p. B3.

Yinan Li went on to become the chief technology officer of one of the largest Internet companies in China.

RDA MICROELECTRONICS: LOCAL ALLIANCES

By 2003 over 40 percent of the chips produced in the world were being shipped to Asia-Pacific countries, and China had become a global hub of electronics assembly. But very few of the chips used in China's factories were produced there. Seven years later China's supremacy in assembly had not changed the situation. In 2010, 96 percent of the chips used there came from non-Chinese companies.[9]

The Warburg Pincus team viewed this as an opportunity to build one or more valuable chip businesses in China to serve the local market. Given the growth of China's wireless industry, the team believed that devices that enabled wireless functionality were interesting products for a startup.

In 2003 the team was introduced by mutual friends to two entrepreneurs who were ideally suited to start such a company. Vincent Tai had been the founder of a company making wireless application chips in Silicon Valley. He then went on to found an electronics distribution company in Hong Kong. Born in China, he had earned a bachelor's degree in electrical engineering at the Georgia Institute of Technology in Atlanta and an MBA from the University of Chicago. His co-founder, Shuran Wei, had earlier co-founded a chip company in Silicon Valley. He had extensive wireless chip experience at other companies in the US. He had a bachelor's degree in electrical engineering from Beijing University and a master's degree from the University of Minnesota.

In 2004, Warburg Pincus funded RDA Microelectronics with Vincent Tai as CEO and Shuran Wei as chief technology officer. Company headquarters were in Shanghai, with satellite facilities in Beijing. The two founders had complementary technical, marketing, and managerial skills and experience. Since the government wanted

---

[9] *IBS Report*, private communication, March 2011.

to encourage the development of a domestic chip industry, RDA was promised (and received) preferential tax treatment from local authorities.

Tai and Wei selected products whose technology they were familiar with for their market entry, in categories where competition was manageable. RDA's chips convert real-world analog signals such as sound and radio waves into digital form. Their chips fall under the categories of RF (radio frequency) and mixed signal (i.e. analog and digital) processing devices and are used in all wireless equipment. Designing them requires highly specialized and relatively rare engineering talent. RDA would be competing largely with mid-sized US companies, not industry giants like Texas Instruments or Intel. They were also avoiding competition with favored Chinese firms: there was no domestic competition.

The two founders believed that a local company would have a major advantage in selling to the rapidly proliferating number of Chinese wireless handset manufacturers. These manufacturers all shared two common traits – limited engineering resources and a tight focus on low-cost manufacturing. Chips were crucial to their success, and they counted on the expertise of the chip vendors' application engineers to help design their products. Given the short product cycles in the wireless industry (as little as six months in the case of handsets), such support presupposes a very close working relationship with chip vendors to make sure that the products meet industry standards. If the supplier is local, collaboration becomes much easier.

RDA was able to hit the ground running because of its business model, which is that of a fabrication-less chip vendor, focused exclusively on product design and marketing. It did not have to build its own chip manufacturing facility. Production of the actual chips is outsourced to factories in Taiwan and the US. As chip factories with the right technology were built in China, RDA used them as well.

Tai and Wei's major challenge was to build an engineering team that could execute their product strategy. Their personal reputations were a great help in attracting talent. So was RDA's focus on leading-edge technology. This attribute drew top engineering graduates from the best Chinese schools, many of them with advanced degrees. With a team of innovative engineers in place, product development went forward at a remarkable pace. Although RDA has licensed foreign technology as needed and available, it also quickly developed proprietary technology for its own use. Throughout this process it has been scrupulous in managing its intellectual property. It had over 100 Chinese patents either issued or filed in 2010.

As a result of its leading-edge products and a marketing strategy concentrated on Chinese handset manufacturers, RDA has experienced very fast growth. Its revenues have increased at a compound annual rate of 197 percent, from $4.5 million in 2006 to $191 million in 2010.

Its customers mirrored its success, quickly making their mark in the world's handset industry. There were 1.2 billion handsets produced worldwide in 2009. Of these, 31.1 percent came from Chinese vendors, most of whom bought chips from RDA. The company has over 500 customers, almost all in China, including all of that country's top manufacturers of handsets. It offers dozens of products. By 2009 it was the second largest producer of RF and mixed-signal semiconductor devices in the Asia-Pacific region in terms of revenues. The fact that such a world-class organization was put together in just five years is testimony not only to the talent of its founders but to the fact that world-class engineering talent is now available in China.

The company has used its expertise in mixed-signal technology products and its rapid development capabilities to diversify into areas outside of wireless applications, such as cable television equipment. In 2010, RDA was the third largest independent Chinese chip company.[10] RDA began generating profits after 2007. In 2010 the company executed an IPO on NASDAQ. Of the various reasons for RDA's success, four deserve special mention:

---

[10] The largest is part of the Huawei group of companies. *IBS Report*, March 2011.

- its ability to develop and deliver products faster than its competitors;
- its outstanding customer service to meet the continuing needs of its customers;
- an aggressive product pricing strategy; and
- the ability to lower prices while maintaining profitability.

RDA is not the only company that can boast of these achievements. In fact, they are basic requirements for all vendors in this industry no matter where they are located. But RDA has the extraordinary discipline and engineering skills to be better at them than its competition.

LOOKING BACK

AsiaInfo, Harbour Networks, and RDA were created with the express intent of focusing on China's telecommunications market. Their stories underscore how important it is for entrepreneurs to combine knowledge of international industry with a familiarity with local business practices in order to to succeed in the global economy. It is instructive to review how each of these companies addressed the circumstances that influenced their success.

The human factor

Foreign credentials. RDA and AsiaInfo were started by Chinese entrepreneurs who combined local savvy and education with additional education and startup experience in the US. For both companies their founders' US education and management experience proved to be an important asset. Their public reports made a point of these attributes. For example, the 2000 IPO offering memorandum of AsiaInfo stated: "Our senior management team, the majority of whom have been educated in the United States or have worked with leading multinational companies in or outside China, have an in-depth understanding of the China market combined with knowledge of best management practices gained from some of the world's leading information technology companies."

Similarly, the 2010 IPO offering memorandum of RDA stated: "We recruit engineers from China's top educational institutions, which graduate a large number of engineers with advanced degrees each year, creating a pool of motivated and qualified candidates for the semiconductor design industry. Our engineering team is led by [four executives] who together have over 60 years of experience in the high-tech industry in Silicon Valley and China."

Cultural adaptability. Fluent in Mandarin and English, and comfortable in the cultures of China and the US, the entrepreneurs who founded RDA and AsiaInfo were able to build business relationships on both sides of the Pacific. Their multicultural backgrounds proved valuable in dealing with foreign competition, negotiating licensing deals, and recruiting engineers who were returning to China from the US. It also proved useful in dealing with investors at the time when an IPO was planned.

Technical talent. When asked what his biggest challenge was in building RDA, Vincent Tai responded, "finding experienced engineers with the level of skill needed to compete with the global players." This is why his company treats training as such an important element of its success. However, this task is eased by the outstanding quality of the graduates from the best engineering schools. The educational system in China continues to improve, with a number of world-class universities turning out well-trained people in all disciplines, including science and engineering. As we noted in the case of RDA, there is an abundant pool of talented graduates available who quickly become very productive under the right management. That is another reason why foreign training and experience in managing new companies is so important in building successful businesses.

State issues

Businesses everywhere are hostage to state regulations. But in a state-controlled economy, regulatory changes come more frequently, particularly in industries like telecommunications. Nimbleness and flexibility in managing such uncertainties is a prerequisite for doing business in China.

For example, regulators influence the pace of deployment of new telecommunications infrastructure, essentially dictating the timing of product availability. Government-mandated changes in timing or technology can be unpredictable. This affects the profitability of vendors to the industry, who can be stuck with an inventory of products that have uncertain market prospects.

As a vendor to the handset industry, then, RDA has to adapt quickly to changing standards so its customers can meet highly fluid handset availability requirements. For example, major handset vendors may begin with fifteen to twenty handset designs. Over the next six to eight quarters they may winnow this number down to perhaps five or six that they will actually produce. But if a small company picks a design that does not make it to market, it has nothing to sell.

Then there are the non-technological quirks. In 2010, for example, RDA's sales took a temporary hit when state authorities cracked down on Chinese handset manufacturers who were not installing the correct software in their handsets or who dodged paying the appropriate taxes.

We should note that situations like these are hardly unique to China. The reality is that selling products to the telecommunications industry has its challenges everywhere. In each country a few dominant service providers establish the rules of the business and the pace at which technology is introduced. In the US, for example, Verizon and AT&T are the dominant service companies, and their rules affect their vendors' ability to sell their products. That is the nature of this market.

No place to hide with inferior products

There are no protected markets for inferior technology in China or any other important developing country, including India. All three of the companies we have covered in this chapter were competing directly or indirectly with global suppliers selling world-class products. Low product quality at a low price is not a winning combination and never formed a part of their strategy. Of course, anyone doing business in China is acutely aware of the intense price competition there. Price is a competitive advantage – if you can deliver competitive products and services at lower prices than others, you have a good chance of success. But industrial customers and consumers alike don't have to settle for inferior products just because they are cheaper. They know that sooner rather than later they will have access to the same high-quality items being sold in the developed countries.

- Harbour Networks' telecommunications equipment was in the same league as what such world-class companies as Juniper Networks or Cisco Systems produced.
- AsiaInfo competition came from multinationals such as IBM and smaller local companies. While it benefited from its partnership with the MPT in the early days, its success over the following years came from delivering high-quality, profitable software and services at a lower price than its competitors.
- RDA's success was due to its ability to serve the local wireless industry better, and at lower cost, than its foreign competitors. Its continued success will require a similar performance not only in its current sector of the market, but in new markets that emerge and can be served by its evolving technology skills.

Pick your competitors carefully

Harbour's original strategy was to serve a highly diverse customer base of enterprises and regional telecommunications carriers. But when, as a result of state policy, its carrier customer base was consolidated into three big companies, it found itself in direct competition not only with Huawei but with the big international vendors selling in China. Lots of capital was needed. This was not a winning situation for a young company with limited resources.

When AsiaInfo entered the market, on the other hand, it was bolstered by joint ventures with the Ministry that regulated the industry. It wasn't fighting the establishment; it was partnering with the establishment. As long as its level of technology, service, and price matched or bettered what others were offering, AsiaInfo was able to compete against all comers.

Finally, RDA entered a market where it competed only with foreign companies. As hundreds of handset manufacturers emerged, a local company with highly competitive products – and better prices – had an opportunity to establish itself as a major vendor.

State subsidies and tax preferences

As mentioned above, China is actively seeking to build innovative industries. National and regional authorities alike offer various financial incentives for companies to locate facilities within the country. Available incentives run the gamut from low-cost loans for the construction and equipping of factories to reduced taxes on profits. These financial inducements are most significant in financing plant construction. They are of much less importance in businesses such as the three companies discussed here, where intellectual property is the key value creator. Of course, lower taxes help companies to retain cash for expansion – but only once a business is profitable.

Patent filing in China and the legal system

Protection of IP is a constant concern anywhere. Chinese authorities are quite sensitive about foreign criticism of their perceived deficiencies in IP protection. The China Patent Office and related organizations have proven very effective in working with participants in such disputes to resolve them.

However, software patents are difficult to obtain, although one can copyright software. Foreign companies doing business in China need to take into account the difficulty of protecting software through the patent system. Disputes over IP where the patents involved are not filed in China are much more difficult to resolve because of the country's complex court system. However, the local courts are very much aware of the need to protect the intellectual property of important companies in their regions. As a result, cases of intellectual theft, such as copying products by competitors, are likely to be vigorously prosecuted in regional courts, with severe penalties imposed on infringing parties.

Exits

In developed countries the most common investment exits are through a company sale or a public offering of securities. The buying and selling of companies within China is common (AsiaInfo acquired a number of companies), but selling a Chinese company to a foreign entity is not easy. Such a transaction is covered by regulations from no fewer than six government agencies. The sale requires the permission of the Ministry of Commerce, and the procedure can be long and complex. This means that selling companies created in China to foreigners may prove to be a problematic exit path.

IPOs, however, are an increasingly attractive exit strategy for Chinese businesses that have reached a significant level of maturity. Of course there are rules you must follow. If the company is majority-owned and controlled by Chinese investors, it can be listed locally. Foreign-owned companies cannot be listed in either Shanghai or Shenzhen, but may be listed in Hong Kong and the US. Both AsiaInfo and RDA are listed on NASDAQ. Both companies have excellent financial systems, enabling them to meet the stiff accounting requirements for US-listed companies with minimal investment.

In summary

One overriding conclusion can be drawn from the history of these three Chinese startups: it is possible for entrepreneurs to build successful high technology companies in China using private equity, even when much of the funding is foreign. Major sectors that state authorities consider strategic are off limits to startups. But the 20 percent to 30 percent of the economy that remains still provides huge market opportunities.[11]

All three of our companies developed world-class products with local engineering talent and with the additional help of licensed foreign technology in some cases. In spite of some key differentiators unique to China, such as the shifting regulatory environment, the ingredients for success there are not all that different from those in the US or other Western countries. Companies that are mindful of the local competitive and regulatory climate can succeed on the basis of competitive products, services, and cost structures.

In the next chapter we will examine an entrepreneurial startup that took a very different approach to doing business in China.

---

[11] Because of the mixed ownership in many enterprises, it is difficult to define the private sector with precision. See R. McGregor, *The Party: The secret world of China's Communist rulers* (New York: HarperCollins, 2010), pp. 194–228.

9   Connecting the wireless networks of the world

> The money from hauling data, things like video and texts instead of calls, is now 35.9 percent of total service revenue [in the US] ... The phone networks carried 341.2 billion megabits of traffic in the first half of 2011, according to the survey, up 111 percent from a year earlier ... Talk, meantime, may be falling slightly out of fashion ... The average length of a call was 1.83 minutes ... As recently as 2007, the average call was near or above three minutes. Who's got time to talk, when there's all that video to watch?[1]

Mobile data service is more than a booming business; it is a global phenomenon. Teenagers text each other on their Droids as obsessively as business people check email and corporate data on their iPhone® or BlackBerry® smartphones. TV stations show video clips of everything from cute babies to the rebellion in Libya, captured and sent by people on cell phones. We take it all for granted. Yet none of these capabilities was available as little as a dozen years ago.

Just as remarkably, Aicent, a Silicon Valley startup founded in 2000 by an entrepreneur born in Taiwan, is a world leader in providing the data interconnections among the international wireless carriers that enable these functions across their networks. For example, if you are visiting China or Indonesia and access your emails on your BlackBerry, the chances are that you are using a network connection managed by Aicent.

Aicent holds interest for reasons beyond its growth and success. It provides an interesting case study of a new model for a startup business: a company that was constructed from the start to meet the challenges of operating globally even as a small enterprise.

[1] Q. Hardy, "More wireless devices than people," http://bits.blogs.nytimes.com/2011/10/12/the-u-s-has-more-wireless-devices-than-people/?scp=16&sq=wireless+networks&st=nyt, October 12, 2011.

Unlike Ness Technologies, the company did not address its domestic market first. Aicent was founded to provide a mission-critical service to the global wireless telecommunications industry. This placed it squarely in the largest and fastest-growing segment of the world economy: in 2010 service businesses accounted for 63.2 percent of global GDP.[2]

Aicent's business depends on the wide global implementation of new wireless technologies, and the rapid growth of mobile computing and messaging. But its success was based on the vision of its founder and the company's execution of its business plan. Having entered the market early, Aicent was in a good position to ride the rising tide of international data traffic. To fully appreciate its story, we need to understand how wireless networks have evolved as platforms for data services.

THE EVOLUTION OF WIRELESS DATA SERVICES

Consumer wireless (cellular) service is so ubiquitous today that one easily forgets how young it is and how quickly it has grown. It only emerged as a major industry in the 1990s, but by 2004 its global subscriber base had reached 1.7 billion. In 2011 that number was over 5 billion. Practically every inhabited part of the planet has wireless consumer service.

Cellular mobile service started with first-generation (1G) analog wireless systems, in use in the 1980s and 1990s. These were designed to provide mobile voice-only telephony, and the handsets were simply portable telephone receivers. There was practically no standardization of technology in those early years. Had the industry stayed analog and voice-only, there would have been no market for an Aicent.

Everything changed with the introduction of 2G systems in 1991. This second-generation technology switched transmission and

---

[2] Statistic from *The World Fact Book*, published by the US Central Intelligence Agency, available at www.cia.gov/library/publications/the-world-factbook/fields/2012.html.

reception from analog to digital, opening the door to data services as well as voice calls. In 1993 text messaging was the first data service to be introduced.

Digital takes over

Three new generations (2.5G, 3G, and 4G or LTE) of digital wireless networks have appeared since then, each representing a significant advance over its predecessor. As carriers deployed these improved networks, handset makers sought to exploit their capabilities, and tempted consumers with ever newer, more sophisticated handsets. Changes came incredibly fast. While analog landline telephones had stayed virtually the same for decades, mobile phones had a model lifespan measured in months.

Early digital handsets provided only telephony and short message service (SMS, the foundation of today's Twitter network). They soon added more data services, such as full Internet access, first announced by NTT DoCoMo in Japan in 1998. Eventually they evolved into today's smartphones. Smartphones have become platforms for entertainment, personalization, and rich media communications. Voice communication is just one of their many functions. Subscribers can use their smartphones to listen to music, connect to the Internet, get GPS-based travel directions, access email, exchange short messages, and send and receive pictures and short videos recorded with cameras incorporated into their handsets.

These devices also serve as gateways to an ever-growing number of personalized applications offered by the networks, such as online payments and social network interaction. Data and video applications dominate the list of features on handsets from companies such as Apple and Research in Motion (RIM), maker of the BlackBerry phone, and those equipped with Google's Android operating system.

Building out the network

Digital wireless networks grew rapidly, thanks in large part to the orderly development of standards by international industry organizations. Carriers seeking to upgrade their networks selected their digital technology from a limited menu of accepted standards. Most carriers, including those in developing countries in Asia and elsewhere, adopted GSM (Global System for Mobile Communications) technology, which had originated in Europe. A smaller group, including a few Asian carriers and Verizon and Sprint in the US, adopted CDMA (Code Division Multiple Access) technology, developed by another California startup, Qualcomm.

Regardless of which system a carrier chose, it was built on digitally "packetized" data technology (discussed in Chapter 5). For GSM operators, the need to offer data services meant adopting the GPRS (General Packet Radio Service) standard. CDMA operators had their own standards, which were not compatible with GPRS. In either case, subscribers could access the Internet from handsets at data rates higher than 100 kbps (kilobits per second).

Carriers deployed data-service-enabling networks in most of the world between 1999 and 2009. As these networks proliferated, smartphone sales grew rapidly, particularly after 2004 when many networks were already in place. Sales increased from 35 million handsets in 2004 to over 500 million units in 2011. Recently they have roughly doubled every year.

Mobile computing arrives

Mobile computing, and the use of data service networks, took a big leap forward with the introduction of wirelessly connected tablet computers in 2010. In 2011, Cisco Systems projected that 15 billion devices would be wirelessly connected globally by 2015. It predicted that mobile data network traffic would nearly double every year.

A good way to appreciate the remarkable growth of mobile computing is to compare it to that of PC-based personal computing. A metric for the two industrial sectors is their comparative sales of hardware and software, shown in Figure 9.1.[3] In 2000 these revenues were $348 billion for PC computing and only $500 million

---

[3] T. McCourt and M. McKee, "The mobile computing revolution," Morgan Keegan, January 28, 2011, p. 4.

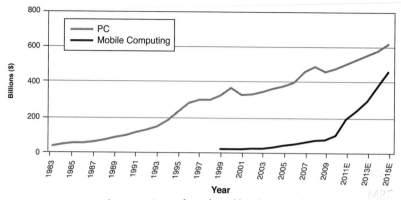

FIGURE 9.1 A comparison of combined hardware and software revenues in the personal computing and mobile computing industries (ref. 3).

for mobile computing. By 2005 mobile computing had reached $20 billion. By 2011, however, PC hardware and software sales had risen to only $485 billion, a 40 percent increase, while mobile computing hardware and software revenues had leaped more than eightfold to $171 billion. This growth was primarily due to mobile network construction and increased sales of smarter handsets.

Data traffic dilemma

As carriers deployed digital networks around the world, they found an increasingly troublesome problem. Global wireless data offered a major opportunity for revenue growth, but the data had to travel easily across all networks. Unfortunately, interconnection among the networks was not transparent, because carrier traffic standards and operating conditions were not uniform around the world.

This situation threatened to undermine the popularity of data services. For example, what if a carrier's customer was outside its coverage zone, or "roaming," in the parlance of the industry? The customer would have to connect through another carrier. Voice calls in this situation were expensive, so the carrier wanted to provide lower-cost data services such as SMS and multimedia message service (MMS). Messaging was the first area of interest for carriers because the earliest popular data services consisted of SMS and MMS messages.

However, because of the disparity in traffic standards, network interconnection required extensive investments in connectivity, followed by rigorous testing, involving the wireless carriers interested in partnering. This was a big change for the industry. Previously, when establishing voice interconnections, carriers had typically negotiated much simpler direct bilateral agreements with each other.

Market opportunities for intermediaries

To address the interoperability problem, in 2000 the GSM Association established standards for GPRS Data Exchange, or GRX. Carriers connected by a GRX-compliant hub could interchange data, thus replacing the complicated, and dedicated, one-to-one technical relationships previously needed to accommodate subscribers who wanted to use GPRS services outside of their home network.

It worked like this. Each carrier would connect its switches, provided with suitable new software, to a GRX computer hub. From there its roaming data traffic would be connected to other carriers with similar termination capabilities. Such a hub and spoke arrangement freed wireless carriers from the cost and difficulties of managing individual connections. CDMA operators also established an interconnection service called CRX.

However, these technology-specific interconnections were not a complete solution. In addition to both technologies needing hubs, carriers that used CDMA technology could not connect their data traffic to those that used GSM technology, and vice versa, without another intervening gateway for standards translation.

Clearly this situation created opportunities for companies that could build and operate interconnection hubs for the international wireless industry. The more carriers that appeared and networks that were built, the greater were the opportunities that arose. This was the business for which Aicent was built. It was designed to serve as a trusted intermediary, providing interconnection for the carriers and eliminating the need for them to establish and maintain bilateral relationships for handling each other's data traffic.

PRECURSOR TO AN IDEA

Lynn Liu, the founder of Aicent, is a serial entrepreneur. Born in Taiwan and educated at National Taiwan University, she came to the US to earn an M.S. in Computer Science at the State University of New York. At the completion of her studies she moved to Silicon Valley where, in 1994, she co-founded GRIC Communications with her husband, Dr. Hong Chen.

The idea behind GRIC was to provide people with low-cost access to the Internet while they were traveling. In the 1990s, when broadband connections were rare, there was a boom in companies called ISPs (Internet Service Providers) who offered dial-up access to the Internet over telephone lines. People would contract for an Internet connection with an ISP that had phone numbers in their local calling area. Since getting Internet access was a local call, they could stay on line as long as they wanted without piling up long-distance phone charges.

Everything changed when these subscribers were on the road. Their regular number became long distance, and they would have to hope their ISP had local numbers in the places they were visiting. Without either a local connection or a toll-free dial-up number, access through an ISP to the Internet became a costly long-distance call, billed by the minute. GRIC offered a number of services, but the most interesting one enabled travelers to access the Internet from anywhere through a local phone call to a local carrier, as long as the carrier participated in the GRIC network. GRIC negotiated the agreements among carriers to permit travelers to access the Internet through a local phone call, thus saving them the expense of timed long-distance calls.

Dr. Hong Chen was chief executive officer of the company, but Lynn Liu was its chief operating officer and head of international market development. Believing that the Asian market offered the greatest growth opportunities, she concentrated on building relationships with regional carriers in Asia. She earned the trust of senior executives of the major carriers in China as well as those in Singapore and Hong Kong. These relationships would prove extremely valuable for Aicent.

Riding the Internet and telecommunications bubble, GRIC had its IPO on NASDAQ in 1999. Despite its modest revenues it reached a market valuation in excess of one billion dollars. Shortly after its IPO, when its value burst along with the market, GRIC was acquired by a competitor. This left Liu free to start Aicent in 2000. She was joined by David Zhang, the former head of technology at GRIC and a telecommunications expert.

The initial funding for Aicent came from Asian venture capital funds. That money lasted long enough for the company to reach significant revenues and attract another investor, Warburg Pincus, which invested in the company in 2005.

AICENT GETS STARTED

Lynn Liu had realized there was an opportunity to build a company to solve the data interconnection problems of the wireless carriers. The GSM industry association had defined standards for its GRX interconnection service. But who was going to manage the interchange hubs it required? She positioned Aicent as a neutral third-party enabler of data traffic interoperability for carriers around the globe, concentrating at first on Asia, where GSM was dominant and she had personal contacts.

Liu planned to establish digital traffic management hubs in strategic locations such as Beijing, Hong Kong, and London, and contract with carriers to route appropriate international traffic through these hubs. Aicent's revenues would come from two sources: fees for message transmission; and payments from carriers for the use of the interconnection links, based on the amount of traffic carried on their behalf. Instead of building her own facilities, she rented the "pipes" that interconnected the data trunks of the various carriers. This kept Aicent's initial costs low, and allowed the company to scale its infrastructure as traffic volumes increased.

It was a bold idea. There were three key conditions for its success:

- the economic build-out of a rented global network to attract the interest of carriers in linking their traffic to the Aicent hubs;
- trust on the part of the carriers that Aicent was capable of delivering a reliable service at an attractive price; and
- enough data traffic to fill the hubs and garner enough revenues to keep Aicent in business.

Without all three of these factors working in the company's favor, there was no business.

Building the network

For Aicent to succeed, it had to quickly establish a dominant position by offering the most routes for data interconnection and the highest reliability. This meant that a special network meeting the most rigorous requirements had to be in place before carriers would commit their traffic. When asked about her strategy in the early years, Lynn Liu says "a business like this needs to have the greatest number of connected carriers – the whole value is in the network. Whoever has the best and widest network has the most attractive one and gets the growth – the winner takes all."

Right from the start, the Aicent technical team, managed by David Zhang, proved itself capable of building and managing the required international access networks. This was owing in part to experience acquired at GRIC, but they also implemented a great deal of novel digital technology to ensure security and reliability.

There were operational challenges too. When dealing with carriers, failure of a link is not an option – 100 percent uptime is essential. That the Aicent team was able to meet this standard of performance was a major reason for the company's eventual success. Compatibility and adaptability were another requirement. Aicent's service had to be compliant with the many existing industry standards; but the wireless industry does not stand still. The company also needed the ability to implement new standards quickly.

Gaining the trust of big carriers

Demanding as these requirements were, building the network was the easy part. It just cost time and money. Overcoming the trust barrier was a much more difficult proposition. What carrier would trust a startup with such a critical service? This is where Liu's previous experience at GRIC came into play.

When simple messaging was the only data traffic, the large carriers, including China Mobile, entered into bilateral agreements with each other for GRX data services. But as new messaging services were introduced, many of the carriers, including China Mobile, sought to avoid investing more time and effort in establishing bilateral contracts, performing engineering tests, and running trials with multiple operators. They shifted to a neutral third-party hub strategy. Outsourcing such services to a trusted outside company made strategic sense, but they had to find the right neutral party. The fact that Liu had already worked with senior executives at the carriers was hugely helpful. She was known and trusted, an important business advantage in Asia, so when she presented Aicent as a vendor a major barrier to achieving credibility was removed. While that level of trust provided an opening for Aicent to build its business, it was still a slow process in the early years. The company had to establish a reputation for quality and reliability. That wouldn't happen overnight.

Liu was successful in securing China Mobile, already the largest wireless company in the world at the time, as an anchor customer. This was a key milestone in the company's development. Aicent created the transport network for China Mobile's data roaming infrastructure. This relationship was critical in helping Aicent to acquire other Asian carriers as clients. By 2005, Aicent had commercial GRX contracts with thirty-four carriers in the Asia-Pacific region, representing a 59 percent market share in a part of the world with 732 million wireless subscribers. By 2010 Aicent had the largest customer base for data roaming services in Asia. It was one of the first to offer these services.

For better support to its Asia-Pacific customers, it has a research and development and customer support center in Beijing, China. Aicent has nearly two-thirds of its employee base in Beijing, where the average engineer costs Aicent around one-third of what it would cost to hire staff in Silicon Valley, the company's headquarter site. This gives the company an important competitive edge over larger competitors who entered the market such as Belgacom, which is based in Europe, or Syniverse, which operates out of the United States. Aicent has another advantage, too. Unlike some of its competitors, it is an independent vendor. Many carriers are reluctant to rely on another carrier to provide their data facilities.

AICENT RIDES THE WAVE OF DATA SERVICES GROWTH

Building a network and earning the trust of big customers were both necessities for Aicent, but logging enough traffic to generate significant revenues was just as important. Here the company was fortunate, though not at first. Carrier data services took a few years to ramp up in volume. While the market was developing, Aicent's revenues remained low, and the company was not profitable but it wisely used its resources to build a customer base. While the business thesis appeared sound, predicting revenue growth is not a science. It took real courage on the part of company management and the investors to continue to support the business while revenues grew slowly.

The turn in revenue growth finally happened in the mid-2000s, jumping between 30 and 45 percent every year. This was because there were finally enough 2G data service-enabled networks in operation to create significant interconnection traffic needs. In fact, Figure 9.1, which charts the hardware and software sales of products that enabled mobile computing (i.e. network deployment), shows that the inflection point at which growth ramped up came in 2003. Carrier network deployment preceded data traffic growth, of course. But when the traffic needs emerged, Aicent was there to handle it, because it had the key infrastructure in place and the staff to handle customer needs.

Since about 2005 the growth in mobile data traffic (and its associated carrier revenues) has been huge. Worldwide mobile data revenue grew from $65 billion in 2004 to $310 billion in 2011. Much of this growth has been due to the popularity of mobile video. About 50 percent of the data being transmitted to mobile devices in 2011 is video. It is amazing to realize that in 2010, global mobile carriers were handling data traffic three times bigger than what the whole Internet handled in 2000. Roaming has also become a very profitable revenue source for wireless carriers, increasing from 12.2 percent of their revenues in 2004 to 21.5 percent in 2009. While voice traffic is still the main revenue source on the new networks, in 2011 data accounted for about 20 percent of the world's mobile carrier revenues, with more growth on the horizon.

Expanding beyond Asia

As handsets proliferated, data services diversified, networks increased their geographic dispersion, and international travel boomed, the need of carriers and their customers to interconnect mobile services across networks, across handsets, and across types of data became more pressing. Aicent was well positioned to grab a bigger share of this exploding market. It had benefited in the early years from the fact that the interconnection market opportunity was too small to be attractive to big companies. By the time the majors began to appreciate the strategic value of such a business, they were in catching-up mode. Aicent already had the network assets to exploit the opportunity and the reputation to sign up new customers.

Aicent, by contrast, was focused on expansion. It began contracting with operators in Europe, starting with one of the major carriers, British Telecommunications (BT). In 2004 BT decided to divest itself of its GRX interconnection service, which had yielded only modest revenues. Accordingly, it invited bids from a number of companies interested in acquiring it. However, BT was not anxious to hand over its hubs to an international telecommunications competitor. Making a deal with Aicent solved this problem, because it was a neutral party. The company also committed itself to leasing BT assets as needed to serve its customers. In effect, Aicent and BT became business partners to the benefit of both. And Aicent gained access to European carriers, complementing its Asian footprint.

In 2005 Aicent acquired an operating base in North America, getting AT&T as a customer. AT&T is the new name of SBC, a spin-off of the original AT&T, which bought its former parent that year and adopted its name. AT&T also owns a majority share of Cingular Wireless, which had acquired the original AT&T's wireless division a year earlier.

By 2011 the company was interconnecting 180 mobile service operators with more than 2.5 billion subscribers, including nine of the ten largest in the world. Its footprint is particularly strong in Asia. It services all of the carriers in mainland China, Hong Kong, Macau, Taiwan, South Korea, Singapore, Philippines, Malaysia, Indonesia, and Thailand. RIM became an important customer, using Aicent's services to connect BlackBerry customers in Asia with its central data center in Canada. On any given day, Aicent's network facilitates over 100 million roaming transactions generated in 114 countries.

New services are constantly being added to its portfolio. For example, the rapid growth of WiFi services around the globe has given rise to the need for roaming agreements, and the company is providing a service that addresses that need.

Aicent's ability to quickly address emerging needs is a tribute to its excellent technology team in Beijing, with support from marketing and customer service teams around the globe. Continuous monitoring of the international network for quality assurance purposes is conducted from the Beijing location.

MANAGING A GLOBAL BUSINESS

It took five years, from 2000 to 2005, for the company to generate the revenue growth it had hoped for. Once that was achieved, it ramped to profitable revenues in excess of $50 million. As is the case with all startups, this lag between investment and revenues is a critical period. How well a company is prepared to make good on its promise depends completely on following a wise investment strategy during this early period – which always lasts longer than any entrepreneur or investor expects.

In Aicent's case its growth was funded with a relatively modest investment. This would not have been possible without the decision to build the company's technical resources in China, where operating costs were much below those in California. The experience of the co-founder of the company provided the basis around which the outstanding technical team in network design and management could be built. At the same time, however, the company's headquarters were maintained in Silicon Valley. This was done in the belief that it would be easier to attract international marketing and senior management talent, as well as future funding, in this location. Lynn Liu acquired a second home in Beijing and was able to manage the company effectively from either side of the Pacific. As she spent a great deal of time with Asian customers and the majority of the company's employees were in Asia, this proved to be a good strategy.

None of this success would have been possible without outstanding financial and operational management. Kallen Chan, the chief financial officer of the company, provided the glue to knit together the operations of the company around the globe from his office in the Silicon Valley company headquarters. Born and raised in Hong Kong, Chan came to the US to attend Santa Clara University, where he earned an MBA. Prior to joining Aicent in 2005, he had held senior financial management positions in several companies in California. He joined the company just when its revenues were starting to grow and profitability was in sight. Along with that growth came a host of financial commitments. How well the needs and commitments were matched determined the fate of the company. It passed this test with flying colors.

The successful operation of a business like Aicent's presents unique challenges. First, the customers are mostly big companies, and many millions of dollars of their revenues depend on Aicent's service. While the fees paid for the service delivered are actually quite small compared to their overall revenues, the carriers are nevertheless very difficult customers because of how critical the service is to their users. Vendors such as Aicent are held to extremely high standards of performance. Second, carriers are also notoriously cost sensitive. Contracts may be renegotiated annually with many of them. Hence, negotiating contract pricing is a major responsibility of the central financial organization.

Third, and equally critical to Aicent's success, is negotiating the best prices for the transport capacity leased from regional carriers in dozens of countries. Aicent rents data transport facilities for its service. Monitoring capacity to determine its actual need and setting prices for its use are central to ensuring a profitable operation.

Finally, the importance of careful long-term planning cannot be understated. The company must lease facilities ahead of customer demand to make sure it has the capacity to meet future needs. This financial commitment carries a degree of risk. So does investment in new technology, equipment, and software, also necessary to meet customers' needs. Getting too far ahead of the demand entails the funding of idle capacity. Being too short-sighted, however, risks not being able to meet customer needs. The job of the financial organization is to work with the operating units to strike the right balance.

LOOKING BACK

Aicent presents us with an interesting case of a company built from the ground up for global operation. It is based on Lynn Liu's recognition of an attractive market opportunity in what established companies thought of as a fringe service. It is strictly service-based, and leases facilities to provide that service. Yet major wireless carriers are totally dependent on it to make data traffic, an increasingly important part of their business, work smoothly. Some of the more striking features of its growth and success deserve a second look.

The advantage and risk of being a first mover. Aicent is not built on proprietary technology, but on providing the most effective service to carriers. This requires an outstanding technology implementation team. Nevertheless, as an innovator in the market, it assumed risk and gained advantages by getting ahead of the large demand wave for its services. Having perceived a growing need for international interconnection services, Aicent correctly assumed that, in order to end up in a leading position, it would have to develop the broadest reach and greatest ability to interconnect data traffic of any company in the field, and would need to offer excellent service well before its competitors. There is not room in the market for many providers of such a service. Aicent had to be in the market early, with a convincing offering, if it wanted to be profitable.

This strategy entailed considerable financial risk. Initially the data traffic being handled by the carriers in the markets served by Aicent did not justify the capacity it was putting in place. This risk was mitigated by placing as much of the technology and network management organization as possible in China, where costs were much lower than in the US. Further, Aicent managed to lease transport capacity under favorable terms. Nevertheless, putting such a network in place well before it was financially justified was a bold step. It did wind up paying off as the company grew in response to the increase in data traffic, but that took several years. During that interim period it had the resources to survive owing to its low operating costs.

The strategic steps taken by Aicent demonstrate the business rationale of a successful startup. The company took risks, but it had investors and management prepared to assume these risks. Everyone knew there were no easy short cuts to success.

The importance of business relationships. Lynn Liu leveraged her prior relationships in the fast-growing Asian telecommunications markets to get her first customers. It is hard to imagine how such a startup, providing a critical service, could have succeeded otherwise. Her contacts were instrumental in winning the initial sponsorship of China's biggest wireless carrier. Other carriers in the region, all of whom were growing rapidly, were open to dealing with a young company because of this prior experience. And of course that impressive start in Asia then made possible the company's expansion into Europe and the US.

An international company from the start. Aicent presents a new model for international business: one that is organized to be local where necessary and multinational where possible. Aicent started in Silicon Valley, but the majority of its staff was in Asia right from the start. Ultimately the staff became multinational. The company operated in many countries where its local representatives had to deal with country-specific issues. Sales teams for each country were recruited locally because of their familiarity with the local carriers. A staff that is familiar with a country and its business environment is best able to deal with local customers.

On the financial side, however, the company was definitely not local. It wisely avoided the common error of decentralizing financial control, which can lead to serious disconnects in pricing, contract profitability, and employee compensation. Aicent maintained strong financial control from its headquarters in Silicon Valley.

There is no doubt that entrepreneurs play a necessary part in building the novel industries required for accelerated economic growth. The big question is, must governments become the patrons of these new industries, and if so, in what ways and to what extent?

In the next chapter we address this issue.

10 Building an economy: Government planning vs. entrepreneurial innovation

"Reconquer the domestic market!" is a rallying cry invented by the government in its effort to reduce France's foreign trade deficit and stimulate citizens to buy nationally-made products in preference to imports.[1]

While globalization has opened up markets everywhere, it has also thrown the inherent tension between government economic activism and entrepreneurial freedom into sharp relief. We now take up crucial questions about the proper role of government on the one hand, and the place, indeed the very future, of entrepreneurship on the other.

In our global economy entrepreneurs are frequently competing with companies supported and directed, and often controlled, by the governments of the countries where they do business. It is hardly an even match: such policies inevitably engender hidden or overt preferences for buying local products.

Clearly, state-controlled economies pose a serious challenge to the basic concept of entrepreneurship and the ability of foreign corporations to operate freely within those economies. By raising barriers to international sales opportunities, they clearly increase the inherent risks of launching new entrepreneurial businesses. Under such conditions, it is fair to ask whether the individualistic and "random" entrepreneurial process, gated by so many unpredictable circumstances, can be counted upon in the future as a significant economic driver. Must governments everywhere become much more involved in supporting ambitious entrepreneurs focused on creating new markets? This is a pressing issue for countries like the

---

[1] J. Gee, "Five year target for France," *Data Processing*, vol. 25, no. 9, November 1983, pp. 37–39.

US, which have a tradition of free markets and limited government support of their industries.

We opened this book on the entrepreneur in the global economy by outlining how governments involve themselves in building local economies. In Chapter 2 we looked at the importance of entrepreneurs in creating new companies and industries. The succeeding chapters tracked the fortunes of twelve entrepreneurs, from David Sarnoff of RCA in the first half of the twentieth century to Lynn Liu of Aicent at the opening of the twenty-first, as they strove to build competitive companies in an increasingly globalized economy.

In this chapter we will ask whether and how governments and entrepreneurs can coexist and cooperate, and explore the ramifications of that question. This covers such topics as, to what extent will governments take on the roles of venture capitalist and entrepreneur, choosing the technologies and building the industries of the future? In what areas is government participation most likely to be healthy and productive? How can entrepreneurs and corporations responding to market conditions make better decisions?

THE HAZARDS OF TARGETING INDUSTRIES

To set the stage, we will review two diametrically opposed views of economic development, as described initially in our opening chapters. They represent the most extreme positions in the argument over industrial policy in the developed world: pure free markets versus heavy state involvement.

There is plenty of public support for an untrammeled entrepreneurial approach. Free-market advocates insist that the US government (and by extension governments in other free-market countries) should stay out of the markets and let entrepreneurs chart their own course. According to these proponents, "The country needs to unleash entrepreneurs, who will only be held back by tax-funded make-work projects."[2]

---

[2] E. Glaeser, "Detroit's decline and the folly of light rail," *The Wall Street Journal*, March 25, 2011, p. A17.

Others question the efficacy of this approach. They believe that the idea that "entrepreneurs are the foundation of the [US] economy" is a myth,[3] and that the US and other free-market countries might be better off with a targeted industrial policy to ensure the growth (and protection) of domestic industries, particularly new ones based on domestic innovations.

A better way to frame the argument is to ask the following question. Is it realistic to believe that government planning, supported by taxpayer money, can force-feed industrial innovations into the commercial marketplace? Can it totally replace the more chaotic but much more flexible and dynamic entrepreneurial process?

As an approach to answering this question, it is worth keeping in mind the observations of Nassim Taleb in his book *The Black Swan*,[4] in which he summarizes the views of Nobel Laureate economist Friedrich August Hayek, a famous proponent of the free market.

> For Hayek, a true forecast is done organically by a system, not by fiat. One single institution, say, the central planner, cannot aggregate knowledge; many important pieces of information will be missing. But society as a whole will be able to integrate into its functioning these multiple pieces of information. Society as a whole thinks outside the box. Hayek attacked socialism and managed economies. Owing to the growth of scientific knowledge, we overestimate our ability to understand subtle changes that constitute the world, and what weight needs to be imparted to each such change.[5]

On a theoretical level, then, there are limits to what can be done with "top-down" economic planning. Hayek suggests that any attempt to dictate a national approach to a dynamic market will be

---

[3] R. Foroohar, "Don't hold your breath," *Time*, June 20, 2011, pp. 22–26.
[4] N. S. Taleb, *The Black Swan* (New York: Random House, 2010), p. 180.
[5] See F. A. Hayek, *The road to serfdom* (Chicago, IL: The University of Chicago Press, 1994), for a statement of his positions.

unsuccessful in the long run. Instead, the most productive strategy for fostering economic growth is likely to be the creation of national policies that focus government on what it does best, leaving private capital and entrepreneurs to areas where they function more efficiently. We will clarify the dividing line between these two spheres by looking at some examples of government actions and their outcomes.

Government as entrepreneur

On the face of it, it seems like a good idea to have the national government fund the creation of industries around promising technologies in the hope of expanding the economy and building exportable products. Proponents of this approach envision using subsidies and other incentives to accelerate the growth of the chosen industries. This would be done in partnership with private industry if possible – and without it if private funding is not available.

This may sound familiar because it is an old idea. We encountered it in our discussion of Colbert, who targeted growth industries for seventeenth-century France. China runs a modern version of the strategy.

Although this approach can achieve quick success, it usually runs into trouble later on. The availability of "easy" state money spawns enterprises with uncompetitive cost structures. They become too far removed from the discipline of the competitive marketplace to achieve profitability. Bereft of entrepreneurial management, companies built on this model risk becoming permanent wards of the state. This actually happened in Colbert's France.

There is a bigger problem with this approach: it too often fails, especially when newer technology is introduced. We can understand why when we contrast industrial development with infrastructure and defense, two functions crucial to economic growth and stability that governments can carry out quite effectively.

Infrastructure (roads, airports, and water and power utilities) is convenient for the citizenry – and absolutely necessary for industrial development. Likewise, defense programs uphold national security – and also spur the growth of industry by underwriting R&D programs. Even the most radical proponents of limiting the power of government would agree that both of these activities are the rightful province of the state. Governments are the only entities with the resources to plan and finance such sweeping programs. They are also dealing with known quantities: it is relatively easy to project infrastructure requirements and forecast future defense needs.

Deciding which new innovative industries to subsidize, on the other hand, is a far less certain undertaking than determining when and where people will need roads and sewers. It is nearly impossible to predict future market trends and competitive threats with any great degree of accuracy. As a result governments are notoriously poor at picking winning new commercial industries for long-range development. Such attempts have often generated disappointing results.

Long-term planning, longer odds
There is another reason why governments have such a poor track record in planning technology industries: the nature of their decision-making process. They are not the only entities affected by this shortcoming. It is common in large corporations as well.

As can well be imagined, thousands of planning meetings take place every day in large organizations around the world, with committees deciding economic and technological matters large and small. Whether these meetings occur in the government bureaucracies of planned economies or in the boardrooms of large corporations, one thing is certain. Lone visionaries, even if present, have little chance to influence the ultimate decision. In addition, most of the people in the room will be far removed from the actual technologies under discussion.

Yet funding decisions must be made, often long in advance. And unfortunately what appears to bureaucrats or board members to be the low-risk approach has a good chance of being the wrong path to take. That is why so many radical innovations come from individuals or small independent teams. They have the freedom to assume risks of their own choosing and the financial freedom to fund programs that balance high risk against high rewards. They also have the flexibility to modify their decisions quickly, without waiting for the next budget cycle.

Planning industrial development is no task for the faint of heart. But countries have to place their bets and take their chances in the competitive global market. The question is how do governments in open economic systems like the US establish policies and fund programs that lead to innovative businesses, without trapping themselves in dead ends.

One would think that a country like China, which has had great success with a planned economy, would have an answer. But even China understands the difficulty of long-term industrial planning. For example, its first five-year plan of 1951 called, among other things, for 6 million tons of cement, 5 million tons of pig iron, and 4.2 million tons of steel. These objectives were achieved because the state paid for the construction of the plants required to produce these products, and the technology was acquired from foreign sources.

But things have changed since then. In what is now the second largest economy in the world, the multitude of industries and priorities are too complex to be sorted out by state planners. Now China's five-year plans target only industries deemed to be of major strategic importance. Hence, the twelfth plan (2011 to 2015) puts great emphasis on broader issues such as employment, energy efficiency, increased funding of research and development, the expansion of top-quality universities, and environmental improvements.[6]

In spite of the pitfalls of planning by committee, critics of the free-market model worry that the transition from innovation to commercialization, when paced by the capitalist profit motive, is too slow in countries such as the US. They call for a more focused

---

[6] "A new epic: China's new five-year plan is at odds with itself," *The Economist*, October 23, 2010, p. 88.

national industrial policy helped along by government funding, which they feel is essential to accelerate the pace.

People who advocate this approach are basing their recommendations on the rapid growth of China and its perceived ability to quickly build industries practically from scratch. In their enthusiasm they tend to gloss over the gap between China's more predictable path of importing existing technology as opposed to the chancy nature of developing innovations.

In defense of government planners, however, they may not be much worse at forecasting the future of transformational technology than the private sector. We will have occasion below to judge the efforts of analysts and technology experts outside the government in predicting which innovations will have a serious impact on the economy. Nor should one assume that government investments in technology never deliver positive results. We will also highlight cases where government involvement has produced truly transformational technology.

However, history is littered with the remains of failed state-funded industrial initiatives.[7] One such case is especially interesting in that it concerns France, a centuries-long bastion of state planning.

Targeting growth industries: A government goes it alone

In 1983, in an effort to develop new growth industries that could compete with foreign firms (see the quote that opens this chapter), the government of France launched a five-year, $20 billion program to stimulate the development of domestic information technology companies. Its program targeted computers, semiconductor components, and industrial software. At the time all of those fields were dominated by the US.

The program also included funding for the expansion of Minitel, a new videotext service pioneered in France. Minitel used a

---

[7] Josh Lerner of the Harvard Business School discusses salient examples in *Boulevard of broken dreams* (Princeton, NJ: Princeton University Press, 2009).

combination of television and the telephone system to interactively provide information to homes and businesses across the nation.

It was not surprising that France should target specific industries for investment. This approach was consistent with the country's history of state industrial planning and financing, starting with Colbert in the seventeenth century. What was surprising was the program's lack of success.

- French computer companies were never able to keep pace with the rapid international progress in the computer industry. The national champion, Groupe Bull (named, ironically, for its Norwegian founder Fredrik Rosing Bull), was nationalized in 1982 and re-privatized in 1994. It has undergone many takeovers, mergers, and name changes, including joint ventures and ownership relations with overseas companies General Electric, Honeywell, NEC, and Motorola. Now called simply Bull, it remains a marginal competitor in need of state support.
- During the semiconductor industry's greatest growth period, between 1980 and 2000, France remained a minor player. Thomson Semiconducteurs, the leading French chip company, merged with Italy's SGS Microelettronica to form SGS Thomson in 1987, but sold its ownership share in 1994. Meanwhile Japan and Taiwan joined the US as major global chip suppliers.
- France developed many niche players in industrial software, but the US raced ahead, and Germany's SAP proved to be a world-class enterprise software innovator.
- Although Minitel was a truly innovative service and did achieve some popularity in France, it was eventually overwhelmed by the success of the Internet – a technology unknown in 1983. The obsolete service was officially terminated in 2011.[8]

Among many explanations for these disappointing results, one key factor, we believe, was insularity. France's program focused on funding domestic companies to execute the turnaround of the computer industry. Its intent was to boost French industry by relying as much as possible on French resources.

---

[8] M. Cochester, "France Telecom will bid adieu to Minitel," *The Wall Street Journal*, July 25, 2011, p.B4.

Another factor was the program's reliance on established (one might say ossified) providers. No new entrepreneurial ventures were in the equation. It was a state initiative, rife with the bureaucratic malaise that such programs commonly entail. The French authorities ignored the example of Colbert, the finance minister who had vigorously recruited foreign entrepreneurs to bring in new technical talent and start new companies in seventeenth-century France.

Contrast this failed effort with what some other countries were doing during the same period, and with the results they achieved.

- Entrepreneurial activity in the US, substantially funded by venture capital, led to an explosion of new businesses, many of which became world leaders in their categories.
- During the same period Japanese companies imported foreign technology under license to get started. They then used domestic product development to fuel the growth of world-class businesses such as Fujitsu, Toshiba, and NEC.
- Taiwan's semiconductor industry began with foreign technology, with RCA a major licensor, giving TSMC and other semiconductor companies the foundation they needed for success.

Targeting growth industries: Government teams with the private sector

When state initiatives to develop new industries fail, it is the taxpayer who foots the bill. Where the government has recruited private capital and entrepreneurs to join such initiatives, however, the economic effects are amplified. Entrepreneurs and their investors are left stranded along with the taxpayers, potentially affecting the availability of funding for other, more promising innovations. Three US government "clean energy" programs illustrate how this can happen.

Clean energy is currently one of the most popular areas for investment, so it was easy to persuade private investors and companies to participate. All the programs were targeted at reducing fossil fuel consumption and controlling greenhouse gas emissions, though in very different ways. Two programs addressed the electrical utility industry, while the third subsidized sales of hybrid electric automobiles.

Of the two programs targeting electric utilities, the first sought to replace non-renewable fossil fuels (oil and coal) in power plants with biomass (wood and other organic materials). Biomass was touted as a "clean" and renewable energy source.

The other program aimed to build a so-called "smart grid" to improve the efficiency of the electrical power distribution network. With a more efficient grid, the electric industry could meet the demand for power with less fuel. Both programs had the worthwhile goal of reducing the amount of CO_2 spewed into the atmosphere by generating plants.

These initiatives were in line with other programs intended to combat global warming and reduce energy consumption, then under way around the world. It is estimated that global funding for such efforts reached $200 billion in 2010, a nearly fivefold increase from $44 billion in 2004. This figure includes private investments as well as government funding.[9]

In the US, however, private funding for energy-related R&D was on the decline. It dropped 50 percent between 1991 and 2005.[10] In response, in 2009 the Department of Energy allocated an incremental $5.4 billion for development of renewable energy sources. Part of that funding went to the biomass program, created to encourage electric companies to use biomass in place of fossil fuels. This was in line with an initiative supported by Congress as far back as 1978 to reduce the country's reliance on imported oil. Private investors invested substantial funds as well, in anticipation of a major business opportunity from a new generation of power plants that could use renewable fuels.

The program's success depended on widespread adoption of the new technology. To make the desired impact on reducing fossil fuel

[9] "Climate change," *The Economist*, November 29, 2010, pp. 59–61.
[10] D. M. Kammen and G. F. Nemet, "Reversing the incredible shrinking energy R&D budget," *Real Numbers*, 2005.

consumption, electric utilities would have to generate at least 25 percent of their power with biomass fuels. Unfortunately, it is more expensive to use biomass than fossil fuels. That means biomass-fueled electrical generation simply isn't profitable without charging businesses and consumers substantially more for electricity. Without increased prices for power, there was little incentive for utilities to make the switch.

Private investors had assumed state regulators would make biomass plants profitable by permitting utilities to raise their electricity rates. They did not take into account the difficulty of forcing through a utility price increase, at least in a democracy. Electricity rates in the US are largely set at the state level by a utility commission. Most commission members are political appointees, and revising rate structures is an inherently political process. Consumers may consider clean energy a worthy cause in the abstract, but when it came down to paying more for electricity, their resistance to price increases was fierce. To complicate the matter, opponents found other good reasons to hinder the profitable operation of biomass plants.

Most state regulators took the path of least resistance, and did not implement mandates forcing the use of biomass fuels. To further frustrate program proponents, operating costs for the new biomass plants that actually got built turned out to be even higher than anticipated.

Finally, with the public increasingly concerned about air pollution from burning biomass fuels, state officials issued costly new regulations to control emissions from generating plants that used the new technology. For example, the Massachusetts Department of Energy Resources decreed that biomass power plants had to increase their efficiency by 60 percent to reduce their level of pollutants. This was not practical. They also required extra filtration of emissions, which increased the cost of building such plants.

With these and other obstacles to profitable operation in their path, by 2010 biomass-fueled electrical generation plants were being phased out as uneconomical. In one case Sierra Pacific Industries of California closed down a 16-megawatt plant because environmental restrictions made it difficult and costly to obtain wood from forests.[11]

Our second program, the "smart grid" initiative, offers another object lesson in the difficulties of forging a public/private partnership to develop a new approach to business. Partly funded by the Federal government, this program had the goal of improving the efficiency of electrical power generation by two means: using new metering technology in homes and businesses; and improving communication and control in the power generation distribution network.

One of its goals was to reduce demand for electricity during peak periods, such as warm summer afternoons when air-conditioning use is at its highest. Utilities have to maintain "peaking capacity" to meet this demand, an expensive resource that otherwise stands idle. If they could even out demand across the day, they would not have to maintain as much peaking capacity, reducing the overall cost of generating electricity.

The "smart grid" initiative called for new electric meters, called "smart meters," as part of the solution. These devices not only record how much power consumers use over the course of a day and billing cycle, but show consumers how much electricity they use at different times of the day. With "smart meters" in place, utilities could institute a policy to charge more for electricity used during peak periods.

Planners assumed that if consumers knew they would be charged more for electricity during peak periods, they would shift chores that require a lot of electricity to times when rates are lower. For example, they might run washers and dryers at night instead of during the day. The architects of this initiative believed that consumers would welcome this scheme because it gave them some

---

[11] J. Carlton, "(Bio)mass confusion: High costs and environmental concerns have pushed biomass power to the sidelines in the US" *The Wall Street Journal*, October 18, 2010, p. R5.

control over the price they paid for electricity and could lead to lower electric bills.

With this noble objective in mind, the Federal government set aside $3.4 billion in 2009 to help fund home installation of the smart meters. Since these new devices have built-in communication capabilities, utilities can read them remotely in real time, and give consumers timely access to data on their electricity use.

Given the tens of millions of homes and businesses where meters can be installed, this represents a multi-billion dollar opportunity. Its enormous potential attracted many companies, including startups, to offer the new smart meters and the communications links needed to connect them to the utilities. Of course the utilities expected that the net cost of the meters (after Federal subsidies) would be passed on to their customers.

It sounded like a good program for everyone concerned: utilities would achieve more efficient power use, consumers smart enough to time-shift their use of major appliances would get lower-cost electricity, and meter providers would rack up sales and profits.

However, it didn't quite turn out that way. In a classic clash between an obvious public good and public unwillingness to pay for it, consumers rebelled. While smart meters have been deployed on a small scale in some states, legal actions in California and Hawaii, among other places, have blocked their mass deployment. Consumers simply don't want to pay for them, directly or indirectly.[12]

Eventually smart meters will very likely be deployed more widely, as they are now in some parts of the US and other countries. But their spread will be at nowhere near the rate anticipated by the promoters of the government's smart grid plan, or by investors in the companies trying to benefit from a national program.

We come now to an example of industrial planning that is more familiar to and more popular with the average consumer: the Federal subsidizing of plug-in electric automobiles. We are not talking about

---

[12] See report in *Bloomberg Businessweek*, September 26, 2010, pp. 44–45.

funding research and development here. (The US Department of Energy did in fact provide low-interest loans to two electric vehicle startups, Tesla Motors and Fisker Motors, for product development, but it is too early to assess the success of this investment.) Our topic is the government rebate of part of the purchase price of electric cars, which is given directly to consumers. About $5 billion has been allocated by the government for this purpose, all in the spirit of reducing oil consumption and helping to create a cleaner atmosphere.

These automobiles exhibit a very limited degree of true innovation. The core enabler is a new generation of a very old product: storage batteries. Advances in battery technology are making such slow progress that one can question whether the cars they power actually represent a new generation of products with long-term value.

Whatever the answer to that question, one thing is certain. With the possible exception of the very expensive Tesla roadster, which claims to travel 245 miles on a full charge, electric vehicle driving ranges are too short to make them credible competitors to gas-powered vehicles. Nissan's Leaf, an all-electric car, requires four to eight hours of charging on a 220-volt circuit to travel 100 miles or less. Its American competition, the Chevrolet Volt, runs only 35 miles on a fully charged battery pack. A built-in gasoline-powered generator extends the Volt's range to 300 miles, but during that operational mode it is not a true plug-in electric. (Fisker's Karma automobile is similar in range and operation to the Volt.)

Given their limitations, electric cars are very much a niche product. Without subsidies it is highly unlikely that they would have been introduced to the general market.[13]

These Federal initiatives show what happens all too often with government plans in a country like the US, where promulgating new industrial standards or forcing people to buy products is not a simple matter of a decree from Washington. Because these initiatives tried

[13] M. Ramsey, "Bumpy road for electrics: Boosters see bright future for battery cars, but some say drawbacks too severe," *The Wall Street Journal*, October 18, 2010, p. B1.

to mandate innovations without taking into account public resistance to their cost or negative consequences of their implementation, they were pre-ordained for failure.

All three programs did some things right: they were conceived for a worthwhile purpose; they displayed a vision, however limited, of the future; and they created new business opportunities for innovators and entrepreneurs. Yet they were by no means as successful in driving new business as the planners or the entrepreneurs who bet on them could have hoped. The energy-related initiatives have been a disappointment, and the success of electric cars is still in doubt. This is all a result of factors outside the control of the Federal government or of entrepreneurs.

Before leaving this topic, it is worth noting that as subsidized industries build constituencies, they have a way of becoming entrenched, leading to misallocation of resources. A case in point is the US Federal program to subsidize the production of ethanol from corn. Started in the 1970s in the midst of the oil embargo, this program was aimed at reducing America's dependence on foreign oil by providing a substitute fuel that could be produced from a major US crop. In addition, ethanol was thought to be far less polluting than oil. Huge private investments were made to build plants to produce it, and its use was mandated by law.

But here is what an original proponent of this program, former US Vice President Al Gore, had to say about it in 2010: "The benefits of first-generation ethanol are trivial ... but it's hard once such a program is put in place to deal with the lobbies that keep it going." Corn producers are strong supporters of this program, and of course the powerful farm lobby is intent on retaining the subsidy. Yet not only is ethanol not delivering the expected benefits, it is now believed to contribute more greenhouse gas emissions to the atmosphere than fossil fuels.[14]

[14] "Al Gore's ethanol epiphany," *The Wall Street Journal*, November 27–28, 2010, p. A16.

WHY LONG-RANGE TECHNOLOGY PLANNING
IS SO CHANCY

So far our examination of the uncertainties of industrial planning has focused on market misreadings by the planners, and on the impediments to progress that a democratic society can place in the path of government initiatives. Now we turn our attention back to the central issue of industrial innovation: selecting new technologies that show promise as the basis of new industries.

People who undertake this task face a different set of issues from the ones industrial planners take for granted. They are dealing with technology in the early stages of development, when much of its potential has yet to be revealed, and before it has been tested in the market.

As already noted, picking winners is very hard. So hard, in fact, that forecasts from experts in the private sector as to which technology will succeed are not much better than those of government planners. As proof, here is a salient example from the not-so-distant past.

In 1995 *Scientific American* devoted an issue to "Key technologies for the 21st century." In his introduction to the survey, Paul Rennie, editor of the magazine, cautioned the reader on the hazards of technology prophecy.

> "The future is not what it used to be," wrote the poet Paul
> Valéry decades ago, and it would not be hard to share in his
> disappointment today. As children, many of us were assured
> that we would one day live in a world of technological marvels.
> And so we do – but, by and large, not the ones foretold. Films,
> television, books and World's Fairs promised that the twilight
> of the 20th century and the dawn of the 21st would be an era
> of helpful robot servants, flying jet cars, moon colonies, easy
> space travel, undersea cities, wrist videophones, paper clothes,

disease-free lives and, oh, yes, the 20-hour work week. What went wrong?

...

Of course, many technologies do succeed wildly beyond anyone's dreams ... In fact, it is tempting to think that most great innovations are unforeseen, if not unforeseeable ... The truth is that as technologies pile on technologies at an uneven pace, it becomes impossible to predict precisely what patterns will emerge.[15]

Rennie went on to assert that technology predictions fail for many reasons. He cited such factors as practicality (the jet-pack looked good in theory but proved unusable in the field) and an overly optimistic assessment of how fast a technology will advance. But the biggest reason why forecasts are inaccurate is that they are, in his words, "simplistic, and hence unrealistic," failing to take into account the challenges a technology will face from market forces, economic conditions, public policies, timing, fashions, and more.

For example, visions of industrial robots taking over the workplace have been tempered by the fact that they are too costly for many applications. Likewise, the exotic (and expensive) materials that experts once thought would replace silicon in semiconductor chips were relegated to niche applications as more advanced silicon chips matched their capabilities.

Looking back at visions of the future

To really appreciate how hard it is even for experts to predict which technologies will shape the future, it helps to look at predictions by some of the smartest people of a prior era. In spite of his cautions about the enterprise of prophecy, Rennie – give him credit for great courage – nevertheless assembled a set of predictions around

---

[15] P. Rennie, "The uncertainties of technological innovation," *Scientific American*, September 1995, pp. 57–58.

several areas of technology. So we will see how the predictions of 1995 compare to the reality of 2011.

- *Information technology.* Only two technologies mentioned in this area have continued to create enormous economic value. Driven by steadily advancing manufacturing technology, microprocessors have evolved in complexity and value creation more or less as indicated by what has become known as Moore's Law. Wireless networks, the second technology, have become an increasingly important part of computer technology. The other five technologies singled out for future importance have not lived up to the hype. These include artificial intelligence and virtual reality.
- *Transportation.* None of the predictions have panned out. High-speed rail systems still use steel wheels and rails, not superconducting schemes, for support. None of the few maglev trains built up to now has demonstrated any significant advantage in speed over a conventional high-speed train. As for customized automobiles, they never happened. Nor have any revolutionary commercial airliners been built. Boeing's 787 Dreamliner, which went into service in 2011, is only an evolutionary advance over previous airplanes. Its development took ten years and billions of dollars in cost overruns.
- *Medicine.* Gene therapy has proven to be a continued investment area, though practical results are still in the future. No artificial organs are even close to replacing the use of transplanted real organs.
- *Machines, materials, and manufacturing.* Here the miss is almost total. Self-assembling materials and high-temperature superconductors are still not commercially significant technologies.
- *Energy and environment.* Solar power is beginning to make an impact in the field of renewable energy, but hydrogen fusion, which attempts to replicate the energy production process of stars, is as far in the future as ever.

A list of the technologies that were not highlighted or mentioned in these visions of the future, but did prove successful, would be just as revealing as the miscast predictions. For example, the forecast of a wireless future envisioned the use of *satellites* for general broadband data communications. In fact, broadband data now reaches consumers through telephone, cable, or fiber optic lines, and through the cellular wireless network. But the biggest miss of all is the fact that the Internet is not featured as an innovation with enormous transformational impact.

It would be comforting to think that the *Scientific American* missed so many of its predictions because it chose visionaries with unorthodox views about the technologies of the future. But that was not the case. The magazine selected highly respected experts to present their views in each technical area.

As a further demonstration of how inaccurate visions of the future tend to be, we will consider a set of predictions from another group of respected experts, also issued in 1995. It was published as a *Technology Forecast* by Price Waterhouse (now Price Waterhouse Coopers), the well-known accounting and consulting firm.[16]

This thick, 650-page tome includes predictions on the likely direction of information technology over the coming years. While its forecasts of evolutionary changes turned out to be right on the money, it notably missed the Internet and its related applications. Also missing is data virtualization – a technology that has revolutionized the use of computer systems in data centers.

INDUSTRIAL PLANNING VS. TECHNOLOGY FUNDING

Up to now we have looked at the difficulties of industrial planning. We have also reviewed the dismal record of planners and prognosticators in accurately predicting which technologies would prove successful in the marketplace. Fortunately, there are positive aspects to the planning process. These include government policies that recognize how important entrepreneurship is to economic development.

As observed before, entrepreneurs do not generate new businesses in a vacuum. They need access to intellectual property developed by others on which to base product offerings. They have

---

[16] Technology Center, *Technology Forecast 1995* (Menlo Park, CA: Price Waterhouse World Firm Technology Center, 1995).

to identify and exploit promising new markets, develop funding sources, and attract talented employees. And contrary to myth, they rely heavily on the infrastructure, resources, and business environment established by government.

Even in free-market countries like the US, the government has more involvement in the development of new industries than most people realize. We saw how David Sarnoff took advantage of cooperation between the US government and private companies in the 1920s to create the broadcast industry as we know it. Without the original government initiative to establish RCA, he would not have had the opportunity.

Of the entrepreneurial innovators we cover in this book, Sarnoff is the earliest by some sixty years. But he took full advantage of government policies and funding, and US entrepreneurs have followed his path right up to the present.

To prove the point, consider a prominent example from our own era: the digital industries pioneered in the US after World War II. Everyone talks about the famous entrepreneurs who created iconic companies such as Apple and Microsoft, but few mention that these and many other enterprises had their genesis in technologies developed under government-sponsored R&D funding.

Many of the companies we discuss in this book replicate the pattern. The technology that underlies RMI, RDA, and SanDisk can be traced to government-funded initiatives if you go far enough into the past. In the case of Ness Technologies, the roots of some of the technologies it commercialized can be traced to work sponsored by the governments of Israel and other countries.

This research was conducted under government funding in universities, national laboratories, and private industry, and originally may have been targeted at applications in the defense and space programs. But somehow the resulting technologies, developed in unrelated settings for different purposes, found their way to the world market. The results were spectacular: the creation of new electronics, computer, and telecommunications industries that have literally transformed the way people live, work, and communicate.

Non-commercial planning produces results

When a controlled economy like China's is slowly backing away from detailed targeting of industries for development, what course should relatively free economies like the US or the UK take? They already do extensive planning and resource allocation in areas of national concern such as defense and infrastructure. Should they increase their role to include general industrial development?

It is not true that free-market governments never become involved in industrial activity. They always get involved during wartime, when resources are mobilized for expanded weapons development and production, and for meeting communications, transportation, and logistics requirements. These projects are generally successful, in large part because the customer base for defense products is well defined, as are the applications.

But peacetime targeting of industries in commercial markets is an entirely different matter. It involves understanding market opportunities, competitive costs, and international trade issues. This is not something that bureaucrats are particularly noted for, as seen in the US government's abortive entrée into environmental projects. Where, then, can government planners make a positive contribution to industrial development? A look at history gives us some answers.

Starting in the 1960s, US government funding of research and development played a key role in developing a number of innovative technologies that revolutionized whole industries. Government planners did not directly target the building of modern US industry, but their role was indirectly important nevertheless. Technologies initially intended for defense and space applications ended up in the commercial world.

Once the technologies were in place, they were seized on by private capital for commercial exploitation. Further development and commercialization of many of these technologies was carried out by privately funded research. The resulting products and services built companies and industries that became the envy of the world.

Cold war R&D

Take, for example, the great entrepreneurial successes that built the foundation for the commercial digital revolution in the US after the 1970s. They were built on core technologies developed under federally funded, defense-related initiatives aimed at increasing the military capabilities of the US in the face of a perceived threat from the Soviet Union. These initiatives were focused on advanced computing technology, semiconductor devices to enable those computers, and such communications technologies as satellites, fiber optics, and lasers.

Another good example of a government initiative with huge (unplanned) commercial impact was the Apollo space program. Launched under the Kennedy administration in 1961, its goal was to land a man on the moon within a decade. Creating the manned space capsule required rapid development of such new electronic technologies as low-power, high-performance computing devices, software, and instrumentation.

This meant creating more and more powerful chips and other devices. As a result, the Apollo program gave enormous impetus to advances not only in rocket technology, life sciences, and support systems, but in microelectronics, displays, and light-emitting diodes (LEDs). R&D contracts to develop these technologies were let to universities, national laboratories, research institutions, and corporations. The technological fallout from that work ultimately infiltrated the commercial marketplace.

By any measure the government's investment in the technology of space flight reaped huge returns. One estimate of the benefit of the Apollo program is that for every dollar of R&D spent, seven dollars came back to the government in the form of corporate and income taxes from new jobs and economic growth.[17]

Building the digital domain

We cannot leave this topic without mentioning the government initiative that yielded the biggest commercial impact, the Internet.[18] Now the universal global medium for communication and commerce, the Internet took almost thirty years from conception to commercial reality. It was started not for a commercial purpose, but to address a specific communications problem among researchers.

The Internet as we know it grew out of a novel network, originally conceived by computer scientists in 1964, designed to let computers communicate. Its creators envisioned it as a communications facility for research institutions. They never imagined that it would spread outside the research community to become a major force in the world economy.

Actual deployment of such a network became possible only because of the independent invention in 1962 (published 1964) of an early version of a packet-based digital communications software protocol, which eventually became the IP (Internet Protocol). As proof of the capricious nature of R&D, the contribution of IP to the Internet came as a result of an unrelated Department of Defense (DoD) research program funded at the RAND Corporation. The rationale for this program was the need for robust military communications to minimize disruptions to the system.

DoD's Advanced Research Projects Agency undertook the actual management of the first network to link research laboratories. This network, called ARPAnet (later DARPAnet), eventually became available to the general public as the Internet. It is noteworthy that AT&T, then the monopoly owner of the US telecommunications

---

[17] www.thespaceplace.com/nasaspinoffs.html, accessed November 6, 2010.
[18] An excellent review of the history of the Internet can be found in J. Naughton, *A brief history of the future: The origins of the Internet* (London: Weidenfeld & Nicolson, 1999).

industry, refused to operate such a network for fear of creating competition for its established voice and data network (so much for visionary thinking in monopolies).

Chips and lasers

Among the other notable outcomes of R&D funded under government defense and space programs were the standard manufacturing process for integrated circuits and commercially feasible lasers. Both innovations were developed at RCA, the company built by David Sarnoff.

Today practically all chips produced worldwide are made in the CMOS process. But it began as a DoD project at RCA in the 1970s. DoD wanted to explore the possibility of creating computing chips with lower power dissipation than the then-current technology could produce. After successful completion of the project, CMOS technology was used to manufacture chips for avionic radar systems, among other applications. It found its way into the commercial market in the 1980s.

Our second example, the development of semiconductor lasers at RCA Laboratories, was a program I headed. The pioneering work on this technology was originally funded in the 1960s by DoD to develop infrared searchlights that could illuminate a battlefield, but would be invisible to the naked eye.

As the technology progressed in the late 1960s and early 1970s, it became clear that it would be possible to use such lasers in fiber optic communications and other systems. RCA announced a commercial laser in 1969 that was based on technology developed largely under DoD funding.

In two earlier books[19] we have described how thousands of entrepreneurs with access to private venture capital seized the

---

[19] See H. Kressel and T. Lento, *Competing for the future: How digital innovations are changing the world* (Cambridge: Cambridge University Press, 2007); and *Investing in dynamic markets: Venture capital in the digital age* (Cambridge: Cambridge University Press, 2010).

opportunity to develop pioneering commercial products around electronic technology that had been partly or fully developed under government funding. For example, several companies were founded to capitalize on the semiconductor laser and its applications. As a result, it appeared in numerous applications over the next few years.

Companion technologies also sprang up that greatly expanded the ways in which lasers could be used. This led to their current status as not only the key to all fiber optic communication systems, including voice and data networks, but as the enabling technology of millions of instruments, DVD players, and a host of other devices.

Government research and commercial innovation
Do these examples of government-funded technologies seeding great industries constitute a unique set of events, or are they representative of a highly effective approach to industrial development? Free marketers and proponents of state control may debate that question, but the fact remains that government-sponsored research and development does eventually migrate into the commercial and industrial markets.

In the US, at least, the government is still a major funder of innovative R&D that has broad applicability outside narrow defense applications. The 2010 US Federal R&D budget of $147 billion covers a vast scope of activities, from medical science to new sources of energy.

Corporate funding of basic research, on the other hand, has waned. Corporations are focused on product-oriented development programs aimed at producing quick results in the marketplace. They are much less invested in long-horizon projects that may or may not produce breakthrough innovations.

One recent study by Block and Keller, published in 2008, offers a view of the sources of industrial innovation in the US between 1970 and 2006. It confirms the increasing importance of government funding for R&D, and the continuing abdication of the field by corporate entities. During this period, as documented in the study, large firms contributed a declining fraction of the innovations, consistent with the decline in corporate research laboratories, while government-funded contributions from universities and national laboratories increased. Block and Keller sum up the situation this way: "If one is looking for a golden age in which the private sector did most of the innovating on its own without federal help, one has to go back to the era before World War II."[20]

SUMMING UP

Government policies play an important role in determining a nation's industrial destiny, no matter what that nation's professed economic philosophy might be. China achieved resounding success in industrializing its economy through a tightly targeted form of "top-down" industrial development.

These policies can change over time to reflect national priorities. In the hopes of generating industry from its own innovations, China is now backing away from its highly prescriptive model to allow a greater degree of "bottom-up" initiative. It may have no choice. In a world where innovation is a key driver of long-term industrial success, government must promote policies that encourage creative entrepreneurship while avoiding, in general, targeting of specific product initiatives.

One such policy is the funding of basic technology development. This approach has paid off handsomely for the US in the past, and will continue to do so in the future. But just generating technology is not enough for economic value creation. The fruits of R&D investments must move into the marketplace. That requires collaborative efforts between those who innovate and companies that can generate successful new products and services around their innovations.

---

[20] F. Block and M. R. Keller, "Where do innovations come from? Transformation in the US national innovation system, 1970–2006," *Information Technology & Innovation Foundation*, July 2008, p. 16.

We are back once again to entrepreneurship as an engine for economic growth. In Chapter 2 we outlined the positive impact that entrepreneurs can have on an economy. They create new companies or rebuild existing ones that drive innovation into the market, where it fails or succeeds on its own merits. If the new company's innovation is successful, it creates significant and lasting value. If the company fails, it makes way for the next company with the next big idea. Firms created by government action, by contrast, tend to persist long after they have outlived their usefulness.

Government can support businesses through creative industrial programs like those of the Fraunhofer Institutes, also discussed in Chapter 2. Under this arrangement the German government helps fund collaborative development between the Institutes and small and medium-sized companies. Normally such companies could not afford an ongoing innovation effort. By sharing a technology development resource, they can stay competitive. If they are startups, this arrangement gives them the opportunity to develop products that can compete in the global market.

Government-funded R&D programs and mechanisms for supporting businesses have proven highly successful as foundations for new companies and new industries. This only bolsters an already solid case for the continued importance of entrepreneurs in taking innovations to market. How entrepreneurial activity should be funded, however, is a source of significant disagreement among economic theorists.

Some point to the level of global competition, and the growing number of countries that directly underwrite industrial development, as reasons for developed countries to fund the creation of new companies. They believe this is the only way they can build an industrial base that will sustain their economies and their continued prosperity. Others maintain that this role should be assumed, as it has been historically, by private companies and entrepreneurs with funding from private sources.

We believe that the dynamic interaction of private investors and entrepreneurs accounts for much of the effectiveness of the entrepreneurial endeavor. However, there is obviously a hazy boundary between government and private financing. That gives each side of the argument some room for compromise.

As to the question of whether entrepreneurs can succeed in the global economy, we have recounted how twelve of them were able to build vital enterprises by adjusting to the demands and challenges they faced both from the market and from various national customs and policies. In the final analysis, debates over the viability of free enterprise are really based on economic orthodoxies. Entrepreneurs deal in innovation, and by definition innovation is anything but orthodox. They find ways to succeed.

In conclusion, here is a summary of what we have learned about fostering industrial innovation and planning an economy.

- Governments can build an industrial economy through subsidies and other incentives to promote new businesses, but only if they bring in proven technology and experienced management, usually from abroad, the way Colbert did in France and government planners have done, to some extent, in China. But that strategy has its limitations – you're always following the leaders and living off their leavings. Ultimately, if you're going to plan your economy for true growth, you have to stimulate domestic innovation. In a controlled economy this means picking winners, and governments are notoriously bad at picking winners.
- Private companies and industry experts may not be better at predicting the next big technology winner than governments (see the examples from *Scientific American* and Price Waterhouse). But the private sector allows the freedom of failure, and also allows successful ideas to percolate to the top as long as an entrepreneurial culture exists and risk capital is available to fund new ventures.
- Government is best at generating innovations through funding of research and development. After that it should let the inventors and innovators plot the course, instead of the bureaucrats. It should only directly support the development of actual products that it needs to accomplish a clear objective within a unique "project," e.g. the space program.

- Established big companies are best at innovation when investing to sustain an existing market. Their weakness is a tendency to stick with evolutionary technology rather than doing higher-risk development for unproven markets. To overcome this weakness, established companies often buy new entrepreneurial companies, which have proven a valuable new market or business thesis. Creating a pool of innovative new companies drives economic growth – which takes us to the next point: where do these innovative companies come from?
- This pool of emerging market creators emerges from a "bottom-up" process of entrepreneurship. Chaotic and visionary innovation plus access to venture capital and markets equals true *economically important* innovation. It requires an environment that supports this kind of activity, including government policies that encourage new business formation.
- More than ever, access to international markets and entrepreneurial skills in operating globally are key ingredients for success in many industries. Government policies must focus on ensuring a fair international playing field for its industries. At a point where corporate scale is needed, industry consolidation takes over, as in the case of RMI (Chapter 5).

One point is clear from our discussion: the creation of innovations is usually not the limiting factor in the development of new products or industries. The biggest barrier to their contributing to economic growth is moving innovations into the commercial market. Here is where extraordinary entrepreneurship, the availability of risk capital, and access to international markets by newcomers and established companies alike are key determining success factors.

Throughout its history the US has created a vibrant and innovative economy on the basis of certain valuable national characteristics. The last word on this topic comes from Joseph Biden, Vice President of the US.

> We owe our strength to our political and economic system
> and to the way we educate our children – not merely to accept
> established orthodoxy but to challenge and improve on it. We not
> only tolerate but celebrate free expression and vigorous debate.

The rule of law protects private property, lends predictability to investments and ensures accountability for poor and wealthy alike. Our universities remain the ultimate destination for the world's students and scholars. And we welcome immigrants with skill, ambition and the desire to better their lives.[21]

These traits will continue to serve well not only the US but any country willing to embrace them.

---

[21] J. R. Biden,"China's rise isn't our demise," *The New York Times*, September 8, 2011, p. A29.

Select bibliography

Appleby, J., *The relentless revolution: A history of capitalism* (New York: W. W. Norton, 2010).

Arthur, W. B., *The nature of technology: What it is and how it evolves* (New York: Free Press, 2009).

Asselain, J.-C., *Histoire économique de la France du XVIII siècle à nos jours* (Paris: Éditions du Seuil, 1985).

Atkinson, R. D., *The past and future of America's economy: Long waves of innovation that power cycles of growth* (Cheltenham, UK: Edgar Elgar, 2004).

Barna, T., *Investment and growth policies in British industrial firms* (Cambridge: Cambridge University Press, 1996).

Belanger, D. O., *Enabling American innovation: Engineering and the National Science Foundation* (West Lafayette, IN: Purdue University Press, 1998).

Berenger, J., *Histoire de l'empire des Habsbourg 1273–1918* (Paris: Librairie Arthème Fayard, 1990).

Bhagwati, J., *The wind of the hundred days: How Washington mismanaged globalization* (Cambridge, MA: The MIT Press, 2000).

Blackwell, W. L., *The beginnings of Russian industrialization 1800–1860* (Princeton, NJ: Princeton University Press, 1968).

Castells, M., *The power of identity* (New York: Wiley-Blackwell, 2010).

Chesbrough, H., Open innovation: *The new imperative for creating and profiting from technology* (Boston, MA: Harvard Business School Press, 2003).

Cohen, S. S. and J. Zysman, *Manufacturing matters* (New York: Basic Books, 1987).

Dickson, C. and O. Shenkar, *The great deleveraging: Economic growth and investing strategies for the future* (Saddle River, NJ: FT Press, 2010).

Dreher, C., *Sarnoff: An American success* (New York: Quadrangle/The New York Times Book Co., 1977).

Frieden, J. A., *Global capitalism: Its fall and rise in the twentieth century* (New York: W. W. Norton, 2006).

Gardner, D., *Future babble: Why expert predictions are next to worthless and you can do better* (New York: Dutton Adult, 2011).

Graham, B., *The intelligent investor* (revised edition by J. Zweig) (New York: HarperCollins, 1973).

Hammen, O. J., *The red '48ers: Karl Marx and Friedrich Engels* (New York: Charles Scribner's Sons, 1969).

Hansen, A. H., *Business cycles and national income* (New York: W.W. Norton, 1951).

Hayek, F. A., *The road to serfdom* (Chicago, IL: The University of Chicago Press, 1994).

Herman, A., *To rule the waves* (New York: Harper Collins, 2004).

Herman, R. T. and R. L. Smith, *Immigrants Inc.: Why immigrant entrepreneurs are driving the new economy* (Hoboken, NJ: John Wiley & Sons, 2009).

Jones, H., *Chinamerica: Why the future of America is China* (New York: McGraw-Hill, 2010).

Kressel, H. and T. V. Lento, *Investing in dynamic markets: Venture capital in the digital age* (Cambridge: Cambridge University Press, 2010).

Kressel, H. with T. V. Lento, *Competing for the future: How digital innovations are changing the world* (Cambridge: Cambridge University Press, 2007).

Lamoreaux, N. R. and K. L. Sokoloff with a foreword by William Janeway, *Financing innovation in the United States 1970 to the present* (Cambridge, MA: The MIT Press, 2007).

Landes, D. S., *The wealth and poverty of nations: Why some are so rich and some so poor* (New York: W. W. Norton, 1998).

Landes, D. S., *The unbound Prometheus: Technological change and industrial development in Western Europe from 1750 to the present* (Cambridge: Cambridge University Press, 1969).

Lerner, J., *Boulevard of broken dreams: Why public efforts to boost entrepreneurship and venture capital failed – and what to do about it* (Princeton, NJ: Princeton University Press, 2009).

Lewis, T., *Empire of the air: The men who made radio* (New York: HarperCollins, 1991).

Lindsey, B., *Against the dead hand: The uncertain struggle for global capitalism* (New York: John Wiley & Sons, 2002).

Lyons, E., *David Sarnoff, a biography* (New York: Harper & Row, 1966).

Magoun, A. B., *Television: The life story of a technology* (Baltimore, MD: The Johns Hopkins University Press, 2007).

Malet, A. and J. Isaac, *XVII and XVIII Siècle* (Paris: Librairie Hachette, 1923).

McCraw, T. K., *Prophet of innovation: Joseph Schumpeter and creative destruction* (Cambridge, MA: Harvard University Press, 2007).

McGregor, R., *The Party: The secret world of China's Communist rulers* (New York: HarperCollins, 2010).

Mokyr, J., *The lever of riches: Technological creativity and economic progress* (New York: Oxford University Press, 1990).

Muller, R. E., *Revitalizing America: Politics for prosperity* (New York: Simon & Schuster, 1980).

Murat, I., *Colbert* (Paris: Librairie Arthème Fayard, 1980).

Naughton, J., *A brief history of the future: The origins of the Internet* (London: Weidenfeld & Nicolson, 1999).

Norbert, J., *In defense of global capitalism* (Washington, DC: Cato Institute, 2003).

Ohmae, K., *The borderless world: Power and strategy in the interlinked economy* (New York: Harper Business, 1990).

Perez, P., *Technological revolutions and financial capital: The dynamics of bubbles and golden ages* (Cheltenham, UK: Edward Elgar, 2002).

Prestowitz, C., *The betrayal of American prosperity* (New York: Free Press, 2010).

Priestland, D., *The red flag: A history of Communism* (New York: Grove Press, 2009).

Prince, B., *Semiconductor memories* (New York: John Wiley & Sons, 1991).

Ridley, M., *The rational optimist: How prosperity evolves* (New York: HarperCollins, 2010).

Roberts, R. M., *Serendipity: Accidental discoveries in science* (New York: John Wiley & Sons, 1989).

Rostow, W. W., *The world economy: History and prospects* (Austin, TX: The Texas University Press, 1978).

Sakaiya, T., *What is Japan? Contradictions and transformations* (New York: Kodansha America, 1995).

Sampson, A., *The new anatomy of Britain* (New York: Stein & Day, 1972).

Sarnoff, D., *Looking ahead: The papers of David Sarnoff* (New York: McGraw-Hill, 1968).

Saul, J. R., *The collapse of globalism: And the reinvention of the world* (New York: The Overlook Press, 2005).

Saxenian, A., *Regional advantage: Culture and competition in Silicon Valley and Route 128* (Cambridge, MA: Harvard University Press, 1996).

Schumpeter, J. A. *The theory of economic development* (New Brunswick, NJ: Transaction, 1983).

Senor, B. and S. Singer, *Start-up nation: The story of Israel's economic miracle* (New York: Twelve-Hachette Book Group, 2009).

Shambaugh, S., *China's Communist Party: Atrophy and adaptation* (San Francisco, CA: University of California Press, 2010).

Simon, D. F. and D. Rehm, *Technological innovation in China: The case of Shanghai's electronics industry* (Cambridge, MA: Ballinger, 1988).

Smick, D. M., *The world is curved: Hidden dangers to the global economy* (New York: Portfolio Penguin Group, 2008).

Stanton, R. P., *Recollections and reflections: A trader's life* (Privately printed, 2009).

Stashower, D., *The boy genius and the mogul: The untold story of television* (New York: Broadway Books, 2002).

Sull, D. N. with Y. Wang, *Made in China: What Western managers can learn from trailblazing Chinese entrepreneurs* (Boston, MA: Harvard Business School Press, 2005).

Taleb, N. S., *The Black Swan* (New York: Random House, 2010).

Walter, C. E. and F. J. T. Howie, *Red capitalism: The fragile financial foundation of China's extraordinary rise* (Hoboken, NJ: John Wiley & Sons, 2011).

Watson, T. Jr., *Father, son, and company* (New York: Bantam, 2000).

Index